CONSUMING PLEASURES

CONSUMING PLEASURES

*Active Audiences and Serial Fictions
from Dickens to Soap Opera*

Jennifer Hayward

THE UNIVERSITY PRESS OF KENTUCKY

Publication of this volume was made possible in part by a grant
from the National Endowment for the Humanities

Scholarly publisher for the Commonwealth,
serving Bellarmine College, Berea College, Centre
College of Kentucky, Eastern Kentucky University,
The Filson Club Historical Society, Georgetown College,
Kentucky Historical Society, Kentucky State University,
Morehead State University, Murray State University,
Northern Kentucky University, Transylvania University,
University of Kentucky, University of Louisville,
and Western Kentucky University
All rights reserved.

Editorial and Sales Offices: The University Press of Kentucky
663 South Limestone Street, Lexington, Kentucky 40508-4008

01 00 99 98 97   5   4   3   2   1

Library of Congress Cataloging-in-Publication Data

Hayward, Jennifer.
   Consuming pleasures : active audiences and serial fictions from
  Dickens to soap opera / Jennifer Hayward.
    p.   cm.
   Includes bibliographical references (p.   ) and index.
   ISBN 0–8131–2025–X (acid-free paper)
   1. Television serials—History and criticism.   2. Serialized
  fiction—History and criticism.   I. Title.
  PN1992.8.S4H39   1997
  791.45´6—dc21   97–16851

PN
1992.8
S4 H39
1997

This book is printed on acid-free recycled paper meeting
the requirements of the American National Standard
for Permanence of Paper for Printed Library Materials.

Manufactured in the United States of America

To Patrick and Nicolas,
Jack Hayward, and Helen Poole

Contents

Acknowledgments

THIS BOOK HAD its beginnings in a doctoral dissertation in the Department of English at Princeton University. Thanks are due to my generous and astute advisers, Michael Goldman and Andrew Ross; I would never have completed the first draft of this book without Michael's profound knowledge of theatrical history and televisual techniques and his enthusiasm for Erica's latest, or Andrew's penetration into lesser-known fandoms and reassuring disdain for conventional projects.

For assistance in completing the research for this book, I am indebted to many sources. Princeton University enabled a year's dissertation research in London under the auspices of a Hyde Fellowship. The College of Wooster has been unfailingly generous in its research funding, providing a medley of Luce Awards, faculty development funding, and a Ralston Endowment Grant to permit me to travel to London, Berkeley, New York, and Columbus to work in a wide range of archives; I would particularly like to thank Susan Figge, Henry Copeland, Stan Hales, and Hayden Schilling for their support and generosity. Thanks to the numerous Newells and to Deb Laney and Michael Casserly in London for their serial hospitality. And finally, I could never have become a soap addict in any meaningful sense of the word without Dan Vigneron, John Hayward, and Helen Hayward, who provided the technology.

David Parker, curator of the Dickens House Museum, was enormously helpful and generous with his time; Andrew Xavier also deserves thanks for his help in locating and reproducing images of Dickens. Thanks to curators, librarians, and staff of the Victoria and Albert Museum and the Colindale Newspaper Library in London, the New York Public Library, and Firestone Library at Princeton University for sharing their knowledge of nineteenth-century serials and newspapers and their collections. Particular thanks are due to Lucy Caswell, curator of the Milton Caniff Archives at Ohio State University, Columbus, for steering me through the riches of her archives. Trina Robbins and Bill Blackbeard shared their homes, comic-strip collections, and unequaled knowledge of comic-strip history, while Dale Messick, creator of *Brenda Starr,* was generous enough to grant an interview. Many denizens of the New York soap world offered humorous and informed perspectives on soap opera production; I owe thanks especially to Jean Passanante, now head writer for ABC's *One Life to Live,* for *almost* landing me a job with the show and for the information she shared; to writer Kathleen Klein and directors Kiersten Sanderson, Joshua White, and Jon Merdin for their insights and expertise; to ABC photographer Ann Limongello for locating and reproducing the photographs I needed; and to the unnamed and unnamable assistant who waylaid viewer mail for me.

To those—too many to name here—who have contributed to this work by reading drafts or engaging in discussions on serial fiction, I offer sincere thanks. Especial gratitude is due to Lorna Lee, who got me through my undergraduate thesis by introducing me to *All My Children,* and to Sarah Zimmerman, with whom I have collaborated in thinking and writing about serial fiction since that time. The friends who taught me the importance of serial reading communities by involving me in intelligent, informed, and always entertaining discussions about soaps and other serials over the years deserve the credit for inspiring this book; among many others, these include Jenifer Ward, Kiersten Sanderson, Susie Dent, Anna Hayward, Patrick and Patricia Lara, and the wonderfully generous and astute Usenet discussion group rec.arts.tv.soaps. Many colleagues have contributed immeasurably to this project in its various stages by reading drafts and providing exhaustive and incisive responses, or by offering help and guidance at various stages of this project; I am indebted to Jay Dickson, Sarah Zimmerman, Ginger Strand, Ivo Kamp, David Parker, Jeff Nunokawa, Ulrich Knoepflmacher, Joanne Frye, Peter Havholm, Michael Budd, and Kelly Coyle. My research assistants Erica Davis, Ayesha Bell, Kate Youther, and Neil Moore were much appreciated for their enthusiasm as well as their concrete labor. I am deeply grateful to Nancy Grayson Holmes at the University Press of Kentucky for her belief in this slightly odd and at times unsynthesizable project and also for tracking me down, despite language barriers and against all odds, in Santiago, Chile. The errors that remain are, of course, entirely my own.

The little balance I have retained while working on this book I owe to those who have distracted me from it: Nicolas (born somewhere in the middle of the final draft) and Patrick Lara, John, Judith, Suzanne, Sam, and Anna Hayward, the great Shaila, Robert and Chris McGee, Donna Regis, and Maryline and Heidi Hutton. For the love and support, for the letters, calls, visits, dinners, and rollerblades—but most of all for producing the ongoing saga that taught me, before I'd heard of Dickens or *All My Children,* to tune in tomorrow—I thank you all.

An early version of Chapter 3 appeared in *Cultural Critique* (Winter 1992–93).

Introduction

*You'd think a hospital would know what protein is. I ask for protein
and they give me corn flakes. No wonder everybody's sick.*
                                        —*Palmer Cortlandt,* All My Children

IN THE LINES just quoted, soap patriarch Palmer Cortlandt succinctly
argues one side of the continued debate over the function of mass culture.
This rather outdated view asserts that the culture industry (like the hospital
café) supplies its own choice of "food" to the starving masses, ignoring audience needs and opinions completely. Forced to fill up on empty calories, the
viewer consequently suffers (like Palmer's daughter Nina, for whom he seeks
the protein) from diabetes. This inability to control blood sugar levels is a
suggestive metaphor, one echoing arguments that, beginning in the nineteenth century and continuing through our own, castigate producers of mass
culture for force-feeding an empty or even dangerous textual "diet" to a voiceless, passive audience.

In their work on the culture industry, Theodor Adorno and Max Horkheimer anticipate Palmer in arguing that "the culture industry perpetually
cheats its consumers of what it perpetually promises. . . . the diner must be
satisfied with the menu" (139). But it is important to acknowledge the limitations of such metaphors. Serials, like other popular texts, require active
participation on the part of consumers. At the very least, a series of choices
must be made: which serial to read or view, with whom, where, while doing
what. Just as Palmer's legendary impatience leads him to ignore the hospital's
complex nutritional regimen as well as the fact that cornflakes were not his
only choice, so disdain for mass culture both produces and results from
ignorance of the complexity of viewer/text relations.

This study of the serial genre as it has developed across time and technologies is intended to increase understanding of these relations. Since the
inception of mass-market culture in the nineteenth century, producers have
relied on the serial form to consolidate and hold a mass audience, thus enabling the profits that make new technologies (cheap mass-produced books,

color printing in newspapers, film, radio, television) viable in a market economy. The advantages of the form for producers are obvious: it essentially advertises itself, providing ever-increasing profits. Charles Dickens perhaps captured the unique attributes of the serial best when he assured his readers, in the conclusion to part 10 of the *Pickwick Papers*, that "we shall keep perpetually going on beginning again, regularly." The complex temporal involutions of this sentence parallel serialization's complex author/audience relations. The choice of subject, "we" rather than "I," reflects the intimate relation of serial readers with their texts. "Perpetually," splitting the verb from its double gerund, stresses the time- and loss-denying temporality of serials as do the gerunds themselves—"going on" enforcing continuity, "beginning again" the eternal rebirth of the serial, and their doubling signaling the inexhaustibility of the text, its celebration of excess. Finally, "regularly" appends, as if in afterthought; in fact it is perhaps the most essential signifier in the statement, since it offers a crucial reassurance. Habit, as any serial producer knows, is perhaps the most important factor in holding an audience.

Roger Hagedorn has theorized, in his article "Technology and Economic Exploitation: The Serial as a Form of Narrative Presentation," that "since the nineteenth century the serial has been a dominant mode of narrative presentation in Western culture—if not in fact the dominant mode" (5). The role of the serial in the last two centuries, Hagedorn argues further, has been that as new media appear, they "have consistently turned to the serial form of narrative presentation precisely in order to cultivate a dependable audience of consumers." Each of the texts in this study supports Hagedorn's point: serialized novels, comic strips, and soap operas all appeared at or near the inception of their respective medium, and all were used explicitly to increase its consumption. Using the serial in this way makes excellent economic sense from a capitalist point of view: "testing" a target audience with a few episodes of a new serial allows producers to expend relatively small amounts of capital and raw materials while gaining large profits from mass sales.

On the other hand, such an argument allows little room for the audience. In Hagedorn's model, serial readers become simply a captive audience passively lured to a form suited to a society that "perpetually defers desire in order to promote continued consumption"; the serial thus "emerges as an ideal form of narrative presentation under capitalism" (12). Although this account is entirely accurate as far as it goes, it silences half of the story. There is no space here for the very real pleasures and satisfactions of audiences; the practices surrounding consumption of serial texts; the functions such texts may serve for the individual and for the community. All of these deserve attention, and the central focus of this study is an investigation of the ways serial audiences use their texts and the processes of collaborative interpretation, prediction, metacommentary, and creation that engage them.

Hagedorn's short article provides compelling though incipient formulations for linking production context and the serial form; however, the only study that treats serials and audiences with the complexity they deserve is Linda K. Hughes and Michael Lund's *The Victorian Serial*. No recent full-length study links reincarnations of the serial across time and technology, a strange absence given that the genre's mass appeal has been repeatedly confirmed since Dickens's *Pickwick Papers* mobilized a mass market for fiction in 1836. The lure of stories told part by part has been known since Scheherazade, but serialization took on new importance after industrialization made mass marketing of fiction possible. Proving itself immensely effective as a means of catching and keeping audiences, serialization was adapted for other fictional genres and eventually crossed media boundaries. Just a few examples are the part-issued domestic novels, mysteries, and detective fiction of the nineteenth century; the comic strips, "chapter-plays" or serialized silent films, and radio mysteries of the early twentieth; and the soap operas, movie series, part-issued novels (most recently Stephen King's best-selling six-part *Green Mile*, with its introductory homage to Dickens), television miniseries, MTV "real world" series, interactive on-line soaps, and AT&T and Taster's Choice television ads of the contemporary scene. By turning commercials into serial episodes, producers of the last two examples highlight a crucial connection between economics and serialization. For producers, the advantage of serialization is that it essentially creates the demand it then feeds: the desire to find out "what happens next" can only be satisfied by buying, listening to, or viewing the next installment. And as discussed throughout this study, methods of maximizing serial profits have been progressively refined as industrial capitalism developed.

Even from this brief survey of serial incarnations, it will be clear that in addition to the common cultural practices of audiences there are certain properties peculiar to serials, whether in prose, cartoon, television, or any other medium. A serial is, by definition, an ongoing narrative released in successive parts. In addition to these defining qualities, serial narratives share elements that might be termed, after Wittgenstein, "family resemblances." These include refusal of closure; intertwined subplots; large casts of characters (incorporating a diverse range of age, gender, class, and, increasingly, race representation to attract a similarly diverse audience); interaction with current political, social, or cultural issues; dependence on profit; and acknowledgment of audience response (this has become increasingly explicit, even institutionalized within the form, over time).

The texts treated in this study have been chosen, with great difficulty and to the exclusion of numberless equally important serial subspecies and texts, for two reasons: each is important in the history of serial development, and crucial evidence of audience response to each has been preserved. The texts are Charles Dickens's novel *Our Mutual Friend* (1864-65), Milton Caniff's newspaper comic strip *Terry and the Pirates* (1934-46), and the soap operas *All My Children* (1970—) and *One Life to Live* (1968—). All clearly manifest the formal characteristics and family resemblances outlined above. All, of course, postpone narrative resolution, for increasing numbers of years as the genre develops; the soap opera might be called the apotheosis of the form in that the text predicates itself on the impossibility of closure. All intertwine multiple subplots (often derived from subgenres as different as romance, adventure, mystery, and crime, again to attract wide audiences). All feature large casts of characters, of seventy or more depending on the serial's scope and duration. All incorporate current social issues, for example the Poor Laws, class displacement, and alcoholism for Dickens; the Sino-Japanese conflict and the US entry into World War II for *Terry*; and AIDS, adoption laws, environmentalism, abortion, and so on for the soap operas. All incorporate audience response in ways increasingly institutionalized within the production process.

As we shall see, these formal qualities tend to encourage particular ways of reading. Intertwined subplots work to unite disparate characters, overcoming differences of class, race, and gender and forging communities within the text that echo the reading communities outside it. Dramatic plot reversals retrospectively rewrite months of narrative, forcing audiences to acknowledge that all perspectives are partial, colored by place and context, and that we must seek knowledge of all points of view before making judgments. Serials also share distinctive (and much derided) narrative tropes: sudden returns from the dead, doubles, long-lost relatives, marginal or grotesque characters, fatal illness, dramatic accidents, romantic triangles, grim secrets, dramatic character transformations. But as will be obvious, none of these are unique to serial fiction; they have roots going back to Greek tragedy and the Homeric epic, among other genres, and recur throughout literary history. The genre is not constituted, then, by purely formal and thematic considerations. Rather, these considerations are inseparable from the unique reading practices and interpretative tactics developed by audiences, practices that include collaborative, active reading; interpretation; prediction; occasional rewriting or creation of new subplots; attempts to influence textual production; and, increasingly often, a degree of success in those attempts.

Because I focus on the (generally neglected) issue of audience and on the serial genre across a wide span of time and space, I am forced to give short shrift to other, equally important issues of serialization: the mechanics of writing against time and to fill a fixed amount of space, the additions and deletions made in consequence of this constraint, the creative and economic pressures on serial authors, the complex negotiations between serial authors and their publishers, and the ways texts are shaped as a result of the serial mode of production. Unlike the questions addressed in the present study, however, these issues have already received considerable attention from scholars of nineteenth-century literature in particular. Readers interested in questions of form and authorship as influenced by serial production will do well to consult the numerous excellent studies of serial composition already available; these include the classic general investigations such as John Sutherland's *Victorian Novelists and Publishers*, J. Don Vann's *Victorian Novels in Serial*, and Norman N. Feltes's *Modes of Production of Victorian Novels*, as well as single-author investigations such as Kathleen Tillotson and John Butt's *Dickens at Work*, Robert Patten's *Charles Dickens and his Publishers*, Edgar Harden's *The Emergence of Thackeray's Serial Fiction*, and Mary Hamer's *Writing by Numbers: Trollope's Serial Fiction*.

Throughout this study, I will emphasize the continuity, across immense differences of cultural context and media, of audience interaction with serial fictions. In their otherwise invaluable contextualization of the reading of Victorian serials, Linda K. Hughes and Michael Lund comment that "we no longer live in the age of the literary serial" (14). This is true only if we feel compelled to emphasize the adjective here. True, the function of literature for nineteenth-century society—as social cement, as focus of discourse—is no longer fulfilled by printed texts. But literature has been replaced by television and to some extent film. In their final section on the value of teaching nineteenth-century texts serially (which, they point out, helps forge reading communities in the classroom, among many other advantages), Hughes and Lund do briefly acknowledge that the "literary serial" has been replaced in the twentieth century by soap operas, movie sequels, and so on, but then virtually dismiss these forms by noting, "Although we would not want to champion all the movie and radio serials in the first half of this century, or the television soap operas, series, miniseries and sequels of the second half, such popular entertainment has prepared students to engage more significant works of literature as serials" (277). Although reimagining the twentieth-century popular serial as mere preparation for reading "real" (literary) serials is an interesting approach, it is not a particularly useful one. Like many academics, Hughes and Lund seem to have allowed their relative ignorance of such popular texts to blind them to any "significance" that may exist. In this they echo only too closely the one-hundred-and-sixty-odd-year history of critical denigration of serial fiction—a history they elucidate brilliantly in their defense of the Victorian serial, making this critical myopia more than usually surprising.

Before turning to investigate serial audiences, a brief history of this critical response will be useful. Although Frankfurt School theorists such as

Adorno and Horkheimer are perhaps the most notorious critics of the culture industry, they are hardly unique in their anxiety over the potentially coercive or mind-numbing effects of mass culture on its audience. Since its inception in the nineteenth century, serialized fiction—like most mass culture—has been assumed to control its audience in insidious and dangerous ways, and has therefore been viewed with suspicion, disdain, and even fear; such reactions become common threads linking denunciations impelled by very different historical, cultural, and political motivations. An early example is this sermon delivered at Rugby chapel in November 1837 (during the run of the wildly popular *The Pickwick Papers*), in which Thomas Arnold warns his boys against the evil influence of their new obsession:

> The works of amusement published only a very few years since were comparatively few in number; they were less exciting, and therefore less attractive; they were dearer, and therefore less accessible; and, not being published periodically, they did not occupy the mind for so long a time, nor keep alive so constant an expectation; nor, by this dwelling upon the mind, and distilling themselves into it, as it were, drop by drop, did they possess it so largely, colouring in many instances, its very language and affording frequent matter for conversation. . . . Great and grievous as is the evil, it is peculiarly hard to find the remedy for it. . . . they are not wicked books for the most part; they are of that class which cannot actually be prohibited; nor can it be pretended that there is sin in reading them. They are not the more wicked for being published so cheap, and at regular intervals; but yet these two circumstances make them so peculiarly injurious.[1]

For Arnold, reading in its serial manifestation is explicitly compared to a laudanum-like drug, one distilled drop by drop into the brain. It is this slow, steady, addictive process of textual progression, not the reading itself, which is perceived as particularly insidious. Clearly, the doctor would indeed ban these books if he could.[2]

In spite of the disdain with which novels were initially greeted, the nineteenth century has been retrospectively mythologized as a time of near-idyllic union of high and low culture. Dickens, among other popular artists, has been perceived as both epitomizing and shattering this perfect moment. Q.D. Leavis, in her *Fiction and the Reading Public*, takes the latter view, attributing the genesis of a cultural falling off to the fact that "the new kind of fiction flourished because it was written for a new, naive public, not that of the old circulating libraries or that could afford to buy Scott but for the shopkeeper and the working man. . . .It is being catered for by a new kind of novelist. The peculiarity of Dickens, as any one who runs a critical eye over a novel or two of his can see, is that his originality is confined to recapturing a child's outlook on the grown-up world, emotionally he is not only uneducated but also immature" (156). Here the mass audience becomes equated not with women as it does so often (as Andreas Huyssens, among many others, has demonstrated) but with the undereducated and immature. This argument is particularly difficult to challenge since Leavis has set it up in such a way that anyone who disagrees becomes one without a "critical eye"—and uneducated and immature to boot.

Arnold's terror of the addictive effects of serial fiction reasserts itself, only slightly transformed, among intellectuals and cultural critics of the twentieth century, most notably with the Frankfurt School's reaction to mass fiction but also with the Italian Marxist Antonio Gramsci, who saw peril in serial novels' sheer proliferation as well as in their possible effects on readers. Ironically Gramsci, whose focus on lived cultural practices and the hegemonic process is a crucial forerunner of contemporary cultural studies, was strongly critical of the serial novel. Gramsci admits that early nineteenth-century serializers such as Eugene Sue, Alexandre Dumas, and George Sand still produced "literature"; presumably Dickens also would have been included in this select group. But he sees serial quality as declining over the course of the century, until by the 1900s, when the "modern serial novel begins," it "nearly always has a most banal form and a stupid content. . . .Now it is a lachrymose literature only suitable for stupefying the women, girls and youngsters who feed on it. It is also often a source of corruption. . . .It may perhaps have influenced the increase in crime among adolescent loafers. . . .In short, the serial novel has become a rather nauseating commodity (36)." [3]

Again we see the serial audience equated with both femininity and immaturity, and the texts themselves with pernicious social influences. But Gramsci implicitly attributes the decline in serial standards to the novels' mode of production, rather than to the mode of consumption that seemed to terrify Arnold, claiming (though without references or examples) that "the great majority of its suppliers no longer write their own works. They distribute 'plots' to the poor devils who have to extract an infinite number of chapters from them." This process, resembling production-line manufacture of fiction, seems especially suspect to Gramsci because it manifests the absence of the creative *individual*, the modernist artist working in isolation. And he goes on to assign responsibility for this decline across the entire cultural apparatus: to the audience, "which often has abominable tastes"; to "the authors, who for speculation open shops for novels as one would open a haberdasher's"; and to "the newspaper editors, full of prejudices and eager to sell their papers at any cost." Gramsci's solution to this shift in fiction production is a fascinating one. He proposes to convince talented young authors, presumably writing "mediocre and self-styled literary novels" in garrets like caricatures of alienated modernists, to produce popular novels instead. And to enable this result, Gramsci (having just thoroughly panned the form) urges that the prejudice against serials be done away with since "this prejudice has consigned the people, who are not always in a position to control the situation, into the hands of speculators whose activity corrupts" (36).

The goals here are essential: Gramsci intends to map popular taste, relate mode of production to content produced, and explore relations between dominant and subaltern cultural forms in dynamic terms as they act upon each other historically, thereby shedding light on new possibilities for the manufacture and function of culture. His understanding of the complex and reciprocal influences of author, audience and producer accords well with his development of hegemony as shaped by both subordinant and dominant groups. However, the ultimate directive is disturbing. Rather than find out directly from readers of this "nauseating commodity" what pleasures or uses they derive from it, Gramsci draws on his own disgust to assume that an undifferentiated "people" simply have "abominable tastes." His solution to the problem he has himself created is in some senses a progressive but in others a reactionary one: he seeks to synthesize cultural dichotomies by proposing that those who still hold to modernism's neoromantic ideal of the struggling, misunderstood, and unpopular artist should be trained to produce a (presumably transformative?) new type of serial for the masses. Although this solution might get authors out of their garrets, it leaves audiences right where they started: as passive victims, forced by the invisible process of hegemonic "secured consent" to consume products developed for them by a dominant culture. But as Raymond Williams (1977) points out in discussing Gramsci's theory of hegemony, however thoroughly a dominant system of "lived identities and relationships" (110) may work itself into our lives, it can never be all encompassing. He stresses that *"no mode of production and therefore no dominant social order and therefore no dominant culture ever in reality includes or exhausts all human practice, human energy, and human intention"* (125, author's emphasis). Therefore, "the full range of human practice" finds expression in other forms of culture outside the dominant: what Williams has described as residual and emergent forms. This book will explore one aspect of emergent culture: the resistant readings of audiences of mass culture, and the effect of these readings on producers of texts.

Gramsci's fears are echoed by a very different kind of critic in 1950s America—this time without any desire to transform the mode of production of mass culture but rather with the goal of censoring it out of existence. Comic censorship was, of course, only one aspect of the wider Cold War policing of the culture industry. In fact, comics scholar Thomas Inge has dubbed its leading crusader, Dr. Fredric Wertham (whose *Seduction of the Innocent* was published in 1953), "the 'Joe McCarthy' of the comic book purge" (117-18). In the second chapter of this book, I discuss the crusade against comics led by Wertham but espoused by parents, educators, psychologists, and other "authorities" newly concerned about the effects of mass media on audiences. Morality campaigns insisting on the evil effects of comics lobbied publishers as well as local and national governments; in Britain, anticomic activism eventually led to an act of Parliament making publication or distribution of (often U.S. produced and distributed) "horror comics" illegal. In the United States, the movement spearheaded by Wertham sought similar legislation. Having already succeeded in forcing newspaper strips to stifle experimentation lest they be censored, the movement next turned to comic books and was successful to the extent that twenty-four of the twenty-nine extant crime-comic publishers folded, while ethnic images simply disappeared from the strips (Hardy and Stern, 9).

More recently, soap operas have been derided as a mindless and archetypal "female" narrative form; and disturbingly, even feminist studies of soaps and other "women's genres" have contributed to this disdain. Tania Modleski's *Loving with a Vengeance: Mass-Produced Fantasies for Women* provides perhaps the clearest example of the extent to which our desire, as academic feminists, to move beyond isolating theorization to achieve real social change can produce a paradoxical inability to respect the "objects" of our efforts, in this case female consumers of mass culture. After acknowledging that soap operas address real social needs (for community, among other things), Modleski closes her third chapter, "The Search for Tomorrow in Today's Soap Operas," with a call for action: "As feminists, we have a responsibility to devise ways of meeting these needs that are more creative, honest, and interesting than the ones mass culture has supplied. Otherwise, the search for tomorrow threatens to go on, endlessly." (108). And similar directives are articulated in Janice Radway's *Reading the Romance: Women, Patriarchy, and Popular Literature*, in other ways an enormously valuable text that spearheaded the movement toward ethnographies of mass-cultural consumers. Toward the end of the book, Radway sounds *her* call for action, but in so doing she distances academic feminists from romance readers, stating, for example, that "I think we as feminists might help this change [in patriarchal power relations] along by first learning to recognize that romance reading originates in very real dissatisfaction and embodies a valid, if limited, protest" (220). The major difficulty in otherwise exemplary early studies such as Modleski's or Radway's is their assumption of greater insight than can be justified into the reasons underlying consumption of mass texts. Before drawing conclusions, we must learn from audiences themselves how they use their texts—what contexts they read or watch in; how they themselves perceive the connection of content, subject matter, characters, or visual techniques to the meanings they come away with. Perhaps even more crucially, we must listen carefully to their responses rather than theorizing about what these readers "really" need. Much more work is needed on both the process and results of ethnographies of readers before we can pretend to determine what texts mean, ideologically or psychologically, to audiences whose specific practices we do not yet understand. Here I align myself with critics such as Lynn Spigel (1985), who in her critique of Modleski suggests a focus on how meaning is "produced in the reading process" rather than existing *a priori*. Spigel also insists on careful attention to the relations between culture and economics, so that rather than demonizing an all-powerful media as creating vacuous, helpless subjects in its own image, we see that hegemony can cut both ways, asking ourselves "how mass culture reacts to (as well as contributes to) the social and historical construction of femininity"— or masculinity or class or race (225, 228).

Radway herself acknowledges problems in her earlier formulation of reading practices in the introduction to the second edition of *Reading the Romance*. She explains that in the course of this project she learned the truth of Clifford Geertz's assertion that all ethnography is subjective. She acknowledges serious problems in her earlier tendency to see her own views as objectively constructed: "I now think that my initial preoccupation with the empiricist claims of social science prevented me from recognizing fully that even what I took to be simple descriptions of my interviewees' self-understandings were mediated if not produced by my own conceptual constructs and ways of seeing the world. . . .Were I writing *Reading the Romance* today, I would differentiate much more clearly between the remarks actually made by my respondents and my own observations about them" (5).

Radway's realization of the bias in her work parallels a recent shift in mass-cultural studies. In the last two decades, critics working to reverse both the long-standing rejection of mass culture and the more insidious rejections of audience agency such as those cited above have sought, in various ways, to assert the relative autonomy of the consumer and to break down hierarchies of high and low culture. Bourdieu's work on taste and cultural capital (1979) has influenced many; for example, in *Textual Poachers: Television Fans and Participatory Culture,* Henry Jenkins draws on Bourdieu's theory of the *habitus* (a cultural milieu produced by education, social context, and hierarchies of taste) to contextualize fan culture, revealing fan activity as impelled not by mindless obsession but by a very different relation to culture and to texts than that legitimized by the conventional middle-class privileging of aesthetic distance. What is more, the cultural capital possessed by fans of mass culture can make their standards and judgments incomprehensible to those not possessing such knowledge. Arguing that fan culture disrupts the boundaries between high and low, causing anxiety to those whose interests are served by the careful maintenance of these borders, Jenkins discusses the vocabulary of fan discourse: "Fans speak of 'artists' where others can see only commercial hacks, of transcendent meanings where others find only banalities, of 'quality and innovation' where others see only formula and convention. . . .Such an account requires not simply an acknowledgment of the superior qualities of a desired text but also a public rejection of the low standards of the 'silly and childish offerings' that fall outside of the fan canon" (17-18).

Jenkins gives these and other fan attitudes and practices as examples of "fans' resistance to the cultural hierarchy" (18). However, as his use of terms like "superior," "rejection," "low standards," and "canon" makes clear, some of the fans he cites tend, not surprisingly, to reproduce cultural hierarchies. For instance, one fan dismisses all but his own favorite TV series as "mediocre" because of "poor writing, ridiculous conflicts offering no moral or ethical choices, predictable characterization, and a general lack of attention to creativity and chance-taking" (17). The terms, the intent, and even the strategy of this fan are the same as those used by defenders of high culture: to set the chosen text over against a mass of undifferentiated, inferior texts by demonstrating its *uniqueness*, its *artistic value*, its status as *masterpiece*.

What we have here, in short, is another example of attempting to dismantle the master's house by borrowing the master's tools. This approach is perhaps necessary or even unavoidable at a certain stage of the construction process. But at a later stage—if we truly want to build a new and different house—we need to find new tools, new terms of discourse. Rather than select our favorite mass texts and argue that they are exemplary, setting them above other such texts as unique paragons of "good taste" to prove them worthy in spite of their mode of production, we could focus on other qualities. We might try to see differences between types of texts as exactly that: a matter of differences of form, content, and intended function. One way to escape the need, so central to the habitus of academics, to evaluate and then canonize particular texts is to focus on function rather than "quality": what do such texts *do* for their readers, what purpose do they serve in readers' lives, what kinds of thought processes, discussions, activities, and meanings do they enable? Of course there are differences between mass-cultural texts: some are more formulaic than others, some more complex, some more innovative. But in this study, I will attempt to resist the urge toward purely aesthetic assessment, instead reading serial fictions' artistic innovations as inseparable from their status as commodity. Creators' innovations, artistic power, and complexity work to increase the texts' value for audiences and arise not in spite of the pressure to catch and keep a mass audience but in many cases as a result of that pressure. As we will see, serial fans contribute to the shaping of their narratives, and creators attest to the creative inspiration this interaction can provide; on the other hand, creators also have the power to resist fan pressure and often do resist to keep texts from becoming too predictable and thus lessen their ability to intrigue and involve their audiences.

This study has its roots in my own fifteen-year involvement with the soap opera *All My Children,* and my consequent desire to understand the peculiar relation between serial audiences and their texts. Throughout the book, then, I attempt to walk the line between fan and critic. Of course, there are dangers here: the too-great subjectivity produced by one's own fandom, the temptation to celebrate the oft-maligned subject of study. On the one hand, it is crucial to acknowledge that positioning oneself as a fan does not necessarily produce an "authentic" view of fan culture. This study, for example, is marked not only by academic privilege and official—rather than popular—cultural capital (a distinction made by Fiske 1992), but more crucially by the necessarily slanted interest with which the study itself has invested my fandom. On the other hand, I share many pleasures with all fans: collaborative interpretation, prediction, suspense, delight in or loathing of particular storylines or characters. I also share a powerful goal with many fans: to work toward increasingly interactive media by proving that mass-cultural consumers *can* have a voice and that mass-cultural producers can in fact enhance their profits by acknowledging the desires of their audiences.

In the last few years, a number of critics—Janice Radway, Constance Penley, Andrew Ross, Henry Jenkins, and Martha Nochimson among them—have begun to break through the limitations of critical distance by acknowledging the agency of consumers and granting serious attention to the ways audiences use texts in their daily lives. In addition, these critics approach fandom either from within—removing the distance implied in the word "critic" by subjecting their own pleasures (no longer coyly termed "guilty") to investigation—or with respect, approaching consumers of cultural productions ranging from New Age belief systems to soap opera not as objects of analysis but as authorities who can introduce us to their subcultures and teach us the practices involved. Jenkins, for example, cites his "active involvement as a fan within this subcultural community [of television fans] over the past decade and more" (4); and Nochimson has worked as a writer, editor, or consultant for five soap operas (5).

In addition to problematizing the "objectivity" of the critic in relation to her texts, this study works toward a revised concept of the serial genre by arguing that it is the specific cultural practices developed by serial audiences across time and technologies—the "shadow economy" of popular culture that fans create, as Fiske has put it (1992)—that consolidate the serial as a coherent genre despite manifold shifts in technology, mechanics of profit-ability, structure, and content. Recent work by Tzvetan Todorov, Jane Feuer, Robert C. Allen, Steve Neale, and others pressures the limits of genre, extend-ing the term outward to include the expectations and desires of audiences as well as purely formalistic categorizations.[4] Steve Neale's "Questions of Genre" cites Ralph Cohen's arguments for the nineteenth-century origin of the term: "Although the concept is clearly much older, the term itself emerges precisely at the time that popular, mass-produced generic fiction is making its first appearance. . . .at the same time, also, there began to emerge a distinct shift in the value placed on generic literature by 'High Culture' artists and critics" (62-63). As we will see, the controversy surrounding the status of Dickens's work bears out this argument. Given genre's inseparability from the high/ low culture dichotomy, Neale points to the need for research on generic formation and circulation across the media—and specifically on the trans-formations each genre undergoes as it crosses formal boundaries. As he ar-gues elsewhere (1980), the term "genre" became in film theory an often de-rogatory signifier for the supposedly formulaic, unimaginative productions of the mass culture industry, a term set over against "auteurism," which is used to signify a much more creative and imaginative product (9 and passim).

In his study of the fantastic, Todorov departs from earlier structuralist criticism in arguing that what is central to the genre is the state of mind it induces: the fantastic, for example, is characterized by "the hesitation that the reader is invited to experience with regard to the natural or supernatural explanation of the events presented" (24). This view at least partially shifts the focus from formal qualities to the role of the reader (although Todorov, in focusing on an abstract reader, projects responses in problematic ways) which in turn leads Todorov to the useful definition of genre as a "horizon of expectations" functioning to help consumers select from the range of avail-able choices so that, for example, texts marketed serially tend to attract audi-ences who have already enjoyed other serials. Conversely, audience expecta-tions guide producers in the kinds of texts they create and the marketing strategies they employ. Fredric Jameson expands the idea of a horizon of expectations in asserting that genres "are essentially literary *institutions*, or social contracts between a writer and a specific public, whose function is to specify the proper use of a particular cultural artifact" (1981, 106). This position helps to explain producers' consistent and long-term reliance on the serial to popularize new media: audiences greet part-issued texts with a sense of familiarity, which eases the transition. Jameson's argument also im-plies, rightly, that audiences have a role in setting the terms of a social con-tract and acknowledges that they wield some influence over the characteris-tics genres develop or abandon over time.

Genre studies can be enriched by a Marxist-informed criticism emphasizing the cultural context of genres as well as the theories that seek to explicate them, while highlighting the material practices surrounding the consumption and production of texts (Williams 1977, 180-85). On the other hand, Jameson's dialectics leads him to argue that once genres become commodified by the culture industry, the generic social contract is no longer functional, and therefore "authentic" artistry must now struggle against the "brand-name system" produced by institutionalized genres (1981, 107). This argument echoes Walter Benjamin's ambivalence over the loss of the storyteller, a loss only partially compensated by the potentially democratizing effects of mechanical production. "The Storyteller" articulates a compelling nostalgia for lost modes of narrative that seems to haunt even critics who would like to appreciate the possibilities inherent in mass culture. After carefully contextualizing the historical, dialectical progress of the rise of the novel as it interacts with the wane of the storyteller, Benjamin anchors this translation of narrative modes from the oral to the written in their historical, material, and existential circumstances: the rise of an information society, the evolving middle class, the increased incommunicability of experience and emphasis on "the solitary individual" (87). As Jameson notes in his essay "Walter Benjamin; or, Nostalgia," Benjamin sees the storyteller's tale and the novel as opposed "in their social origins (the tale springing from collective life, the novel from middle-class solitude)," in their content (the tale drawing on collective experience, the novel on individual and unique experience), and ultimately in their attitudes toward death (1971, 78).

Leskov, the subject of "The Storyteller," provides the fulcrum to demonstrate the dialectical rollover from craftsperson to manufacturer, art to technology. Like Dickens, who referred to the writing process as "weaving" and was virtually obsessed with retaining an intimate relationship with his mass audience, Leskov is portrayed as a writer seeking to preserve an organic model of storytelling. The dialectic described here is instructive, of course, in its contextualization of writing, a practice often imagined as removed from material concerns. It is perhaps even more interesting in articulating Benjamin's profound ambivalence toward industrialization and the culture industries it produced. In emphasizing the unprecedented material conditions of novel production and consumption, Benjamin focuses on the absolute departure from hearing a story to reading a novel: "A man listening to a story is in the company of the storyteller; even a man reading one shares this companionship. The reader of a novel, however, is isolated, more so than any other reader" (100). He then goes on to compare the desire for novel reading to an out-of-control (and destructive) force of Nature: "In this solitude of his, the reader of a novel seizes upon his material more jealously than anyone else. He is ready to make it completely his own, to devour it, as it were. Indeed, he destroys, he swallows up the material as the fire devours logs in the fireplace. The suspense which permeates the novel is very much like the draft which stimulates the flame in the fireplace and enlivens its play" (100).

Beyond the destructive metaphor chosen to depict the reading process—a metaphor that conveys mourning for a storytelling mode Benjamin sees as lost forever—one aspect of the comparison particularly stands out: the consuming interest fanned by the draft of suspense, its purpose to both postpone and anticipate one's own death by "warming" oneself, as he puts it, with fictional deaths. Benjamin's analysis initially seems to work well in explaining the eventual extension of serial runs from two years to decades: the warming suspense is increased, while the ultimate death—the end of the text itself—is deferred, sometimes forever. On the other hand, exploration of serial readers' relationship to texts, to their producers, and most crucially to fellow readers contradicts both Benjamin's view of novel reading as a destructive and solitary process and Jameson's fear of the "brand-name system" working to harden generic texts into inauthentic, unresponsive commodities.[5] As we will see, serial audiences often emphasize the importance of an interactive, responsive text and of the pleasures of collaborative reading; in this sense, serials actually revert to Benjamin's storytelling paradigm of an interactive interpretative process, one that influences the narrative produced.

The mass serial has undeniably been increasingly commodified since its inception in the nineteenth century, but as Benjamin himself predicted in a more optimistic mood, this process has proved in some ways paradoxically liberating to both audiences and the collaborative creative process. Over the wider span of serial history, built-in means of assessing audience response have become essential components of serial production, and fans have found new ways of communicating with others—through on-line discussion groups, to name just one example—to form interpretative communities. On their side, producers, out of necessity, have increasingly turned to a collaborative productive process, forming creative teams to handle the high volume of serial production, asking audiences for their suggestions to ensure high sales or ratings, and even (in some on-line serials) providing "alternate" episodes for readers not satisfied with the standard episode and easy e-mail buttons for readers to write to characters or forward their ideas directly to creators.

In his recent work on soap opera (1989), Robert Allen strongly emphasizes the role of audiences in defining genres, explaining that "genre theorists have until fairly recently presumed that their classification of the world of literature was also based on features objectively and indisputably existing in the text itself. . .[but] genre describes not so much a group of texts or textual features as it does a dynamic relationship between texts and interpretative

communities" (44). Once regarded as distinct entities to be treated in isolation from each other, text, production, and consumption have become increasingly intertwined, their borders blurred by the realization that, as John
Fiske contends with regard to television, "there is no text, there is no audience, there are only the processes of viewing" (1989, 57). Mass culture does
not exist without its audience, which may subvert, revise, or challenge meanings in ways not intended by producers; and that audience expectations
shift over time and across technologies will become apparent through the
cumulative evidence of this book. My texts provide a case study for recent
testing of the borders of genre, since they reveal ways in which a single
"family" of fictions has mutated while remaining linked by key resemblances
over a wide temporal and cultural span, and offer evidence of the impact
audiences can have on generic development.

   This is not to celebrate serial fiction as a utopian form but simply to
suggest the need to revise long-standing misperceptions of serial audiences
as well as the ways in which its lessons (negotiated as they may be) offer
directions for increasing audience involvement with all forms of mass media. Although Raymond Williams's call, at the end of *Television: Technology
and Cultural Forms,* for decentralization of communications systems—in favor of locally based but internationally linked public-owned television stations, for example—still needs to be realized eighteen years later, a system of
international communities of media audiences, exchanging information and
working together to affect the narratives created by existent networks, has
already developed on the Internet, Prodigy, and other computer networks.
The pleasure and power of these communities are discussed in the last chapter of this study.

For clarity, each of the three chapters to follow opens with an introductory
section establishing the material practices surrounding production and consumption of the serial incarnation under discussion and also locating the
theoretical issues involved in its transmission and reception. The section
beginning the Dickens chapter focuses on the technologies enabling the rise
of mass-produced fiction, as well as on the demographic shifts creating a
mass, middle-class audience. The comic-strip chapter begins by exploring
the role of strips in developing visual techniques concurrent with the incipient film industry as well as in boosting sales for the ruthlessly competitive
American newspaper industry; it also examines the influence of Taylorism
on cultural production. And the soap opera chapter first establishes the rise
of radio and television soaps, the history and stereotypes behind their status
as a "female" narrative form, and the role of recent technologies like VCRs in
influencing both production and consumption of serials. The remainder of

each chapter addresses three subtopics: context (establishing the immediate conditions of production and reception of the specific text under discussion), text (reading a particular novel, comic strip, or soap opera to establish shared serial qualities such as structuring devices and narrative tropes), and audience (providing evidence of audience attitudes toward the text, shared reading and communal interpretation, and audience interaction with the production process). The specific topics addressed within each chapter are briefly described below.

In the London of 1837, just before the first part of *Pickwick* was issued, various factors—notably industrialization and the consequent mass influx to urban centers—combined to produce demand for new forms of leisure activity. At the same time, new technologies in printing coexisted with increased awareness of the potential profits of lowering the cost per unit of published material to increase demand. As the first author to adapt continuing narrative to an industrial-capitalist economy with his runaway success *The Pickwick Papers* in 1836, Dickens played an essential role in developing an entertainment industry and is thus more central for my purposes than other nineteenth-century serializers such as Gaskell, Thackeray, Trollope, and Braddon. Not coincidentally, Milton Caniff and Agnes Nixon, creators of the comic strip and soap operas that form the core of Chapters 2 and 3, acknowledge Dickens as the founder of the mass serial and credit him with developing the techniques on which they rely. Dickens is also one of the form's most active apologists. To cite just one example, he asserted: "that I hold the advantages of the mode of publication to outweigh its disadvantages, may be easily believed of one who revived it in the Pickwick Papers after long disuse, and has pursued it ever since" (postscript to *Our Mutual Friend*, 821). In addition to this primary motivation for choosing Dickens, he has become such an industry that letters, journals, and articles attesting to the influence of readers on his writing process have been saved. These are invaluable in providing evidence of the intersection of artistic and commercial imperatives as well as of the theory and practice of serialization from both producers' and consumers' perspectives.

Of course, quite a lot of work has been done on Dickens as a serial novelist, as well as on the Victorian serial as a narrative form.[6] The author's recurrent references to the warmth of his relationship to his readers and his capitulation to specific readers in altering planned outcomes (the fate of Little Nell, the ending of *Great Expectations*) coincide with tales of readers rowing out to the steamer carrying the "death of Little Nell" installment of *Old Curiosity Shop* and with anecdotes insisting on a community of readers so deep that Dickens was discussed by members of every social class from bootblacks to Queen Victoria, so wide that illiterate factory workers gathered

to have installments read to them. Such legends perpetuate a Dickens mythology. However, the Dickens industry has produced very little in the way
of concrete, extended investigation of the intersections between producer
and consumer. In the first chapter, I focus on Dickens's role in creating a
market for part-issue fiction, examining the discourse surrounding the rise
of his serials and of serial fiction in general. I then investigate one particular
text: *Our Mutual Friend*, chosen because as Dickens's last completed novel it
marks his ultimate inscription of themes and narrative strategies, doubling
of identity for example, which have become peculiarly central to the serial
form. The novel also reveals Dickens's responsiveness to the interests and
demands of his audience as well as to social issues of the time.

In the second chapter, the comic strip takes precedence over other early-
twentieth-century serials such as the magazine novel or the serialized film
because its unique combination of visual and written narrative sets it in sharp
contrast to my other two examples. While the magazine novel is a continuation
of the nineteenth-century serial and the "chapter-plays" can be seen as direct
predecessors to soaps, the newspaper comic strip is unique in technique,
intended function for producers, and response of readers. Milton Caniff was
chosen over his contemporaries for his contributions to the development of
the adventure comic, for the international scope of the strip, and most of all
because Caniff is, as far as I know, exceptional in having saved thousands of
reader letters. These letters are now part of the Caniff archive, an extensive
collection of largely uncatalogued material that also includes original drawings and proofs offering direct evidence of the uses audiences made of the
text and of Caniff's responsiveness to, even reliance on, his readers.

Early comics tended to feature animals or children and were primarily
humorous. Later strips, from the thirties on, became much more "serious"
and dramatic, concerning themselves with romance, adventure plots, or the
efforts of a superhero to right social wrongs. To suit its altered content, comic-
strip art changed from impressionistic fantasy to a realistic "documentary" style.
Paralleling this stylistic development, comic narrative changed from one-
frame situation cartoons (in the eighteenth-century sense) to continued narratives experimenting with the point-of-view shots and angles of vision also
under development in the incipient film industry. By 1934, when *Terry* began, comic-strip art had shifted from the highly individual creation of a single
artist to a streamlined assembly-line process involving a writer, artist, outliner,
inker, colorist, and dialogue writer. The demands of the form required this
production process since no one person could consistently produce the strip
a day that audiences demanded in order to maintain their interest.

The heterogeneity of Caniff's audience is also of interest for this study.
Because soap operas have become the paradigmatic serial in the public mind,
the genre is often perceived as essentially female, and many critical studies

have only reinforced that view by ignoring other, male-centered serials such as comic strips. In this context, the Dickens chapter will usefully be born in mind as exposing the lack of gender essentialism in the serial form; we know from contemporary journals and letters, as well as from reviews and sheer volume of sales, that both men and women read Dickens in apparently equal numbers. The lack of gender bias in the first mass serializer contrasts with the gradual (market-driven) gendering of later serialized fictions. Adventure comics were often targeted for adolescent males and are widely perceived as a "male" narrative form, while soap operas were first created for a female audience and are still perceived as women's shows. These stereotypes can and should be challenged, however. The producer of *Terry* explicitly insisted that Caniff include a range of characters to appeal to both genders and to a range of ages. In a sample of 10,147 Caniff fan letters, 31 percent were from females (Morrison, 29-34); similarly, one-third of the soap audience is now male.

In the third chapter, I assess the increasing role of audience activity in shaping television soap operas. The soap serves as my final example because it has become the epitome, in the public mind, of the serial. The shows *All My Children* and *One Life to Live* were chosen because of my own long history with them and their extraordinarily active and long-term fans. What is more, Agnes Nixon, who created both shows, is known for her commitment to exploring ground-breaking social issues. Originally created to capture the middle-class female consumer sought by soap and food manufacturers, soaps now attract a much wider audience: a recent estimate counts 60 million soap viewers per week.[7] By 1981, the weekly profits of a single show, *General Hospital*, were over 1 million, and net yearly profits across the networks amounted to over $700 million.[8] These profits are generated by a medium whose costs per episode are one-fifth those of prime-time, and they have led directly to soaps' improved image in recent years. New demographics have also changed production strategies since audiences are now estimated at 30 percent male and 20 percent black (to name just two of the populations not traditionally targeted as soap viewers). Shifts in gender roles, race, and sexual preference as well as in content, pacing, and even visual style of shows all directly reflect network awareness of the increasing diversity of soap audiences. As a form originally produced for a female audience, the "femininity" of the soap audience and the valuelessness of the product have long been a critical cliché. However, the fact that soap production is also historically female-dominated tends to be ignored, and the influence of female producers and creators will be discussed in Chapter 3.

Each of these chapters participates in ongoing reconstruction of genre theory by tracing the cultural history of a particular form and the material contexts of its production. Each also assesses audience contribution to genre formation by specifying the practices surrounding consumption of serial texts: how they are read, used, and interpreted; whether audiences feel investment in or control over texts, and if so, how much; and whether audiences have any say in the ways texts represent social issues.

In addition to these intertwined fields of focus, a more slippery—but perhaps even more crucial—area of questioning underlies this study: that of technologies of representation. Fiction that continually seeks to enlarge its own audience, "to grow by what it feeds on," must by virtue of its own imperatives incorporate those Others whom most cultural representations elide. Because of their long runs and large casts of characters, serials can and do include more representation of marginalized figures than most fictions. This fact has been true since Dickens's time, but in the late twentieth century the quantity and tenor of such representations changed markedly, most notably since Nielsen and other ratings systems prompted producers to attend to the specific demographics of their audience. Serial history inscribes a narrative of the absence, stereotypical inclusion, and gradual visibility of populations marginalized by race, class, gender, and sexual preference. Thematically, then, this study reveals historical transitions in identity politics within cultural productions; it exposes ways in which others are first elided, then silenced, and finally included (to some extent) in continuing mass-produced texts.

Audiences' social practices play an important role in helping to produce the narratives picked up and then naturalized by the mass media. To complete the circle, serial fictions, as mass-produced texts reaching audiences that in some cases number as high as one-fourth of a nation's population, in turn work to shape the social practices of their audiences. The trajectory of serial development reveals, for producers, ever more rationalized and segmented production processes as outputs increase; and for consumers, steadily rising confidence that their preferences will be listened to, coupled with a contradictory decreasing sureness about who exactly is in control of production and thus of responding to their desires. But producers now work actively to determine audience desire, by means of focus groups, quantification and analysis of viewer mail, and other strategies. Serialization's persistent tracking of audience response marks one of its most compelling characteristics. Because of their continued accountability to consumers, serials may offer cultural models for material transformation—models that come not from the directives of academic critics, not from marginal pockets of cultural resistance, but from within mass culture itself as a result of the influence of fans' voices over time. By engaging with the history of serial production, then, we join the process of creating a past that allows a viable future. It is time to stop mourning a lost authenticity and start acknowledging—and working to increase—the real power that audiences can have over mass culture.

1

Mutual Friends
The Development of the Mass Serial

Please, Sir, can I have some more?
    —*Dickens,* Oliver Twist

The appearance of a new tale by Mr. Dickens is an event of too great importance in the literary world—that part of it, at least, which indulges in fiction—to be passed over without comment . . . This part is, however, doubtless, by this time in the hands of thousands of delighted readers, and thousands more of eager applicants and candidates are pressing to secure its next perusal. We will not unfairly interfere with their pleasure by giving the slightest insight into the nature of the mysteries wherewith the wizard is at present dealing. We will not even recommend its perusal, as everybody who reads a novel at all is sure to read this without recommendation, and as soon as he can lay his hands upon it. [London Sunday Times, May 8, 1864]

As IS OBVIOUS from this review of *Our Mutual Friend*, popular serial novels became phenomena on the level of the O.J. Simpson trial or the first heady season of *Twin Peaks*. The sheer volume of discourse surrounding such fiction, which mobilized suspense and desire in highly profitable ways, enabled it to change the shape of the novel while creating a new genre that persists across time and technology to the present.

Like later serials, the novel in parts appeared just when a new technology needed to consolidate a mass audience in order to prove its viability. Although the narrative advantages of telling stories over a period of time have been known since storytelling began, the economic advantages became apparent in the 1720s and 1730s, when histories, encyclopedias, the Bible, and similar texts were sold in penny and twopenny parts, and sales boomed in consequence.[1] But "boomed" in an eighteenth-century context means little when compared with sales of later serials. The printing, papermaking, and distribution technologies necessary for cheap mass runs had not yet been invented, and low literacy rates and the concentration of the population in rural rather than urban environments precluded an audience larger than a few thousand per serial run.[2] In the early nineteenth century, urbanization, higher literacy, and the concept of leisure led to increased demand for reading matter; industrialization made possible a proliferation of consumer goods at lower prices; and transportation technologies, rapidly growing networks of shops (even in small towns), and the growth of advertising permitted the dispersal of these goods throughout the nation and abroad. But mass audiences somehow managed to ignore the page-turning potential of Harriet Martineau's *Illustrations of Political Economy* (1832–34) and similar serialized works. The market was clearly ripe for a new attraction. Seeing the possibility of greatly increased sales, publishers began to take an active role in the creation of books, commissioning authors and artists to produce a particular nexus of plot, character, and image to satisfy perceived demand.[3] Dickens's *The Pickwick Papers*, commissioned by the publishers Chapman and Hall, will serve to illustrate changes in the production context of fiction.

Stephen Marcus has called Dickens "the first capitalist of literature" in the sense that he worked within apparently adverse conditions to take advantage of new technologies and markets, creating, in effect, an entirely new role for fiction.[4] In *Charles Dickens and His Publishers*, Robert Patten quotes Oscar Dystel (president and chief executive of Bantam Paperbacks) on the three "key factors" in his development of a successful paperback line: availability of new material, introduction of the rubber plate rotary press, and development of magazine wholesalers as a distribution arm. As Patten points out, parallel factors operated in the Victorian era: a plethora of writers, new technologies, and expanded distribution. And as methods of papermaking, printing, and platemaking increased in efficiency, so did means of transportation. By 1836, a crucial network of wholesale book outlets in the Strand, peddlers, provincial shops, and the royal mail—made possible by the development of paved roads, fast coaches, and eventually the national railway system—had been consolidated. The final task facing early publishers was, then, to develop the newly accessible market for their commodity. By lowering prices, emphasizing illustrations and sensational elements, and increasing variety of both form and content, publishers created readers within the largest demographic groups: the rising middle and working classes, where readers had essentially not existed before.[5]

When Chapman and Hall commissioned a series of sporting stories to accompany sketches by the popular illustrator Robert Seymour, they launched the first true mass-market serial and thus changed the concept of serialization, making it the primary form of publication for the next fifty years.[6] The first number of the serial fell flat, selling only four hundred parts, perhaps owing to the relative anonymity of its author (at the time, Dickens was twenty-four and known only for his "Sketches by Boz" series). After number 2, the overworked Seymour committed suicide. This event was fortuitous for Dickens (who has since been accused, a little unreasonably, of having impelled the suicide by demanding changes in a sketch) since it left him in virtual control of the project.[7] A new illustrator, R.W. Buss, was quickly hired to complete number 3. Buss's drawings were disastrous, Dickens defiant, profits nonexistent. Given this dismal scenario, many publishers might have cut their losses by abandoning the project. Chapman and Hall instead forced Dickens to accept a reduced rate of 10 shillings per installment and prefaced the third number as follows:

> We announced in our last, that the ensuing Numbers of the Pickwick Papers, would appear in an improved form: and we now beg to call the attention of our readers to the fulfillment of our promise.
>
> Acting upon a suggestion which has been made to them from various influential quarters, the Publishers have determined to increase the quantity of Letter Press in every monthly part, and to diminish the number of Plates. It will be seen that the present number contains eight additional pages of closely-printed matter, and two engravings on steel, from designs by Mr. Buss—a gentleman already well known to the Public, as a very humorous and talented artist.
>
> This alteration in the plan of the work entails upon the Publishers a considerable expense, which nothing but a large circulation would justify them in incurring. They are happy to have it in their power to state, that the rapid sale of the two first numbers, and the daily-increasing demand for this Periodical, enables them to acknowledge the patronage of the Public, in a way which they hope will be deemed most acceptable. [reproduced in Waugh, 24]

What had actually happened was that all but two of Buss's prints were, as he himself put it, too "wretched" to be used, and therefore text had to be substituted. Faced with the production reality of negative profits, a fledgling writer, and an incompetent illustrator, the publishers created a *trompe l'oeil* facade. And more important for my purposes, they chose to do so by purporting to respond to "a suggestion . . . from various influential quarters," thus highlighting a defining quality of serial fiction: its ability to (at least pretend to) respond to its audience while the narrative is still in the process of development. Chapman and Hall also demonstrated ingenuity in disposing of their piles of unsold monthly parts. Since sales in the provinces had been negligible, they sent the parts to provincial booksellers *without charging in advance*, telling the booksellers to sell on consignment and simply return the numbers not disposed of. In the first month, 1,450 of 1,500 copies were returned, but within a few months the method was a huge success, establishing an essential new distribution system (Patten 66).

Concurrently with these marketing advances, Dickens transformed the narrative from a standard series of bumbling sportsmen's sketches into a picaresque based in London but depicting urban infiltration of the country. The fifth number introduced a working-class character, Sam Weller, and his father. Audiences responded well to Dickens's humorous but sympathetic textual representation of these urban characters. Sales soared after Sam appeared on the scene, and readers apparently wrote Dickens to "counsel him to develop the character largely—to the utmost."[8] And Dickens, already showing the true responsiveness to his audience that contrasts so markedly with the simulated responsiveness of Chapman and Hall, answered by making Sam central to the *Pickwick* adventures.

The author's and publishers' narrative, advertising, and distribution techniques, innovative from an entrepreneurial standpoint, proved overwhelmingly successful. By number 5, *Pickwick's* circulation had increased to forty thousand per number, where it stayed throughout the run. As Norman N. Feltes is careful to stress in his *Modes of Production of Victorian Novels,* this success is generally attributed to literary genius, lucky accident, and marketing ability, combining to explode upon the literary world. But, Feltes argues, the historical processes that shaped and determined the material production of *Pickwick Papers* are as important as "genius, luck, and the shrewdness of Chapman and Hall" (3). The series' success certainly depended on a combination of perfect timing, insight into the potential of advertising, Dickens's great comic skill and ability to reflect his audience, and fine-tuning of the narrative to respond to audience desire. But all these factors could not have arisen simultaneously without the particular nexus of economic, technological, and ideological conditions existent in the 1830s.

Of course, this revolution in the production and distribution of narrative did not go unchallenged. From early in Dickens's career, reviewers formed an important part of the serial equation. As Kathleen Tillotson notes (1954), the era of *Pickwick* marks the beginning of serious criticism of novels. Thus the genre as a whole was still considered artistically and morally suspect, which meant that early reviewers were especially reluctant to acknowledge serials, the dregs of this debased genre, as worthy of notice. In addition to the reasons already noted for the prejudice against serials, a more covert cause was that, as Tillotson points out, "reviewers were not quite disinterested; part-issue put them in a difficulty. If they reviewed the novel during publication, they risked premature judgment; if they waited for completion, their criticism might well be superfluous" (39). The economically driven need to review the highly popular and profitable serials effectively forced reviewers into the reading community not as experts but as equal participants. On the other hand, reviewers' livelihood obviously depended on the reading public's continued interest in serials. Therefore their relation to the new form was bound to be ambivalent at best. The involuntary suspension of reviewers' critical superiority seems to have produced considerable anxiety amongst critics of the new genre; many reviewers for upper-class quarterlies refused to review serials at all.

Critics tended to reflect the agenda of the type of periodical (patrician or reformist, elitist or popular) for which they wrote and consequently chose very different analogies and metaphors to describe the serial phenomenon. In addition to imposing the discourse of addiction on serials, for example, upper-class critics described serial fiction in industrial terms. In 1839, two years after the run of *Pickwick* and concurrently with that of *Oliver Twist* and *Nicholas Nickleby*, the conservative *Quarterly Review* directly parallels the new form of fiction with the system of industrial labor in its review of *Oliver Twist*: "The works of Boz come out in numbers, suited to this age of division of labour, cheap and not too long . . . in fact, Boz is the only *work* which the superficial acres of type called newspaper leave the human race time to peruse."[9] As late as 1843, after Dickens was an acknowledged literary phenomenon, serialization still aroused protest and controversy. For example, in that year the *Quarterly Review* continued its attack by grimly congratulating itself (at least sixty years too soon, as it happens) on the early demise not only of individual serialized novels but of the serial as a mode of publication. Of Dickens, the reviewer says, "His longer works owe much, we are afraid, much of their popularity to their having been published *in numbers*. . . . we are inclined to predict of works of this style both in England and France (where the manufacture is flourishing on a very intensive and somewhat profligate scale) that an ephemeral popularity will be followed by early oblivion" (71 [March 1843]: 504). The industrial metaphors continue here: like the earlier use of "division of labour," "manufacture" again establishes the connection between mass-produced fiction and the Industrial Revolution while also imposing an implicit lower-class coding on serials; "profligate" adds a suggestion of eventual (and well-deserved) ruin, as well as absence of the capitalist virtues of thrift and investment. Just as manufacturer's money carried a stigma, so manufacture of fiction implied—and still implies—absence of artistic value.

Despite their anxieties over the form, by the mid-1840s most reviewers were forced to admit that serialized fiction was defiantly healthy, on the agenda for at least a few more runs to come. Periodicals as disparate as the upper-class *North British Review* and the working-class *Sun* cite (with fury or with approbation) the serial's ability to transform readers' attitudes. In 1845, the *North British Review* moves beyond earlier predictions of the form's demise to bemoan its moral repercussions. The reviewer delivers a sermon on the evils of installment fiction, one worth quoting at length since it summarizes mid-century arguments against the form. After an extensive laundry list of Dickens's faults, the review concludes:

> The form of publication of Mr. Dickens's works must be attended with bad consequences. The reading of a novel is not now the undertaking it once was, a thing to be done occasionally on holiday and almost by stealth. . . . Useful as a certain amount of novel reading may be, this [serialization] is not the right way to indulge in it. It is not a mere healthy recreation like a match at cricket, a lively conversation, or a game at backgammon. It throws us into a state of unreal excitement, a trance, a dream, which we should be allowed to dream out, and then be sent back to the atmosphere of reality again, cured by our brief surfeit of the desire to indulge again soon in the same delirium of feverish interest. But now our dreams are mingled with our daily business. . . . the new number of Dickens, or Lever, or Warren . . . . absorb[s] the energies which, after the daily task, might be usefully employed in the search after wholesome knowledge. [3 (May 1845): 85]

This lambasting reveals the reviewer's central assumptions. Novel reading may be "useful," but only if it is done by stealth so as not to interfere with the utilitarian accumulation of knowledge and so as to preserve the strict separation of daily business and unconscious release. As so often with serials, it is their disruption of boundaries—between fiction and reality, dream and business, manly sport and womanly indulgence—that really seems to upset the reviewer. He is not alone in expressing this fear, one echoing Arnold's and other clergymen's sermons, numerous letters to the press, and an almost infinite amount of more recent criticism of mass audiences, of which a representative example (to be discussed in the final chapter) is the pervasive perception of soap opera fans as unable to separate character from actor, fiction from reality.

As we will see shortly, a number of critics from cheap newspapers such as *News of the World* praised this interpellation of fiction and "real life"; however, upper-class critics such as Arnold and the reviewer above found it profoundly disturbing, seeing particular danger in serials' unprecedented intersections with the rhythms of everyday life. Later, conservative critics turned to explicit economic analogy to emphasize the threat posed by the serial habit. In 1851, the *Prospective Review* discusses Dickens's *David Copperfield* and Thackeray's *Pendennis*, two serial *bildungsroman* running simultaneously. The review gravely informs readers that "the serial tale . . . is probably the lowest artistic form yet invented. . . . In it, wealth is too often wasted in reckless and riotous profusion, and poverty is concealed by mere superficial variety, caricature, violence, and confused bustle."[10] Compare this upper-class use of "wealth" and "poverty" as metaphors for literary content and structure with the *Working Man's Friend*, which just a year later appropriates economics for the purpose of explicit social critique, arguing that Dickens is universally read because poverty, "the common lot and natural birthright of the masses, is itself a bond of communion with the many. In the depths of this poverty the author of the Pickwick Papers has discovered his wealth" (Aug. 21, 1852, 326). Poverty becomes here not a metaphorical but an actual condition. Wealth, on the other hand, as a much less likely reality for most of this reviewer's audience, is apotheosized into metaphor, although certainly Dickens's huge profits are implied as well.

Early in Dickens's career, then, the more expensive quarterlies attempted to conceptualize the serial phenomenon in material terms by means of familiar, disparaging models of addiction and industrial production. Clearly these models do have interesting reverberations with regard to serials, which are inseparable from the system of production that impels them and which may insert themselves into the patterns of our daily lives in ways that resemble addiction. Equally clearly, our present ways of thinking about and perhaps even of using mass culture have been shaped by the persistent metaphors of addiction and industrial manufacture applied to mass culture in the nineteenth century. Indeed, as Terry Lovell notes in *Consuming Fiction*, panicked critique of new cultural forms is a time-honored tradition. She cites eighteenth-century terror of the novel's potential effects on morals and reading practices: "The moral panic it occasioned in the last quarter of the eighteenth century was merely the first of a series which occurred whenever a new cultural commodity made its debut. It was repeated in very similar terms in the twentieth century over cinema and then television, both of which were attacked as culturally debased and as tending to corrupt" (8). The period Lovell discusses here, 1770 to 1810, was dominated by the Gothic craze and also saw the rise of the novel as commodity. By the time the serial appeared, new fears surrounding industrialization joined to the traditional moral panic Lovell describes to create new terms of critique for the novel.

By the 1850s, installment fiction had become economically entrenched in the system of fiction production. Since there was no point in continuing to slam an undeniably thriving mode of publication, debate as to the origins and value of the serial form began to decrease, while arguments as to the role of fiction in general, and the political effect of this fiction in particular, increased. As Dickens's work became more explicitly political, then, so did the extratextual discourse surrounding it. Praise of his treatment of social issues in working- and some middle-class periodicals contrasts, predictably, with denunciation of his social and political ignorance in upper- and other middle-class reviews and quarterlies.[11] Disparate as they are, though, most of these later critiques have in common an at least tacit acknowledgment of the measurable influence of fiction on political life.[12] The conscious political goals of the industrial novels led Dickens's contemporaries to see fiction as wielding considerable influence by the 1850s, and authors understandably reinforced this view. "If the world is to be set right," remarks Mr. Bold in Trollope's *The Warden* (1855) after reading the first number of "The Almshouse," a novel by "Mr. Popular Sentiment" (i.e. Dickens), "the work will be done by shilling numbers."

By 1864, when Dickens began *Our Mutual Friend*, the power of the novelist had been consolidated to the extent that Justin McCarthy could argue, in a piece entitled "Novels with a Purpose,"

> The novelist is now our most influential writer. If he be a man of genius his power over the community he addresses is far beyond that of any author. Macaulay's influence over the average English mind was narrow compared with that of Dickens; even Carlyle's was not on the whole so great as that of Thackeray. . . . The influence of the novelist is beginning, too, to be publicly acknowledged of late much more frankly than was once the fashion. For a long time his power over society, except as a mere teller of stories and provider of easy pastime, was ignored or disputed. It was, indeed, something like the power of women in politics; an influence almost all-pervading, almost irresistible, but silent, secret, and not to be openly acknowledged. [*Westminster Review* 82 (July 1864)]

To reduce his/her threat, the early novelist is feminized here; by contrast, the contemporary novelist is explicitly masculine. In this narrative of the professionalization of authorship, "feminine" subversive power that used to act covertly (and therefore dangerously) can be vanquished once "masculine" power is admitted openly. Acknowledgment of authorial influence becomes "frank" and therefore respectable, manly, and positive; the author can be hailed as "a man of genius" rather than feared as the woman behind the man.

Nineteenth-century serial fiction aroused, then, strong reactions among critics. Depending on the class whose interests they were paid to express, critics feared its addictive potential and democratizing or mechanical tendencies, or lauded its reflection of the lives of its readers as well as its redefinition of traditional narratives of power. They rejected the marginalized voices whom Dickens allowed to control narratives or praised the author for seeing such subjects as worthy. And some critics, regardless of class, feared serial intersection with everyday life. Overall, the controversy surrounded Dickens's serial fiction is indicative first of the perceived threat and power of a fictional form uniquely intertwined with "real life," and, second, of Dickens's own ability to become the ideal mass-market author, creating a highly profitable niche by tackling controversial social and political issues from a platform of profoundly conservative "family values."

Nineteenth-Century Readers of Serial Fiction

Whatever their attitude toward the serial, almost all reviewers admitted the strong influence of the novel on the "spirit of the age," and in its appreciation of this rich web of associations between the nineteenth-century serial and its cultural context, Hughes and Lund's *The Victorian Serial* is unparalleled. The authors work to re-create original readers' experience of Victorian texts, drawing on contemporary reviews to stress the multiple ways that serial texts interacted with other kinds of reading as well as contemporary events to produce texts much more closely tied to the news, scandals, seasonal changes, and materiality of everyday life than we now realize.[13] Among other connections between nineteenth-century serials and their cultural context, Hughes and Lund note that both the Victorian age and its serial fiction privileged an "expansive vision of life," an optimistic view that reflects both faith in the meliorist imperative of constant improvement in living conditions, and belief in Christian and imperial ideologies of moral and spiritual progress (1). Both also altered inherited notions of time. While technological revolutions such as the railway collapsed time and space, discoveries by geologists, archeologists, and biologists conversely worked to extend time by situating nineteenth-century life as a mere pinpoint in a vast expanse. Similarly, the serial paradoxically both compressed and expanded traditional ways of reading, since the practice of part-issuing three or four chapters or a fragment of a poem worked to satisfy the desire of "increasingly rushed readers" for narrative, while enforced pauses and long duration worked to intertwine fictions with the everyday lives of audiences and to allow unprecedented degrees of growth and change among characters (5). And finally, Hughes and Lund agree with Norman Feltes in seeing the serial as paralleling nineteenth-century capitalism in that both require an investment of time and money—along with the confidence that such expenditure will be rewarded in the long run—and both privilege abundance, even excess, such that serial "richness of detail and expansion of the text over time suggested a world of plenitude" (4).[14] I would add to their analysis the fact that both serial novels and capitalism institutionalize delayed gratification, while the serial re-creates fiction in capitalism's image by providing what is essentially a payment plan for narrative, thus simultaneously increasing audience and profits and lowering costs.

While reflecting their age's belief systems and participating actively in its debates, nineteenth-century novels served multiple functions for readers acclimatizing themselves to a rapidly changing world.[15] Like newspapers and other periodicals, novels provided information, showing readers how to act in social situations. Novels introduced disparate classes to each other, showing the increasingly juxtaposed "two nations" how others actually lived and thus helping to promote mutual understanding and to catalyze social change. Novels explored difficult social issues and attempted to move toward solutions. Novels helped to make coherent a radically new social and physical landscape; by organizing random, apparently senseless social relations and economic facts into narrative trajectories, authors imposed a shape on inchoate and therefore terrifying changes. Among the first textual representations of the living and working conditions of the new urban middle and working classes, novels helped displaced populations orient themselves by representing and thereby rendering visible their lives. Serialized novels served all these functions particularly well since they appeared over months or years and thus could parallel the seasons, political changes, and passage of time that affected readers' own lives. What is more, parts were often written at the last minute, just before they appeared in print, and could therefore shift to reflect the external world.

The activation of a mass middle-class readership worked with serials to provide a powerful means of forging shared interests, values, and demands—a means that the nation, fragmented into geopolitical and class factions, had lacked. Andrew Blake concludes his study of the intersections between developing Victorian ideologies and Victorian novels by stating that novels were concerned with "the reproduction of society: with the integration of the new wealthy, new powerful, and new respectable groups into the already-existing ruling class culture, and the modification of that culture to include within it many new ideological elements associated with those groups. . . . The novel was an arena of public information, of public debate, and of 'interpellation,' helping by its concerns to form society by helping to form individuals as members of that society" (134–35). Blake's study centers on the work of middle- or upper-middle-class novelists such as Trollope and Thackeray and on the responses of similarly positioned readers and journalists for publications such as *Blackwood's Edinburgh Magazine* and the *Fortnightly Review*. His conclusions posit Victorian novels as conforming to bourgeois ideologies and as seeking to secure consent for these ideologies from their readers. However, Blake is careful to refute simplistic "dominant ideology" theories by citing, among other problems, the fact that such theories require us to believe that the "ruling class" shares "a single set of ideas and values"—a belief clearly reductive in the extreme. In addition, Blake cites recent studies of working-class resistance to and contestation of dominant ideologies as proof that theories of indoctrination of a passive working class by an active ruling class are reductive as well. Therefore he replaces such social-control theories with a Gramscian concept of hegemony, noting that critics have a tendency to simplify the term by ignoring the fact that hegemonic consent is necessarily and permanently in *process*, never an established status quo of dominance and control but always an ongoing negotiation for acceptance and consent.[16]

The unique reading practices serial fiction inspires worked to strengthen this hegemonic process of textual interpretation. By involving a community of readers in collaboratively interpreting and to some degree shaping a text, serials incorporate a space for critique and thus defuse the text's potentially coercive power. What is more, the communal reading process of serial consumption serves important social functions in addition to those discussed above. Though many critics were frightened by novels' potential influence over their readers, none denied that the texts, and serial novels in particular, were becoming increasingly central to nineteenth-century urban communications. As the popular *Illustrated London News* put it in 1853: "'What do you think of *Bleak House*?' is a question which everybody has heard propounded . . . and which . . . formed, for its own season, as regular a portion of miscellaneous chat as 'How are you?' One obvious distinction is, that a great number of people who ask how you do, make a practice of neither waiting for, nor listening to, your reply. . . . But, on the contrary, those who inquire for your ideas about *Bleak House*, think of *Bleak House*; and, if they do not really want to know your opinion, want you at least to know theirs."[17] This commentary emphasizes one of the most important gifts of serial fiction: it cements social bonds, providing neighbors or workmates who might otherwise have no interests in common with an instant topic of conversation. Dickens's homey, voyeuristic writing style reinforced a sense of intimacy with the characters, a masquerade that allowed readers to gossip about "people" both discussants knew intimately even though they may well have had no close ties in "real" life. Exchanged opinions about a serial community of fictional characters essentially took the place of shared gossip about a common circle of acquaintances. In default of the latter, the former worked to provide not only a necessary sense of connection, but perhaps more importantly a space for the exchange of ideas about shifting social values.[18]

In defining what can be said to have emerged from the mid-nineteenth-century explosion of the novel, Raymond Williams sees *community* as a central focus. Taking into account the radical social, political, and economic changes transforming life in the nineteenth century, Williams points to the consequent need to create models of "what it means to live in common." In place of close-knit rural villages, where individual lives were intertwined with extended families, communities, labor, and fellow laborers and where even the relationship with management and landowners was a visible one, industrialization produced entirely new relations to the workplace. Workers were reconstructed as faceless units of production with no direct relationship to the end product, to those in control of the production process, or to each other. And urbanization compressed people with neither familial nor occupational ties into closer and closer contact; early urbanites in many cases shared nothing but poverty and profound alienation. As Dickens himself said of Londoners, "99 percent are strangers to everybody."[19] Novels provided a community of "friends" to discuss with neighbors and co-workers and thus helped to mitigate this condition, as did the thematization of "community" found in many nineteenth-century fictions.

Andrew Blake's view of the novel as a site of negotiation and development of shared cultural values is echoed by some nineteenth-century reviewers who were clearly well aware of the novel's political functions. This view is borne out by celebrations of Dickens in working-class periodicals proclaiming him "the Champion of the People." For example, *People's Journal* introduced its feature "The People's Portrait Gallery" by choosing Dickens as its first subject because "we propose that our Portrait Gallery shall be a gallery of the true nobility of England—a gallery of God's and the People's nobles. We hold no man noble merely because some ancestor of his some time killed a great number of his own species . . . was the favorite of some silly King, or the tool of some king's base minister. Nobility from such sources is a strange abuse of the term" (vol. 1 [June 3,1846]). Dickens, among the first middle-class authors to include lower-class characters in major roles rather than as walk-ons or comic relief, encouraged his readers to take crossings sweepers and factory girls seriously. Little Jo, Lizzie Hexam, Betty Higden, and many others are constructed with the powerful rhetorical tools of nineteenth-century sentimentality and melodrama, thereby helping to shift perceptions of who "heroes" and "heroines" could be.[20] Of course, these same lower-class characters often follow the reassuring "poor but happy" or "poor but hardworking" models, thereby failing to challenge conventional perceptions of class; and center stage, in a Dickens novel, is almost always reserved for the middle classes.

The *People's Journal* review quoted above goes on to connect the politics of the novels with their structure and cast: "There are two great schools of novelists which may be termed the feudal and the popular. . . . It has been well remarked that the feudal school, like the feudal system, must not only take its hero from the privileged class, and make all the other characters move in subordination to them . . . according to their station on the artificial sliding-scale of society. . . . But the popular school has no tether . . . it can afford to have as many heroes as it pleases. Every man, woman or child is its hero or heroine." ·

In sharp contrast to the *Prospective Review*'s complaint about the "reckless and riotous profusion" of Dickens's serials, this reviewer praises the form's potential to be politically progressive *even on a structural level*, arguing that almost every character of every one of Dickens's novels can be perceived as hero or heroine of at least one part-issue section. Clearly this pushes the point a bit, since many of Dickens's novels do have well-established heroes and heroines. However, the basic impulse behind the argument—that serial fiction structurally encourages a large cast of characters and multiple story lines and therefore subverts the conventional narrative focus on a single hero and/or heroine—increasingly holds true as the genre develops. In contemporary serials, of course, this reviewer's anticipation has become reality. Virtually every character of a soap opera has his or her time in center stage (and if this never happens, the character will eventually be dropped from the cast), while formerly central characters take the background for a time. No wonder upper-class readers were wary of the rise of the mass serial; no wonder lower-class readers were popularly supposed to lap up stories that transformed people of their own class into heroes and heroines.

Assessing the reactions of working-class readers themselves presents problems, however. In the chapters on comic strips and soap operas, I am able to draw directly on the voices of a range of readers and viewers thanks to the existence of letters, discussion groups, computer bulletin boards, and the like. The voices of nineteenth-century serial audiences are infinitely more evasive. Since Dickens burned his letters, we have little direct evidence of reader response to his novels. We do have numerous anecdotal accounts, from Dickens as well as others, attesting to the fact that readers believed him responsive to their suggestions and demands; we also have a few firsthand accounts from readers themselves. But most evidence is indirect and must be inferred from the many reviewers and friends who speak of Dickens's close relationship with his audience; his own letters, some clearly indicating responses to suggestions from readers; his letters to friends such as Forster and Bulwer Lytton, indicating he had taken their advice in making plot or character changes; and, finally, his prefaces and other authorial addresses that attempt to make contact with the audience.

By far the largest source of evidence of the ways readers received serials is the rich store of serial reviews in cheap daily and weekly newspapers, and for lack of more representative accounts, these will form the basis of my analysis of responses to *Our Mutual Friend*. They are invaluable in providing access to some of the voices, public rather than private, engaged in creating the discourse surrounding fiction as it was issued part by part. Of course, reviewers are hardly "typical" readers but rather are professionals paid to provide a mass readership with advice. What is more, in our present state of scholarship anonymous reviewers in cheap papers generally remain unidentified. Still, reviewers of serial parts were subject to the same conditions of reading as the general audience, and therefore they engaged in typical activities such as prediction, response to the author, and attempts to influence the direction of the narrative. As dominant (because professional and public) voices, they also participate in the process of shaping readers' expectations about the fictions they consume. For these reasons, reviews can help in deepening our understanding of the process of reading Victorian novels in their original context as well as of the relations between serial texts and their audiences.

A number of researchers in search of an audience have elaborated on the considerable difficulties involved. Jonathan Rose, while calling for historically grounded studies of the ways books interpellate with the lives of actual readers to replace speculations about the ideological effects of texts *on* such readers, notes that firsthand accounts from readers below the upper classes are almost nonexistent since their (comparatively rare) letters and journals are much less likely to have survived than those of the aristocracy. Rose also admits that even the extant working-class autobiographies do not provide unproblematic evidence. Their authors are not necessarily representative of their class, for one thing. Moreover, their texts are shaped by conventions of the autobiographical form, by context, and by the intended purpose of such texts (to prove that members of the working classes can educate themselves, to provide encouragement to others); they are also prone to embellishment, forgetting, or misremembering. Therefore, while these texts— especially when used in conjunction with other data— remain valuable resources, an accurate history of nineteenth-century reading audiences is hard to come by (51–52).[21]

To complicate the question of audience still further, not only the authentic response of readers but even the existence of certain populations of readers is open to question. The long-standing legend of Dickens as "author of the people" has been rightly challenged in recent years by historians and literary scholars arguing that the working classes could neither read nor afford his monthly parts. As late as 1850, almost a quarter of the population could neither read nor write, and price was as prohibitive as illiteracy. Dickens's reputation as "the people's author" is ironic when we consider that the 2d for his weekly magazines or even 1 1/2d for the "Cheap Edition" weekly parts of his novels (not to mention the shilling for his monthly parts) was virtually out of reach for employed working-class families surviving on ten or fifteen shillings a week.[22] As George Ford, in his classic *Dickens and his Readers*, explains, "Perhaps the largest group among those loyal early Dickensians was one about which it is most difficult to obtain information. Dickens himself credited the extensive sales of Macaulay's history and Tennyson's poems to working-class readers, and it is likely that his own sales were similarly assisted. Below certain economic levels, however, the evidence becomes scarce. Diaries, letters, autobiographies, and essays—even if written—rarely survive" (77).

Despite the dearth of firsthand information from serial readers, though, there is some evidence, mostly either implicit or anecdotal, that the working classes found ways around both poverty and illiteracy, and that one of the most important of these was the practice of communal reading. We can pick up indirect evidence about reading habits from articles of the time. For example, an 1858 *Household Words* piece, estimating the reading public for penny journals from sales figures, states that "reckoning only three readers to each copy sold" the readership becomes three million; the implication here is that readers pooled together to buy texts and that three readers per copy was the absolute minimum.[23] We can infer, from the fact that even a shilling part could cost a London laborer a full day's wage (Altick 1957, 286), that the working classes must often have read communally if they were to read at all. Given the economic constraints on urban working and lower middle classes, it is therefore unsurprising that many of the extant accounts of reading practices stress communal readings. The value of these readings becomes a recurrent theme in accounts of serial consumption and is repeatedly emphasized in both public and private discourse. A number of working-class autobiographers confirm the prevalence of family readings: for example, Charles H. Welch tells us, "It was quite a feature of home life to assemble in the parlour on a Sunday evening, while Dad read a chapter or two from one of Dickens' novels" (41).

As they became an important part of shared family pleasures, serials helped organize leisure time. In "The Commercialization of Leisure in Eighteenth-Century England," J.H. Plumb focuses on the rise of "leisure" and the development of a printing industry as contributing to a revolution in consumer attitudes. Its "explosive social possibilities," he argues, began to manifest themselves in the eighteenth century, after revolutions in printing and papermaking technologies had combined to lower the price of printed material (266). Newspaper advertisements and articles helped to institute the idea of leisure as inseparable from consumption; "work" was newly distinct from home life, public and private spheres were diverging. The spread of a reading public both accelerated and responded to this shift. As we will see in the later firsthand accounts of serial audiences, the importance of serial fictions in audience lives does seem to depend heavily on the ritualization of its consumption, which often helps to mark off work time from leisure time. For example, many communal Dickens readings took place at Sunday tea, comic-strip audiences talk about the importance of comic reading during coffee breaks or on Sunday mornings, and soap viewers attest to the invaluable role of taped shows in providing a transitional space between work and home lives. Thus serial fiction meshes with the changing needs of its audience over two centuries while satisfying the continuing need for ready-made communities of "mutual friends."

That novel reading became an important means of constructing leisure time and family life can be seen in the fact that reading aloud became a Victorian institution which took place even among the middle and upper classes not forced into it because of illiteracy or poverty. Its prevalence must therefore be seen as the result of cultural as well as economic factors, especially since it anticipates later serial audiences' marked preference for reading their texts communally.[24]

In addition to family readings, the value of serials in forging communities is attested to by the prevalence of reading groups, which satisfied both economic and social needs. Anecdotally, we are told that during *The Pickwick Papers'* serialization a group of about twenty workers clubbed together not to buy shilling parts (which they could not afford) but to hire them at twopence per day from a local library. They then gathered in a locksmith's shop where a literate club member read the installment to the others (Collins 1972, 6). Similar stories are told by informants ranging from Dickens's mother-in-law's charwoman to Henry Mayhew. *London Labour and the London Poor* is especially valuable in providing one of the few first-person records of how illiterate populations managed to consume texts; Mayhew's "Literature of the Costermongers" section tells us: "It may appear anomalous to speak of the literature of an uneducated body, but even the costermongers have their tastes for books. They are very fond of hearing any one read aloud to them, and listen very attentively. One man often reads the Sunday paper of the beer-shop to them, and on a fine summer's evening a costermonger, or any neighbour who has the advantage of being 'a schollard,' reads aloud to them in the courts they inhabit" (65). David Vincent, among others, proves the prevalence of communal readers by citing as evidence groups of workers who pooled together to buy texts.[25] Communal readings made so much sense in meeting the needs of an impoverished and partly illiterate population that they were eventually institutionalized in the Penny Reading movement that swept the country in the 1860s. Dickens rode that wave into shore, as he rode so many others, by instituting readings from his own works at about this time.

Economic exigencies thus reinforced the tendency toward collaborative interpretations of serial fiction. Another reinforcement came from the fact that part-published novels and poems intertwined in unprecedented ways with the lives of their readers. As narratives that unfolded over time, they were read over months or years, which encouraged both a sense of intimacy on the part of readers and an interweaving of current events, political issues, even seasonal changes on the part of authors. Dickens's characters could seem closer to readers than many of their fellow workers or neighbors, and readers could watch these characters struggle with poverty, joblessness, homelessness, death of loved ones, and so on. Much of the power of serial fiction was a consequence of its sheer duration: readers became familiar with the characters whose doings they followed week after week or month after month for a year or two. As the *National Magazine* expresses it, "The characters and scenes of this writer [Dickens] have become, to an extent undreamed of in all previous cases, part of our actual life. Their individualities, whether mental or external, are as familiar to us as those of our most intimate associates or our most frequent resorts" (Dec. 1837, 83). However, this intertwining of text and reader was not always greeted with applause. Not only did it heighten the suspense fostered by the serial mode of publication, but many critics found the unusually close relations between serial readers and their texts disturbing.

Since the most expensive texts were still three-volume novels, available only to those who could afford either their purchase or a circulating-library subscription, less affluent readers were forced to consume Dickens installment by cheap but anxiety-producing installment. Even library membership was economically circumscribed; only the rich could afford a three-volume ticket, while less well-off subscribers were restricted to a single volume at a time and thus could not guarantee their ability to finish a novel. That middle- and upper-class readers sometimes chose to evade the close intersection of part-issue fiction and everyday life, with the anxiety this intersection produced, can be seen in the journals and diaries some readers have left us. From these, we can see that class hierarchies directly affected not only what people read but the *way* they read as well as their degree of freedom in determining this process. For example, Henry Crabb Robinson, a London barrister and man of letters, records in his journal entry for September 5, 1841 (midway through *Barnaby Rudge*'s serialization): "Finished all of *Barnaby Rudge* yet published . . . I will read no more till the story is finished . . . I will not expose myself to further anxieties" (578). Robinson was true to his word: he does not mention the book again until recording, on March 2, 1842, "I finished this morning *Barnaby Rudge*, a novel full of talent and wisdom" (612). But not full of anxiety—because he read with power over the text. To achieve the same goal, a less affluent reader would have to buy the novel part by part while resisting the temptation to read the parts as they accumulated, or borrow or buy a full set of parts at the end of the run. Both are unlikely scenarios.

This contrast in the material conditions of reading raises provocative questions. Why did upper-class readers like Crabb Robinson, who could afford to buy the completed text rather than the parts as they were issued, refuse to get caught up in the novel as it unfolded over time; why did he resist the kind of "addiction" subsequently deplored by privileged observers of lower-class reading and viewing habits? These questions may be partially answered by D.A. Miller's theorization of the sensational. In *The Novel and the Police*, Miller discusses the role of the body in Victorian fiction: "Nothing boring about the Victorian sensation novel: the excitement that seizes us here is as direct as the 'fight-or-flight' physiology that renders our reading bodies, neither fighting nor fleeing, theaters of neurasthenia. The genre offers us one of the first instances of modern literature to address itself primarily to the central nervous system, where it grounds its characteristic adrenaline effects: accelerated heart rate and respiration, increased blood pressure, the pallor resulting from vasoconstriction" (147). Miller may be claiming too much for the sensation novel—surely other Victorian literary forms, melodramas most obviously, also produced physical effects—but his argument is nevertheless crucial in understanding how such novels were received. As we will see in the Chapter 2, the symptoms Miller charts are exactly those cited by Dr. Fredric Wertham and Dr. Louis Berg as proof of the nefarious neurological effects of comic strips and radio soap operas. In default of actual censorship, the mechanism often chosen to limit consumption of physically stimulating materials is to lower their prestige, creating a barrier of snobbism between at least the "privileged classes" and the consumption of pornography, sensation novels, action-adventure movies, and so on. What is more, the emphatic physicality of such literature is a contributing factor to and thus inseparable from its intersection with everyday life. Miller's discussion of sensation fiction concludes that "by a kind of Cartesian censorship, in which pulp-as-flesh gets equated with pulp-as-trash, the emphatic physicality of thrills in such literature allows us to hold them cheap" (147). Miller is exactly right in his insight into the mechanism of this equation, but for my purposes it is important to emphasize the increased suspense produced by serialization as well. If the sensation novel produces physical effects when read today, how much stronger must these have been with the added factor of enforced pauses to increase suspense and long duration to increase identification with characters?

As the publishing industry developed, Victorian publishers and critics expanded their range of potential consumers by distinguishing an elite from the growing mass of readers. This strategy necessitated different marketing strategies for different audiences, a concerted effort to distinguish fiction that affects the body from fiction that affects only the mind. Serial fictions, being the cheapest form, often fell to the bottom of the heap along with penny dreadfuls and the like (although readers distinguished between weekly newspaper serials like Reynolds's and the more prestigious monthly or weekly part- or magazine-published narratives like Dickens's, Gaskell's, or Thackeray's).

Perhaps as a consequence of their ghettoization, less "respectable" novels often incorporated subversive themes. Sensation novels of the 1860s have been shown by Ann Cvetkovich and Jane Tompkins, among others, to have had considerable political motivation and influence, albeit of a general kind. They inscribed a broader politics of class, race, gender, and restrictions on sexuality rather than the specific politics of industrial power relations impelling the "social problem novels" by authors such as G.W.M. Reynolds, Charlotte Brontë, Dickens, Benjamin Disraeli, Elizabeth Gaskell, and Charles Reade in the 1840s. These broader issues include, for example, Wilkie Collins's interrogation of received ideas of "knowledge" and "evidence" in *The Moonstone*, as well as Elizabeth Braddon's subversion of accepted constructions of the "perfect lady" by creating, in *Lady Audley's Secret*, a heroine who wields all the signifiers of the Victorian Angel in the House—fluffy blond ringlets, childlike beauty, artistic accomplishments, gentleness and deference, even charity toward the poor—but who proves to be "actually" wicked, adopting these conventional signifiers as protective cover to conceal her real desires and to enable their fulfillment.

As we conclude this discussion of Dickens's readers, the author's own vexed relationship with his audience demands analysis. Dickens occupies an anomalous position in the history of serialization. On the one hand, he was instrumental in developing mass-produced fiction, and thus became a kind of manufacturer of narrative for a vast and faceless public. On the other hand, probably more than any writer of his time he insisted (sometimes against all evidence to the contrary) that his relationship with that public was interactive, even intimate. Part of this contradiction can be attributed to his position as part of the first generation of "professional" writers, with all the anxiety this distinction entails. In addition, Dickens himself was very much a product of the Industrial Revolution: as a kind of social migrant, he contained class contradictions within his own persona. Born into the lower middle class and plunged into the working class when his father went to debtor's prison and he went to work at age twelve, he was ultimately raised above the middle class by his own prodigious energy.

His productivity was, he repeatedly insisted, dependent on his relationship with his readers and with the urban landscape. He is widely recognized as an innovator in the process of developing the complex and constantly negotiated author/audience relationship so characteristic of continued fictions, not just because he was produced by the historical moment when technology made large-scale publication and mass readership a reality, but because of his obsession with "that particular relation (personally affectionate and like no other man's) which subsists between me and the public."[26] Preternaturally tuned in to the ethos of the new urban culture, the practice of the *flaneur* was apparently indispensable to his writing; his notorious hourslong walks fueled both urban obsession and imagination.

As Walter Benjamin explains in "Some Motifs in Baudelaire," his interrogation of this nineteenth-century obsession with crowds and with the city, the crowd itself becomes a prime subject for nineteenth-century writers: "It became a customer; it wished to find itself portrayed in the contemporary novel, as the patrons did in the paintings of the Middle Ages. The most successful author of the century met this demand out of inner necessity" (120). Although Benjamin refers here to Victor Hugo, his remark could apply with equal force to Dickens, whose "inner necessity" has been well documented. The author himself validates Benjamin's theory in his explanation, to John Forster, of his inability to write well at his Broadstairs seaside retreat: "I can't express how much I need these [the streets of London]. It seems as if they supplied something to my brain, which it cannot bear, when busy, to lose. . . . the toil and labour of writing, day after day, without that magic lantern is IMMENSE!!" (Forster, 423). Despite his own desire to forge an imagined bond between author and audience, seeing himself as a kind of Benjaminian storyteller symbiotically producing fiction in collaboration with his audience, Dickens's relation to his work and to his readers should not be mystified. Dickens not only wrote after that retroactively imagined bond had been irreparably broken; he was amongst those contributing to the breaking. Dickens's interaction with his audience was not as personal or direct as the mythology he so actively fostered would imply. Like the exchange between any producer and consumer in an industrial economy, it was a highly mediated one. His refusal to acknowledge the degree to which he simply produced a commodity can be seen in the fact that he worked strenuously to bridge the gap of alienation by means of perpetual strolls through London, talks with readers, and public readings. His texts also worked to bridge the gap by means of various ideologies of connection: idealization of home, family, innocence, childhood, romantic love. As we will see in his novel *Our Mutual Friend*, Dickens's compulsion to maintain a close, personal relation between himself and his readers is paralleled by a textual compulsion to forge relationships—often through the power of sentimentality—across classes: between wellborn John Harmon and his former servants the Boffins, indolent Eugene Wrayburn and hardworking Lizzie Hexam, the upwardly mobile Boffins and the poorhouse-bound Betty Higden, and so on.

Despite these attempts to reconcile Others, gaps are apparent in the contradictions, absences, and disjunctions of all Dickens's texts, and never more so than in this last completed novel. Dickens was very much aware of his role as chronicler, victim, and (he hoped) reformer of the sociopolitical abuses consequent upon the shift to an industrial economy. London, his "magic lantern," was so necessary to him not because of its ineffable muselike powers but because of its concrete conditions, which he perceived from a multitude of angles: social, topographical, economic, political, sexual. And while romanticizing the bonds of sympathy between himself and his readers, he remained strongly and insistently aware of the economic conditions that determine the material relations between author, readers, and publishers. We will now turn, for elaboration of the structures and tropes that organize serial fiction and of the audience that reads, discusses, and helps to shape it, to Dickens's last completed novel, *Our Mutual Friend*. The novel was chosen for this study because the text, arguably Dickens's most complex, reveals the author's working through of serial tropes and techniques still in use today. In what follows, I will first provide a context for and overview of the novel, next discuss the general expectations of its reviewers in relation to plotting, character presentation, and authorial responsibility, and finally focus on two specific subplots to more closely interrogate Dickens's plotting strategies and readers' response to them.

Case Study: Our Mutual Friend

In August 1863, Dickens wrote to Collins, "I am always thinking of writing a long book, and am never beginning to do it." The wonderful sliding temporality of this statement indicates that the novel had been brewing for a long time—since at least 1855, when Dickens entered in his Book of Memoranda, "Found Drowned. The descriptive bill upon the wall, by the waterside."[27] This bill, in manifesting the ease with which one can become anonymous, encapsulates the instability of identity invoked by the concept of "personation." It also invokes shades of the confusing class mobility and displacement so central to this novel as well as to the nineteenth century as a whole.[28] Between 1862 and 1864, Dickens refined the original narrative impulse: "LEADING INCIDENT FOR A STORY. A man—young and eccentric?—feigns to be dead, and *is* dead to all intents and purposes external to himself." To this he later added, "*Done Rokesmith*." The motivation for this novel about rebirth, in which many characters shed old identities and appropriate new ones, intertwines richly with the nexus of social and political concerns of the 1850s and 1860s, which led to Dickens's fascination with the theatricality and fraudulence of social life as conflated with the novel's themes of inheritance, doubles, drowning, death, and dust. These themes also reflect the inherent structure of the serial genre, which because of its temporal extension and interpretative gaps is uniquely situated to explore shifting identities.

As its title implies, and as serial structure insists, *Our Mutual Friend* is a collective novel. The "friend," generally assumed to be John Harmon, could also be read as referring to many other characters. Veneering constantly dubs new acquaintances his "best friends in the world"; Twemlow spends the novel desperately attempting to deduce his relationship to those who claim friendship with him in order to appropriate, by proximity, the power of his cousin Lord Snigsworthy. The ubiquitous Wegg, or Headstone, or Boffin could also be considered "mutual friends." More important, though, the title instantly invites us, as readers, into a novelistic community. These characters are *our* friends—a relation contemporary readers acknowledged, as we will see in the reviews—and the community within the text echoes, even as it serves to consolidate, the community of readers.

With its clear social and moral agenda, the novel also sets the standard for later serials in other media by addressing contemporary social problems. The controversial poor laws, inheritance laws, and the marriage market that allows women to be left in wills "like so many spoons"; scapegoating of Jews, Ragged Schools, and indeed the entire educational system; and perhaps most important the interlinked problems of conspicuous consumption and invisible destruction (the Veneering plate glittering for all to see while Betty Higden creeps off to die alone) are all tackled by the novel. As is clear from the last example, the novel's vision of the world is both melodramatic (constructing a clear opposition of good and evil, and relying on excessive representation to make its moral point) and sentimental (appropriating culturally resonant icons such as poor but good hero, dying child, or virtue assaulted). These narrative tropes are wielded in the service of social change on the one hand, social stability on the other; melodrama and sentimentality both function by critiquing existing power relations and proposing other ideologies (of connection, family, the power of love) in their place. Within the Dickens world, both modes often work to enforce new types of social control, proposing a restrictively idealized model of family, gender, and class relations and of personal responsibility as the answer to all social problems.

As well as being Dickens's last completed novel, *Our Mutual Friend* was the first since *Little Dorrit* to be issued in monthly parts rather than serialized within a magazine (as *Great Expectations* and *A Tale of Two Cities* had been). By the 1860s, magazine publication appeared to conform better to the demands of an age increasingly wishing to consume small doses of reading matter at frequent intervals and in a form enabling purchase of several kinds of entertainment at once, all for a penny or two. So while magazines and newspapers proliferated and circulations increased, by 1864 part-issue novels were virtually dead. Investigating Dickens's decision to revive the form, John Sutherland provides "the standard explanation" that "the novel in monthly numbers gave him a sense of intimate contact with his public." This certainly makes sense given that, as we have seen, Dickens was obsessed with re-creating at least a facsimile of the apocryphal storyteller's intimacy with his audience. But Sutherland additionally speculates that purely material considerations influenced Dickens's decision to revert to what even he had called "the old form" as early as 1941: "As an economic strategy, the novel in numbers spread payment at all levels of production and consumption, allowing a larger investment in time and money by the involved parties . . . [and] ever higher scales of remuneration. Thackeray, Trollope, Ainsworth and Lever had the greatest rewards of their writing lives from their novels in numbers."[29] These arguments are persuasive, since letters to Forster and others show that Dickens's reading tours (in which he persisted even after it became clear that they endangered his health) were impelled by the same pair of desires: close contact with his public and large profits. But there was another, perhaps even more central motivation for reversion to part-issue: space restrictions in magazines, especially in weekly serialization, enforced a simplified narrative with a smaller cast of characters. Given the complexity and multiple subplots of Dickens's late novels, then, a return to the space and leisure afforded by independent monthly parts made sense.[30]

Chapman & Hall agreed to Dickens's decision, and the book proved an excellent bargain for the author though not for the publisher. Sales of the monthy number dropped from forty thousand to twenty-five thousand by the end of the run, and thus *Our Mutual Friend* was a failure in comparison to its predecessors *Great Expectations*, which ran weekly in *All the Year Round* (1860–61) and outsold the *Times* by the end of its run (Patten, 300), and *Little Dorrit*, which was issued in monthly numbers (1855–57) and earned Dickens the highest profits of his career (Patten, 251). Still, Dickens profited nicely from *Our Mutual Friend*, despite its relatively low sales. As Chapman points out in a note included with Dickens's accounts on October 24, 1864, "In spite of the last half year being about the worse [sic] in my recollection, I am glad to see that it has not so much affected the enclosed accounts."[31] Before issuing the novel, the publishers had contracted to pay a £6,000 advance and additional half-shares of the book's profit. Dickens thus made a total of £10,611, while Chapman and Hall cleared £4,000, with more on the way from reprints (Sutherland 1976, 42, 60).[32] These profits may have been at least partly the result of Chapman and Hall's capitalist caution. The publishers' accounts to Dickens reveal that in preparation for the novel's release, the firm (no doubt concerned about the return to part-issue) conducted an unprecedentedly extensive advertising campaign, issuing over 1 million bills and 145,000 catalogues and plastering virtually all of England (including omnibuses, steamboats, and train stations) with posters. Before the serial had even begun, then, Chapman and Hall had invested over £1,000.[33] But they took care to compensate themselves for this expense. Sales aside, each part also contained a larger paid advertising section than any of Dickens's other novels—320 pages altogether.[34]

So Dickens's central motivations—obsession with his audience, preoccupation with profits, and continued development of narrative techniques—most likely interacted to shape his decision to revert to the "old form," a decision that satisfied both economic and artistic goals. On the one hand, the producer clearly regarded his books as commodities, products marketed so as to reach the widest possible audience and make the highest possible profit. On the other hand, the author believed strongly in the artistic worth of serial fiction as well as its power to positively affect both individual and social behavior. He turned to the more leisurely and commodious form of part publication rather than magazine publication to give himself more space to work out his serial designs while increasing his sense of communication with his audience.

This need for interaction with readers manifested itself partly in incorporation of what soap producers now call "socially relevant story lines." He drew these from news stories and government blue books, or simply from endless walks through London. The importance of setting Victorian novels within the rich and fragmented narrative of Victorian discourse has been amply demonstrated.[35] Contextual framing becomes even more crucial in the case of part-issued fictions of any period, not only due to serial emphasis on social relevance but because serials appear literally side by side with other texts; even when issued in independent parts, novels would be absorbed concurrently with the month's magazines and newspapers.[36] From its first sentence, Dickens makes clear the multiple goals and genres he will encompass in *Our Mutual Friend*: "In these times of ours, though concerning the exact year there is no need to be precise, a boat of dirty and disreputable appearance, with two figures in it, floated on the Thames, between Southwark Bridge which is of iron, and London Bridge which is of stone, as an autumn evening was closing in" (1). The first two clauses work simultaneously to elide temporality—"there is no need to be precise"—and to locate it—"these times of ours." This assumption of a shared temporal if not geographical reference creates intimacy between author and audiences (and also, for Dickens fans, echoes the subtitle of *Hard Times: for These Times*). The elision of the exact year reaches out toward future audiences in its anxiety to include us while simultaneously recalling the "once upon a time" of fairy tales. By encompassing such a range of effects, Dickens's novels managed to be both contemporary documents of social conditions and imaginative re-creations of ongoing social structures, testimony of a very particular place and time and fantasy interventions in a self-perpetuating, mythologized social system.

The opening sentence of this novel also introduces a central character: the Thames, hemmed in both by the multiple clauses of this sentence and by London itself as metonymically expressed by two of its bridges. Our setting, forbidding and dirty, elides the human beings who attempt to dominate it and reduces individuality to the anonymous "two figures" trapped within multiple clauses. This first sentence establishes many of the themes of the novel to come: dehumanization, poverty, the city as subject with human beings demoted to objects, the tenuous "professions" improvised, out of necessity, by the underclass, the implacable Thames flowing beneath it all.

The opening illustrates the Dickensian storytelling techniques Sergei Eisenstein credits as inspiring Griffith's development of montage in "Dickens, Griffith, and the Film Today" (214–15 and *passim*). We get a composite picture of this river world, beginning with a placard establishing the date of "these times of ours"; then a close-up of the boat revealing its dilapidation; pull out to a medium shot (two silhouettes just discernible); cut to the surrounding architecture to establish place and mood; zoom in to capture the textures of iron and stone; and finally a long shot, containing all these elements as background but focusing on the sky above them—the veiled, faintly lurid orange of a smoggy London sunset. In the next paragraph we zoom in even further, to pick up voices and details.

Inhabiting this montage of place and atmosphere is a vast range of characters, of which thirty-two can be called central, ranging in age from birth to death, in class from pauper through member of Parliament to aristocracy, in morality from pure, sentimentalized angel to manipulative villain. The novel alternates between subplots drawn from differing genres: the mystery of the search for the missing heir, John Harmon, the identification of a drowned body as Harmon himself, and the search for his murderer; the romance of John Rokesmith's blocked love for the mercenary Bella Wilfer; the farce of Bella's "education"; the social comedy of the Boffins' attempt to "live up to" their sudden wealth and of the Veneerings' attempt to disguise the origins of theirs; the social realism of Lizzie Hexam's desire to improve living conditions for herself and her family and of Betty Higden's desperate evasion of the workhouse; the revenge tragedy of Bradley Headstone's pursuit of Eugene Wrayburn and so on. All these plots become entangled with increasing complexity as the novel progresses.

The novel also contributes to Dickens's development of techniques and tropes now definitive of the serial form. Due to their sheer length and duration, serial narratives encourage plot and character developments such as returns from the dead, radical character transformations, and long-concealed secrets. Although all these tropes of course have a long and distinguished history in literature, they become thematically central to serial fiction and will be recognized as typical of the kinds of "cheap ploys" for which soap operas are denigrated. *Our Mutual Friend* centers on two sensational events: the discovery of a drowned body, presumed to be that of the missing heir to the fortune; and the simultaneous appearance of a man with no apparent past and a variety of aliases. This double focus works to interrogate notions of identity and to map its borders in relation to social context, issues central not only to *Our Mutual Friend* but to the popular press of the 1860s: In 1864, the *Spectator* featured an article entitled "Personation," which opens:

> Novelists, weary of love and bigamy, are making a run just now upon personation. Two novels, each of them very good in its way, Miss Braddon's *Henry Dunbar* and Mr. Jeaffreson's *Not Dead Yet*, have this as the main element in their plots, and as inferior writers always imitate the successful we are pretty sure by December to have a whole crop of personations. The situation is, indeed, a most tempting one. No *bouleversement* of position, not even the old device of changing children at nurse, can be so full of suggestion as that which is created when a man with a history professes to be another man also with a history. [June 4, 1864, 656]

In predicting a surge in tales of forged or mistaken identity, this reviewer is quite accurate. Through the next decade, a number of novels would use this as a central theme; just a few examples are Braddon's *Lady Audley's Secret* and Collins's *Woman in White* and *The Moonstone* as well as, to a lesser extent, his *No Name*. This phenomenon cannot be seen as simply a matter of imitation of successful novels but rather reflects the obsessions of the time.

As Richard Altick establishes in *The Presence of the Present*, the rise of the sensation novel as an acknowledged genre is closely linked to the proliferation of newspapers and the overwhelming popularity of newspaper serials like Reynolds's *The Mysteries of London*. This popularity, in turn, led to a focus on news stories as inspiration for fiction, as manifested in the sensational murders, robberies, lawsuits, and will cases appropriated by novelists (and, to a lesser extent, poets and essayists) as either direct or indirect inspiration for their fictions. Altick cites Charles Reade's letter to the *Times* in 1871, which claims that "for eighteen years [the paper] has been my preceptor and the main source of my works,"[37] as well as Wilkie Collins's *No Name*, in which a character slyly attacks critics of the "unaccountableness" of sensational events when she explains, "I know a great many excellent people who reason against plain experience in the same way—who read the newspapers in the morning, and deny in the evening that there is any romance for writers or painters to work upon in modern life."[38]

Although Dickens occasionally took pains to deny that newspapers influenced his writings (as when he publicly refuted Sir James Stephen's accusation that he simply stole plot elements from news events as they occurred, adding the destruction of Mrs. Clennam's house in *Little Dorrit* to the novel only in response to the collapse of a number of houses in Tottenham Court Road),[39] his novels certainly reverberate with the news of the day. In the years just previous to and concurrent with publication of *Our Mutual Friend*, cases of doubles, mistaken identity, and false appropriation of identity packed newspapers as well as sensation novels. Many of these cases echo the circumstances of John Harmon's return from the dead, exposing a powerful source of anxiety: the numbers of men who had been sent off to the colonies to make fortunes and who returned virtually unrecognizable. In this vein, *Reynolds's* ran the story of the "Personation of a Brother in Wales," which described the deception of a sailor who claimed to be the man a family had sent to Australia years ago. Although the man had not done his homework— knew nothing about the town, its inhabitants, the locale, even the house he had supposedly grown up in—he nevertheless passed as the prodigal son for three days, answering all queries such as his mother's "if he was her son he was greatly altered" by saying that the world had greatly altered him (Jan. 22, 1865, 6).

A different type of identity confusion appears in a *Lloyd's Weekly London Newspaper* story entitled "Mistaken for an Ambassador." A man arrived late one night at a Parisian hotel, was ushered to a room, and awoke the next morning in an enormous suite with breakfast awaiting him. He became alarmed by this unwonted luxury, and asked the waiter why he had been given a suite. The waiter replied,

> "I thought monsieur was an ambassador. We always put them au premier."
> "Ambassador! why?"
> "Because monsieur wore a black coat." [Jan. 3, 1864, 6]

Whatever this story's basis in reality, its inclusion in *Lloyd's* reveals its importance for 1860s society, when clothes no longer necessarily advertised their wearer's class status. Cheap manufacture of fabric as well as ready-made clothing meant that anyone could choose to "dress up," thus transgressing class boundaries in ways many found disquieting.

More subversive still were accounts of women passing as men; for example, the *Sunday Times's* "A Strange but True Story" tells of a Dr. Barry who died after forty-two years in the British army, during which time he had made an excellent reputation as a surgeon and had served in Malta and Corfu. Once dead, he was found to be a woman. The article ends: "This is all that is as yet known of this extraordinary story. The motives that occasioned and the time when commenced this singular deception are both shrouded in mystery. . . . There is no doubt whatever about the 'fact,' but we doubt whether even Miss Braddon herself would have ventured to make use of it as a fiction" (May 27, 1865).[40] This closing comment emphasizes the thin line between fact and fiction—a slippage of which journalists were clearly well aware. While manifesting anxiety over the elision of gender and class borders, all these accounts indicate the work done by newspapers as texts engaged in the process of forging nineteenth-century identities.

That novelists did not simply copy sensational news stories but rather responded to anxieties and obsessions circulating in the culture that produced them can be seen by the evidence of *Our Mutual Friend,* which began serialization just a month *before* the publication of the review predicting "a whole crop of personations" by December. Neither readers nor reviewers could know as yet that concealed identity would be the novel's central theme, but Dickens's memoranda prove that he certainly did. John Harmon, Eugene Wrayburn, and Rogue Riderhood all miraculously survive drownings, and the first two are "reborn" with new and improved personalities. Characters also transform themselves, in all kinds of ways. Just three of the many examples are Harmon, who, presumed drowned, reappears as another man and continues in that guise for most of the book; Noddy Boffin, who changes from jolly old man to evil miser and back; and Bella Wilfer, who develops from a willful, selfish girl to a devoted, selfless wife (much to the chagrin of many twentieth-century readers; from a twentieth-century perspective, she seems much more "realistic," and certainly more interesting, before being apotheosized into one of Dickens's "ideal" girl-wives).

For his part, Dickens had long been interested in such issues, appropriating elements from the Gothic and stage melodrama and developing them for the purpose of exploring the serial possibilities of identity.[41] Many of Dickens's novels feature at least one (usually central) character cut off from or ignorant of his or her parentage or class. Oliver Twist is perhaps the prototypical figure in this regard. His story initially seems to support the democratic/capitalist ideology that any individual can succeed if he or she is bright and honest, but ends by reverting to class essentialism by revealing Oliver to have been a "gentleman" all along—a fact that retroactively "explains" the puzzlingly perfect English he speaks despite his utter lack of models for such speech patterns.[42] *Our Mutual Friend* marks both a shift and a heightening in Dickens's use of the trope of displacement in that virtually everyone in the novel is cut off from his or her original family, class, or identity. Indicative of this trope is the proliferation of orphans in the novel: John Harmon, Sloppy, and little Johnny are orphans right from the start, while Lizzie, Charley, and Jenny Wren become so. Moreover, many characters (including Handford/ Rokesmith/Harmon, Boffin, Bella Wilfer, Lizzie Hexam, Eugene Wray-burn, Bradley Headstone, Rogue Riderhood, Fascination Fledgeby, old Riah, Jenny Wren, and her "bad child" Mr. Dolls) are not what they first seem to be. Each conceals a "true" identity or motivation at some point in the novel, undergoes a radical transformation of personality and/or social level, subverts conventional stereotypes, or in some cases manages all three.

The novel's central theme of displacement also meshes with another plot device much in the news: the idea of inheritance, a will imposed from beyond the grave that can make or break one's chances in life. In the post-script to *Our Mutual Friend*, Dickens defends himself against accusations of the improbability of Harmon's will by noting that "there are hundreds of Will Cases (as they are called), far more remarkable than that fancied in this book" (893). And he is certainly right. Papers of the time teem with head-lines like "A Pauper Heir to an Immense Fortune," "Singular Will Case," or "An Eccentric Bequest."[43] This cultural obsession with the disposal of money can be assumed, on the most obvious level, to stem from the radically in-creased social mobility of the nineteenth century. Money increasingly de-fined status, producing a preoccupation with inheritance: was the source tainted "trade" or respectable "old money"? More subtly, the idea of a will and a claimant, like the notice "found drowned," implies issues of identity. As discussed earlier, the radical shifts in the ways individuals located their class and personal allegiances made for interrogation of the processes by which such locations occurred. Dickens's John Rokesmith created himself anew through his time in the colonies, during which he acquired his own capital, escaped his past and his family, and—on his return—rejected his former identity in order to evade that patriarchal will that would fix his identity even as it made him rich. His story brings to life the struggle be-tween the (old) safe, assured identity and the (new) terrifying but exhilarat-ing "freedom" to determine oneself—or be lost in the process. In this, Rokesmith uncannily resembles the Tichborne Claimant. Just a year after *Our Mutual Friend* completed its run, issues of identity, class, disappearance, and inheritance fused in the "family romance" of the Claimant, an Australian butcher who was recognized as Sir Roger Tichborne by the dowager his mother. The Tichborne trials of 1871–72 and 1874 provided a public locus for debate on the status of identity, class, and inheritance (as well as inspira-tion for plays and novels focusing on a spurious claim to inheritance—Trollope's *Is He Popinjoy?* (1874–75) for example, just as the O.J. Simpson trial provided a forum for debate about the role of race, gender, violence, and fame in 1990s North America.[44]

Not only does the mistaken identity plot reverberate with a range of news stories of the day, but, as alluded to above, it is also ideally suited to the structural exigencies of serial fiction. In the only full-length study of Dickens's serial techniques, Archibald C. Coolidge (1968) argues that part-publication continually tempted the author to "give his stories only the crudest kind of structure" (8). I argue that, on the contrary, serial publication forced Dickens to develop storytelling techniques that led not only to a tighter structure within novels but to a unique thematics for the novel. The most important of these techniques are the interweaving of multiple story lines and the transformation of characters over time. Coolidge does acknowledge that because of the difficulties forced on him by serialization, Dickens essentially developed a new kind of text; however, he sees this new text as increasingly centering on a "single, passive protagonist" as Dickens's career advances. In fact, the opposite is true. As a rule, Dickens's novels move, post-*Pickwick*, from a primary focus on the development of a single figure or travails of a single family (perhaps the clearest examples are *Oliver Twist, Nicholas Nickleby,* and *David Copperfield*, all issued 1837–50) to exploration of increasingly complex interactions between multiple heroes and heroines widely divergent in class, character, and circumstance (*Bleak House, Hard Times, Little Dorrit, A Tale of Two Cities,* and *Our Mutual Friend,* all issued 1852–65). A notable exception to this development is *Great Expectations* (1860–61), but its focus on a single protagonist, relatively small cast of characters, and single central plot can be explained by the fact that Dickens felt compelled to run the novel weekly in *All the Year Round* to revive its flagging sales, and the shorter parts of weekly serialization severely limited the scope of the novel. The multiple focus and multilayered structure of the longer monthly serials Dickens preferred, on the other hand, anticipate strategies used by twentieth-century serials running for years or even decades.

The *People's Journal* review cited earlier points up the political implications of this structure: "The popular school has no tether . . . it can afford to have as many heroes as it pleases. Every man, woman or child is its hero or heroine" (3 June 1846). For the first time, lower-class characters are allowed a central place in fiction. There are philosophical implications as well, since intertwining multiple subplots involving figures of widely different classes and narrative concerns implies a communal world, one centered not on the individual but on the relation between individuals. As Raymond Williams has argued in *The Country and the City*, over the course of his career Dickens developed "a new kind of novel" that could embody the contradictions inherent in industrialized London life: "the coexistence of variation and apparent randomness with what had in the end to be seen as a determining system: the visible individual facts but beyond them, often hidden, the common condition and destiny" (154). Williams rightly connects Dickens's vision of London not to the local instances or descriptions the author provides but to the novels' *form*, "their kind of narrative." Dickens's "new kind of novel" enabled him to convey the complex London environment and re-create the paradox at the heart of industrial life, the contrast between the chaos of urban existence and the apparent economic determinism control-ling the destiny of its inhabitants. Williams cites many tricks that help in achieving this dual focus, such as the use of devices allowing many charac-ters to be recognized, with seeming randomness, through "some fixed phrase, seen in some fixed expression: a way of seeing men and women that belongs to the street," as well as structural techniques providing alteration of mul-tiple subplots that in turn created a polyphony of voices, each in pursuit of its own subplot and alienated from the rest. In the early chapters of a novel, characters "do not so much relate as pass each other. . . . [t]hey speak at or past each other, each intent above all on defining through his words his own identity and reality." Eventually, however, the lives of these individuals begin to intertwine, and "unknown and unacknowledged relationships, profound and decisive connections, definite and committing recognitions and avow-als are as it were forced into consciousness" (155).

What I find most interesting in Williams's theory is that while he is undoubtedly right in concluding that Dickens's trick of isolating the indi-vidual within a crowd reflects his larger awareness of the paradoxical com-munity-in-alienation of urban industrial life, this trick is also necessary to serial fiction. Characters must, above all else, be easily recognizable—by tags of speech, idiosyncratic gestures, and so on—so that audiences remem-ber them from month to month. Gaffer Hexam, for example, is introduced as bearing "a certain likeness to a roused bird of prey"(3), and the unusual description sticks in the mind so that when we see a character with a "ruffled crest" of hair and hear the tag "bird of prey," the first river scene is recalled to mind. Similarly, Mr. Twemlow, who appears infrequently but serves a crucial thematic function in the novel, consistently puts his hand to his forehead and thinks, "I must not think of this. This is enough to soften any man's brain" (usually, "this" has something to do with the social habits of the "mush-room man" Veneering). The gesture simultaneously fixes Twemlow in our minds and furthers the thematization within the novel of the startling shifts in social relations produced by the "mushroom" class of the nouveau riche. Once characters have been established, their lives can intertwine with the complexity that is structurally necessary to serial fiction. Because of its long duration and reliance on interconnections between characters, serial fiction is virtually forced to depict a complex and diverse world. This quality in turn encourages intersection with the lives of its audience and emphasis on growth and change in its characters. Thus the form is a peculiarly reassuring one in the industrial age of increased disconnection from or absence of total-

izing narratives of belief. Williams does not emphasize the influence of serialization in achieving "profound and decisive connections" between characters; however, it is the process of reading a novel over nineteen months that
enables the gradual intertwining of formerly alienated characters and plots
to become infinitely more persuasive than a reading of a week or two could
possibly achieve.

A look at the architecture of the first two numbers of *Our Mutual Friend*
will reveal its careful structuring to maximize the benefits of serial issue and
will also illustrate Williams's description of the ways that interrelations are
"forced into consciousness" (see Table 1). Most obviously, each section, con-
sisting of three or four chapters, alternates plot strands, narrative modes,
and moods to provide a variety of class setting, theme, tone, and even voice.
In opening the novel, Dickens first establishes distinct and utterly discrete
social worlds, each contained in its own chapter and using only one intersecting or shared character, Charley Hexam. In chapter 1, he introduces us
to the grimy, menacing social realism of the river world, in which Gaffer and
Lizzie Hexam pursue a gruesome calling that readers would recognize as
factual since there were numerous articles about the profession in the popular press. In chapter 2, we observe the satirically exaggerated Veneering social circuit. In chapter 3, Charley Hexam infiltrates the Veneering milieu,
bearing news from a very different one: the river world, which is apparently
only acknowledged within Veneering purlieus for its entertainment value.
And finally, in chapter 4 of this first part we are entertained by the comic-
sentimental poverty of the Wilfers, with Bella, its heroine, clearly destined to
play a leading role in the action. After building these separate subplots and
establishing a distinct genre (realism, satire, comedy) to suit each one, Dickens
proceeds to show how entangled his characters, levels, and even narrative
modes actually are. In the opening two chapters, we do not yet see the connections, but one of a serial's central lessons is that as we come to know all
sides of a story, apparently irreconcilable perspectives become intertwined
(though this is *not* to say that they ultimately form a coherent whole). Dickens
hints at this lesson as early as chapter 3, when Mortimer and Eugene de-
scend from the solipsistic, glittering Veneering circle to the dark, "realistic"
level of the Thames, death, and Lizzie. The encounter between the two will
change the lives of all who meet there.

Reviewers As Readers

The intersections between the range of worlds Dickens created were significantly strengthened in the original reading context by the fact that most

Table 1. Storyline Alteration in *Our Mutual Friend*

Chapter	Topic	Mood
1. "The Cup and the Lip"	Lizzie and Gaffer Hexam, as they drag a body out of the Thames.	Dark: horror, suspense
2. "The Man from Somewhere"	The "bran-new" social set of the Veneerings; presents, in guise of dinner-party entertainment, the background of John Harmon and his father's dust-heap fortune and eccentric bequests.	Light: comedy, satire
3. "Another Man"	Charlie Hexam, who comes to find Mortimer Lightwood and brings him to the river to encounter John Harmon's supposed body (here the two worlds intersect); introduces a new twist in the form of "Julius Handford," desperate to see the body but mysteriously reluctant to disclose his own identity.	Dark: suspense, mystery
4. "The R. Wilfer Family"	Bella Wilfer, who was willed to John Harmon by his father, and her comic, exaggerated family.	Light: caricature, comedy, sentimentality
Number 2		
5. "Boffin's Bower"	Wegg and Boffin; also the crucial theme of reading (false versus accurate) and interpretation.	Light: humor
6. "Cut Adrift"	Develops character of Lizzie, and separates Charlie from her.	Dark: pathos, realism, sentimentality
7. "Mr. Wegg Looks After Himself"	Mr. Venus the taxidermist (as we know from his correspondence with Marcus Stone, Dickens explicitly searched for "a character" at this point in the novel); sets up, vaguely and mysteriously, Wegg's plotting.	Dark: grotesque

readers of the novel discussed each part with others, collaboratively reinter-preting and predicting future plot twists. Serial reviewers formed one voice in the total community of readers, and some clearly took active pleasure in guessing the outcome of mysteries. In what follows, I draw on reviews in four of London's cheaper newspapers to demonstrate the ongoing response Dickens received to *Our Mutual Friend* as it was published. Reviewers clearly felt themselves entitled to specify their expectations and to strongly encour-age Dickens to comply with them; thus their voices reveal the views of a sector of the novel's audience as well as the ways the author may have shaped his novel as a result of this response.

Before we discuss these issues, a brief overview of each paper will be useful. The papers are *News of the World*, the *Weekly Times*, the *Sun*, and the *Illustrated London News*. *News of the World* and the *Weekly Times* were both intended for the lower-middle and working classes, as estimated by price (2 pence and 1 penny respectively); by advertisements for cheap patent medi-cines, cheap passages to the colonies, cheap daily excursions ("Brighton and Back for 3s [shillings]"), and so on; by articles, including leaders on political questions of pressing interest to the working classes, updates on the Work-ing Men's Clubs and Friendly Societies, and so on; by the amount and type of sensational stories such as "A Mother Hanging her Child" and "Murder by a Lunatic"; and by entertainment reviews provided for the Polygraphic Hall, Madame Tussaud's, and music halls. The *Sun* had a reputation as a politically progressive paper; the *Newspaper Press Directory* of 1864–65 says of it, "Lib-eral in politics, Free-Trading in Commerce. . . . In regard to literary criticism, also, it has long enjoyed considerable respect: the tone of these criticisms frequently contrasts curiously with its extreme political opinions, addressed as the latter are to the masses." In the subjects of its articles and the types of advertisements and reviews included, the *Sun* is similar to the *Weekly News* and the *Weekly Times*.

By contrast, the *Illustrated London News* targeted upwardly mobile lower-middle- and middle-class readers, as we can see by its price (5 pence) as well as the types of advertisements it carried (for silver and furniture makers, India shawls, and Family Arms painters rather than patent medicines and the latest sensation novels) and the content it tended to include (leaders on political questions of the day; "Foreign and Colonial Intelligence" divided by country); a social column, including news of the Royal Family; and reviews of the more expensive periodicals such as *Blackwood's* and *Fraser's* as well as of "straight" drama rather than music hall.

On May 2, 1864, the *Sun* provides the following review of Part I of *Our Mutual Friend*:

The "two green leaves" dear to us all by reason of so many delightful recollections are putting forth anew, this once, appropriately enough in the spring-
time. . . . As an opening chapter, this first one of "Our Mutual Friend" is
wonderfully striking. It influences the reader, like a glance from the Ancient Mariner's eye: we needs must listen. In its way, as an introduction to a
serial story, it is equal—more than this we could not possibly say of it—it is
equal to that opening chapter in the graveyard by the marshy flats, giving
at once a landscape and a haunting interest to "Great Expectations." . . .
Already, in truth, there is abundant promise in this Part I. of an enthralling
story. The ravelling of the thread of it into a most intricate plot is, to our
mind, in these thirty-two pages, even now pretty well accomplished.

This reviewer, clearly attuned to serialization's specific narrative demands,
points out how Dickens manages to introduce us to a labyrinthine cast of
characters while producing suspense of mood and situation such that "we
needs must listen." After a long extract from the Veneering dinner party, the
review continues: "The chapter coming next, chapter three, that is, entitled
'Another Man'—as the one before it has been typically called (in reference to
the plot) 'The Man from Somewhere'—carries us onward into the intrica-
cies of that labyrinth the readers of 'Our Mutual Friend' are happily destined
now to track out through all its manifold windings during the next nineteen
months consecutively." Especially intriguing here is the recurrent notice given
to the pleasures of serialization. Besides the comment above, this review
includes others such as, "We may now most cordially congratulate Mr. Dickens
upon the brilliant commencement he has made of his new serial fiction—as
we may certainly congratulate his countless readers upon the treat before
them."

Of part 2, the *Sun* tells us, "Another delightful number here introduces
us to several new characters," and proceeds to describe Mr. Wegg and the
others, with profuse extracts. Of the scene in which Lizzie Hexam sends her
young brother Charley away (just before their father's arrest for murder) to
prevent his career from being destroyed, we are informed that "we read it
through a mist that often makes the letterpress indecipherable." This
conflation of the materiality of text and body occurs again in the conclusion:
"Altogether a capital installment, as full of good things as a Christmas plum-
pudding" (June 1, 1864). Tears and letters blur together, words are ingested
like plumcake.

But the *Sun* becomes progressively less enchanted as the story proceeds.
On Feb. 2, 1865, we are told of number 10 that "Half the story of Our
Mutual Friend has now been told. And yet—. . . . We have not, to this
moment, the merest glimmering ghost of a notion as to the pattern into
which all these numerous and complicated threads of the narrative will be

found to have been woven, by the period of the work's completion, nine months hence." This dissatisfaction with the novel's complications was echoed by many other reviewers, even as it predicts the critical response of the next sixty-odd years. *News of the World*, for example, discussing Bella's shabby treatment of John, speculates that "possibly this selfish young woman may, in the course of the story, become transformed; and John Harmon may come into his own" (Jan. 8, 1865). Similarly, the paper asserts of number 15 that "it must be premised that Rokesmith is rightful heir to the property the golden dustman possesses, and this will explain a remark made by the secretary in conversation with his employer" (July 9, 1865). Earlier, though, the same paper complains, "We do not clearly perceive Old Betty Higden's connection with the story of 'The Mutual Friend,' nor, indeed, is the progress made in the chapters before us very intelligible; but this may arise from the author's desire to keep his subject under a veil, so as to prevent the interest flagging. The object, as it appears to us, might have been secured with a little less fogginess of style" (May 7, 1865). In other words, Dickens has failed to live up to at least this reader's understanding of the serial contract: authors should not intentionally mislead the audience but should provide enough clues to enable intelligent and alert readers to anticipate future developments and take pleasure in correct guesses.

In addition to manifesting desire to participate actively in the ongoing construction of the serial, reviewers state their expectations about the way a plot should work. Toward the end of the serial run (number 12), the *Sun* uses a common metaphor—that of weaving, often cited by Dickens himself—to describe its sense of the way the novel should work itself out in the next seven parts:

> Without as yet seeing the merest glimmering of a way out of the labyrithine [*sic*] mazes of the plot of *Our Mutual Friend* as that tortuous labyrinth has been here elaborately arranged in all its, as yet, bewildering involutions— we can nevertheless perceive through the medium of one apparently slight and casual disclosure (a disclosure already here in this notice of ours distinctly particularised) the possibility of the seemingly inextricable puzzle of the plot being explained, after all, to be about the simplest thing in the world, and to be so explained, moreover, by no more than one or two touches of the masterhand. The disclosure here referred to being no other, of course, than that revealing to us quite incidentally, that the object of Mr. Venus's affections is identical with Pleasant Riderhood. A touch or two more like that, and all the now apparently scattered and divergent threads of the plot—threads many of them as yet seemingly woven into the pattern quite separately and independently one of another—would be brought together meshed and knotted into one symmetrical and homogeneous device. As it will be, in fact—we may rest perfectly well assured. [April 3, 1865]

This statement links two central demands of these readers of nineteenth-century texts: that the novel must be complex enough to constitute a "puzzle," and that all subplots must ultimately be woven together. Note also that the *Sun* reviewer cleverly slips in parenthetical proof of his/ her own astuteness in picking up clues.

On the other hand, *News of the World* does not share the *Sun's* confidence in Dickens's commitment to the serial contract. It complains of number 18, "We are within two numbers of the conclusion of this romance, and are still without a clue to any adequate motive for the action of its principal characters; and a great deal of explanation will have to be afforded within a small space" (Oct. 8, 1865). As we will see, Dickens's solution to this difficulty—to expose a "plot" that, unbeknownst to us, has governed the actions of the Boffinses and Rokesmith—did not satisfy all reviewers. However, his summary disposal of many other characters (the Veneerings, Lammles, Wegg, Venus, and so on) is apparently perfectly acceptable, conforming as it does to nineteenth-century and especially to Dickensian conventions of closure. Interestingly, even reviewers who do *not* manifest the faith of the *Sun* reviewer in Dickens's ability to tie up loose ends nevertheless seem to hold such closure as the standard. The *News* reviewer clarifies these expectations earlier in discussing of the novel. Of number 12 he or she describes the Wegg/Venus/Boffin subplot relating the search for and discovery of a missing will and then explains that "the interest of the narrative is heightened by the above-mentioned discovery, for it cannot now be foreseen how the rightful heir to the property . . . is to arrive at his own. Some new discovery will probably be made, whereby 'poetical justice' will be done to all" (April 9, 1865). And in the review of number 16 the ideal of poetical justice, this time without the ironicizing quotation marks, is again held up as a model: "As this story approaches its conclusion, we become more interested than hitherto in the fortunes of its prominent characters. We observe the approach of poetical justice, and can foretel who will be made happy and who condemned to punishment at the end" (Aug. 6, 1865).

Thus reviewers of *Our Mutual Friend* articulate definite expectations about plotting and closure for the novel. In general, all insist on perfectly constructed plots, with clear alteration of subplots, gradual interweaving of characters from different subplots, and loose ends neatly tied in the final double number of a serial. This insistence on "satisfying" closure is in many ways antithetical to the serial form, but Dickens could hardly complain since by the time of this novel's creation he had already played a major role in shaping these expectations. Comparing Dickens's novels to the serialized adventure tales that immediately preceded *Oliver Twist*, Lance Schachterle refers to Dickens's famous statement in *Oliver Twist*—"It is the custom on the stage: in all good, murderous melodramas: to present the tragic and the comic scenes, in as regular alternation, as the layers of red and white in a side of streaky, well-cured bacon" (102)—in explaining that "earlier serialists solved the problem of providing variety simply by using the rough-and-tumble of adventure as an excuse to bring in new characters as needed, but the cumulative force of their serials was consequently impaired. Dickens, by alternating between the streaks of the bacon, provided a pleasing change of pace in his novel, but not at the cost of abandoning the order imposed by a tightly constructed plot" (12).

Dickens developed, of course, many other serial techniques in addition to final closure and alternation of subplots. For example, while he claimed to scorn the cliffhanger techniques of the penny dreadfuls in his novels, in his later works he nevertheless continually and unapologetically made use of such techniques himself.[45] To name just one example, the final sentence of the first part of *Our Mutual Friend* reads "if Mr. Julius Handford had a twin brother upon earth, Mr. John Rokesmith was that man" (43). This not so subtle signpost works to involve readers in two ways: by forcing retroactive interpretation of the first number (these men are doubles? why? how?) and by encouraging prediction of the next number (how will the plot resolve itself? is Handford actually Rokesmith?). What is more, despite the fact that *Our Mutual Friend* demonstrates Dickens's increased privileging of serial resistance to closure over against conventional novelistic resolution, in his final double part Dickens apparently capitulates, either to his critics or to the force of habit and tradition. The novel's conclusion parallels that of many Victorian novels in becoming essentially a litany of the marriages and progeny of "good" characters, the decline or death of "bad" ones.

These serial techniques, most still central to serials today, were developed in response to critiques like those discussed above as well as to the indisputable evidence of sales figures. Like contemporary soap opera producers, he "tried out" characters and plot shifts, enlarging their role if they proved to appeal to readers. To list just a few examples, he greatly expanded Sam Weller's role in *Pickwick Papers* when sales jumped to forty thousand after Sam's first appearance. Again, his periodical *Master Humphrey's Clock* (1840) was intended as a miscellany of stories and sketches loosely linked by the conceit of a group of storytellers, but when sales dragged he first reincarnated Mr. Pickwick and the Wellers and when that failed, expanded one of the stories (*The Old Curiosity Shop*, which appeared as a sketch in the third number) into a novel and allowed it to take over the periodical (Bentley, Burgis, and Slater, 161–62). And poor reader response to *Martin Chuzzlewit* caused Martin himself to be sent off to America in an attempt to revive sales figures in 1842–44, while later in the novel, the linguistically entrancing night nurse Sairey Gamp proved so popular that her part was considerably expanded.

In his eagerness for some sense of interaction with the readers of his novels, Dickens also constantly used his friends as a test audience, checking plots and characters with them. For example, he asked whether to kill off Paul Dombey and Little Nell and notoriously took Bulwer Lytton's advice in revising the planned ending to *Great Expectations* so as not to depress readers too much (Shattock, 165). He also took suggestions for odd or unique characters. Mr. Venus appeared in *Our Mutual Friend* when Dickens, needing to replace the too-long chapter 7 (now chapter 10, "A Marriage Contract," concerning the Lammles) with something shorter, was casting around for an eccentric character and a hint of menace to add interest to the novel and carry readers through to the next part; his illustrator Marcus Stone happened on an eccentric taxidermist and brought Dickens a description (J. Hillis Miller, 176).

As well as changing texts to enhance popularity and therefore increase sales, the author also responded to readers' complaints about stereotypical or unfair portrayals. As we know from letters Dickens himself wrote, Miss Mowcher, the grotesque chiropodist in *David Copperfield*, was based on the woman (also a chiropodist and a dwarf) who treated Catherine Dickens's feet; not surprisingly, she objected to being portrayed in print as a kind of sideshow freak. The author responded to her complaints by transforming the projected role of the character to a much more positive one and allowing her the honor of being responsible for the arrest of the obsequious and corrupt Littimer. At times Dickens extended the concept of seriality by using characters in one novel as responses to criticism of another, earlier novel, as when he introduced Riah the "positive" Jewish character in *Our Mutual Friend* to make amends to a Jewish friend who pointed out the massive injustice Dickens had done her already maligned race by creating the evil Fagin.

After studying the manuscript and number plans of *Our Mutual Friend*, a few critics have speculated that planned plotlines were altered in the course of writing the novel. F.X. Shea (1968) draws on evidence in the original manuscript as well as on comments and emphases in the number plans to argue that as originally conceived, the plot to cheat the Boffinses out of their inheritance from old Harmon was to have been carried out by the Veneerings or the Lammles rather than by Wegg and Venus and thus would have had considerable force as a critique of the criminal greed of the upper classes: "but having made, under conditions of haste and precipitancy, an alteration of his plans he became enmeshed in the developing plot and was unable to recover his original scheme" (170–81). Shea may be right in his conjecture, but newspaper reviews can help us judge the motives for such changes; their evidence suggests another—or at least a concomitant—possibility. Dickens may have changed his plans not because of the careless "haste and precipitancy" conjectured by Shea but as a deliberate and well-considered response to the clearly stated desires of his audience. Reviewers repeatedly expressed loathing for both the Veneerings and the Lammles; on the other hand, they were amused by and interested in Wegg right from the start.

As early as the first number, the *Illustrated London News* (whose resistance to satire of the upper classes may derive from its extensive middle-class readership and upwardly mobile aspirations) tells us, "Happily, we have not seen much of the Veneerings as yet, and we hope to see no more of them than is absolutely necessary to the plot" (May 7, 1864). The reason for this distaste is that "nowhere, perhaps, is he [Dickens] more thoroughly himself than on the great river, with its silent metamorphosis and perpetual combinations of the most heterogeneous objects into a picturesque whole. In the polite world he is out of his element; the rich grotesqueness in which he exults is out of harmony with all the surroundings of the drawing-room." And this critique persists throughout the paper's early reviews of the novel. By the third number it becomes even more pronounced: "The literary merit of the number is very unequal. Mr. Dickens is perfectly at home with Mr. Boffin, and nothing can be better than his description of the struggling curate's house. But as soon as he approaches the Veneerings a spell seems to fall upon him, and his humour becomes extravagantly forced and tedious" (July 9, 1864). As late as the fourth number, the *News* is still harping on the issue: "For the whole of a long chapter Mr. Dickens is in 'society,' where, as usual, he is awkward and ill at ease. May good satirical hits are made, but only with a disproportioned expenditure of labour: everything is forced. Removed to the river-side, Mr. Dickens is himself again" (Aug. 6, 1864).

The *News of the World*, though not as extreme as the *Illustrated London News*, also praises working- or lower-middle-class characters (for example Bradley Headstone, Miss Peecher, and Jenny Wren in the review of number 6), and its criticisms focus on Dickens's satire of the upper classes. For instance, also in the review of Number 6 we are told that the chapter focused on the Veneerings, Twemlow, and their circle and "devoted to the purchase of a seat in Parliament, and the pretence of canvassing the doctors, is not equal to the other contents in the number" (Oct. 9, 1864). And in reviewing number 15, the *News of the World* comments laconically, "There is another chapter in this number wherein those galvanised figures, the Podsnaps, the Veneerings, and others, dance and jibber with an unsuccessful effort at comicality" (July 9, 1865).

The Lammles, for their part, become more popular with some reviewers later in the novel when they are counterpointed by the innocence and humor of Georgiana Podsnap and also become more clearly intertwined with other characters. However, early mentions tend to be disparaging. The *Sun*, for example, complains of number 7 that "the two preceding chapters of this November number of 'OMF' have to do with the very dreariest and worldliest of the mere hangers on of the great system of Podsnappery," meaning the Lammles and Fascination Fledgeby (Nov. 4, 1864). And the *Weekly Times* claims that in creating the Lammles, Dickens "indulges in conceits so absurd, and his creations of characters are so extravagant, that nothing less than a blind admiration of Dickens's writing for Dickens's sake can tolerate" (Nov. 20, 1864). The *Illustrated London News* continually disparages Dickens's ability to depict these characters, right to the bitter end; on their ultimate appearance, in number 16, the reviewer tells us that "the Lammles retire from the scene at last, leaving it as unaccountable as ever why they should have come on" (Aug. 5, 1865).

Silas Wegg, on the other hand, is greeted with immediate appreciation. The *Illustrated London News* tells us when Wegg is first introduced in number 2 that "in this instalment of his serial . . . [w]e have four new personages . . . Mr. Wegg will probably be the popular favorite among them" (June 4, 1864)— and perhaps this critical approval helped to make him so. *News of the World* is not quite so enthusiastic, finding Venus and Wegg to be "rather ingenious than agreeable"; but the reviewer does choose to quote from Venus and Wegg's chapter as the "most comprehensible" since the other chapters include the reviled Veneerings (June 5, 1864). And by number 13, this reviewer attests that while "there are other personages whom the reader is careless about . . . [t]he most striking figures are the Boffinses and Silas Wegg of the wooden leg; and when these actors leave the stage we are not regardful of the rest, but anxiously look for the reappearance of the favourites" (May 7, 1865). For its part, the *Sun* gives Wegg a full share in the enthusiasm it invariably accords the lower-class characters, implying that readers will identify strongly with this new figure since he is easily recognizable as "realistic." All the papers concur, then, in approving Dickens's depictions of lower-class characters. On the other hand, willingness to tolerate caricatures of upper-class life seems to depend on the class context in which a reviewer writes. As we have seen, the middle-class *Illustrated London News* is particularly vocal in its disapproval of Dickens's liberties with the "higher orders."

Given the consistently negative response to characters planned as central and the enthusiastic praise of others brought on as afterthoughts, if Dickens did change plot projections in midstream—and Shea's evidence is quite suggestive—he may have done so consciously and not with the carelessness Shea implies. It is true that portraying the scheming, upwardly mobile Veneerings as the innocent Boffins' would-be fleecers would have had more force as social critique than did the creation of a vicious lower-class villain, Wegg, but Mr. Veneering's buying of a seat in Parliament, the Lammles' attempt to sell Georgiana to the highest bidder on the marriage market, and Fledgeby's gleeful manipulation of stereotypes about Jews to cover his own usury do not exactly show the upper classes in the most positive light either. What is more, readers' praise for the lower-class characters proves the extent to which Dickens and other popular authors had succeeded in rendering the middle and working classes appropriate subjects for "serious" fiction. Instead of judging Dickens's flexibility as a weakness, then, we could see such changes as representing one of his—and serial fiction's—great strengths. The ability to alter narratives in response to the success or failure of subplots or characters is seen as negative because we have constructed ideologies of the "true" artist and writer as governed only by individual genius and never by the demands of the marketplace. This view is, of course, elitist, alienated, and above all unrealistic. There is no inherent flaw in a kind of "just in time" production of stories; neither does this method preclude the inspiration of creative genius. Instead, both market forces and artistic gifts can work together to produce texts crafted by an individual or creative team but flexible enough to respond to good and relevant ideas from outside, whether in the form of audience response, news events, or other sources. As Benjamin shows us in "The Storyteller," the interaction of author and audience has long been a central feature of the art of narrative creation, and within mass culture only producers of serials have the luxury of long-term and ongoing response from the audience during the process of fiction production.

Reviewers had a clear, pragmatic role as mediator in the author-audience relationship: their job was to tell readers which serials were worth an investment of time and money. Reviewers remained quite conscious of this fundamental purpose, as shown by the fact that in reviewing the first number of *Our Mutual Friend*, three of the four newspapers allude to the novel's potential readership. On May 2, the *Sun* closes its first review by announcing, "We may now most cordially congratulate Mr. Dickens upon the brilliant commencement he has made of his new serial fiction—as we may certainly congratulate his countless readers upon the treat before them." On May 7, the *Illustrated London News* assures readers that "this first number has fully satisfied our expectations, and will repay the eagerness with which it will be universally perused". On May 8, *News of the World* "promise[s] our readers that they will also be amused and interested in the perusal." Finally, on May 22, the *Weekly Times* laconically notes that "the commencement of a new tale by this popular writer will be sufficiently noticed by a simple announcement of the fact." Except for this last—the *Weekly Times* reviewer loathed the novel for the first half of its run and seems to have born a grudge against Dickens as well, as we will see—each of these reviews explicitly acknowledges its primary purpose: to let readers know whether or not to invest in the new serial.

In the reviews to follow, readers remain firmly at center stage. They are advised as to the best and worst passages in each number and told which are the strongest and weakest chapters; their probable reactions are anticipated; they are counseled as to the moral or political weight of particular subplots. The implicit bond between readers and reviewer is reinforced by the cozy "we" used in many reviews, as in the *Illustrated London News* quote above. It is important to note that reviewers assert their identity with readers because this implies a hesitancy to assume the role of expert: when it comes to serials, all readers are equal. Every paper's reviewer employs the collective "we" at least at times during the run of this and other novels, making absolute pronouncements such as the *Sun's* "the reader will therefore have the mournful task of taking leave of one who has so long fascinated and charmed his leisure with his inimitable productions" (review of *Denis Duvall*, May 2, 1864) or the same paper's comment that "as an opening chapter, this first one of 'Our Mutual Friend' . . . influences the reader, like a glance from the Ancient Mariner's eye: we needs must listen." (May 2, 1864). As the last quote demonstrates, the *Sun* reviewer is particularly prone to imply identity with the reader, tossing off comments such as, "The very corner of the street where he [Silas Wegg] passes the chief part of his existence—don't we know it?" (June 1, 1864) or "Several new characters are introduced to our notice in this latest instalment. . . . And foremost among these ought at once to be particularised a little creature destined, or we are very much mistaken, to be embalmed with tears of love among our tenderest recollections" (Oct. 3, 1864).

The *Illustrated London News* is equally willing to predict readers' responses, though less apt to assume an identity of response between reader and reviewer. Characteristic comments include, "The search for the drowned man in the first chapter will not readily be forgotten by any reader; it occupies less than four pages, and yet, somehow, claims a larger picture in the memory than the other twenty-eight" (May 7, 1864). Again, of number 17 the reviewer assures us that "the interest excited by the personages in this story is comparatively so tame and languid that the reader passes indolently over what appears to him a mere battle of the kites and the crows" (Sept. 9, 1865). So the *Illustrated London News* takes the conventional approach in assuming and predicting readers' responses. However, this paper does depart from the practice of other reviewers in allowing some autonomy to the reader. Of the controversy over the title, the reviewer hints that "Mr. Dickens's explanation of his title Our Mutual Friend . . . does not give, as might have been expected, satisfaction to everybody. What it is our readers may see for themselves" (July 2, 1864); the last two sentences allow for both divergence of opinion and an independent reading experience. Similarly, of the last double number this reviewer tells us, "If the progress of this story has frequently been feeble and languid, the conclusion at least is all that could be desired. We will not spoil the reader's pleasure by acquainting him with the surprise in store for him, but merely observe that it will be found to compensate in some degree for that premature revelation of the main feature of the plot" (Nov. 4, 1865). Thus this reviewer whets readers' appetites by providing plot teasers but takes care not to spoil the suspense Dickens so carefully develops.

News of the World reveals an interesting double split in its relation to readers. For the most part, it keeps its distance, simply acknowledging the review's pragmatic function as advice to potential consumers. Thus, of part 1 the review asserts, "We promise our readers that they will also be amused and interested in the perusal" (May 8, 1864); of part 15 it assures us that "the reader will be better pleased with the little love affair, which occupies the larger number of its pages, between John Rokesmith, the golden dustman's secretary, and pretty Bella" (July 9, 1865); and of number 17 it warns, "Some readers may consider that the incident is made too terrible by the finding of the battered body of the victim" (Sept. 10, 1865). However, when forced to confront unfamiliar narrative techniques, the reviewer suddenly assumes the position of the reader, as in this review of number 5: "The 'first book' of this extraordinary tale is concluded in the present number . . . and we rise from the perusal of this instalment in a state of utter unconsciousness of what it is about. If it were Mr. D's object to puzzle his readers, he has succeeded in doing so. We have been wandering with a considerable number of persons without caring much for any one of them; and who or what they really are, it would puzzle a conjurer, not in author's confidence, to tell" (Sept. 4, 1864). And again, when reviewing number 7, the reviewer admits, "The reader is perplexed by the words and behavior of Mr. Eugene Wrayburn, who had previously made a somewhat favourable impression, but who now seems to be acting a rascally part towards a poor girl" (Nov. 6, 1864). In both these extracts, the reviewer becomes the reader in moments of doubt, with no claim to higher insight into the text and with equal likelihood of being confused, misled, or annoyed.

Possibly because of its initial disgust with Dickens, the *Weekly Times* consistently refuses the stance of the expert. It introduces the novel by asserting blandly, "Of course, with the first number, we are left to conjecture as to the plot, and are unable to say anything about it" (May 22, 1864). This is a neat trick; by stating the obvious, the reviewer cleverly evades the professional responsibility of higher insight into texts, insight that may well be proven false in just a few months. A similar stratagem is used in the review of Number 2, where we are told: "There is a mystery, but we must not expect to have it unravelled yet" (July 3, 1864). Interestingly, though, by the time the *Weekly Times* has come round to considering *Our Mutual Friend* a fine piece of writing it also adopts the inclusive "we" that serves to identify reviewer with readers, as in the following: "Georgiana is a style of character we often meet with in the world, and it is this individualizing of types that gives Charles Dickens such a hold of the great mass of readers of fiction" (Aug. 13, 1865).

So reviewers developed a range of roles for themselves, from authoritarian predictor of reader response to equal participant in the reading experience. Moreover, a simple equation of reviewer's attitude with class of paper cannot be made. While establishing themselves as "just your average readers" in some ways, reviewers for these papers have definite expectations of the text, and they make these very clear. All expect Dickens to highlight lower-class characters. All also concur more or less explicitly in wishing Dickens to stay away from portrayals of the wealthier social circles, though their motivations seem to vary from a desire to keep the upper classes free from caricature to a lack of interest in the doings of that class and a concomitant desire that Dickens increase representations of the middle and lower classes. We saw evidence of these preferences in the consensus that Wegg and Venus were preferable to the Veneerings and the Lammles.

In addition to revealing specific expectations regarding plotting and depiction of classes, reviews articulate distinct standards of style. Among the most consistent of these is the demand that the author create "realistic" story lines. This expectation exposes one of the most interesting contradictions among serial audiences, one that has persisted from the nineteenth century to the present. Audiences often demand satisfaction of the most traditional expectations of storytelling (coherent plots, interweaving of characters and themes, and narrative justice). Simultaneously, however, serial audiences expect and appreciate narrative modes as diverse as social realism, fantasy, camp or self-reflexivity, and comic relief. These expectations produce what can now be termed, in the case of soap opera, a postmodern awareness of the serial as a fictional construct composed of a juxtaposition of contradictory genres (comedy, sentimentality, melodrama, social realism, farce, mystery). The roots of these seemingly contradictory demands can be seen in their incipient stages in criticism of *Our Mutual Friend*.

In expecting that Dickens will focus on middle-class characters and include sympathetic walk-ons of the lower classes—while repeatedly urging him to avoid "caricatures" of the upper classes—reviewers connect these strategies with narrative realism. As might be expected, however, definitions of exactly what constitutes "realism" seem to vary considerably from reader to reader, class to class. Dickens's friend John Forster, for example, ascribed *Pickwick*'s popularity to the author's creation of "real people" who echoed readers' own urban lives: "That a number of persons belonging to the middle and lower ranks of life . . . had been somehow added to his intimate and familiar acquaintance, the ordinary reader knew before half a dozen numbers were out." Similarly, a *National Magazine* reviewer explicitly links Dickens's productions with the domestic space in which they were often consumed: "To furnish our readers with a guide to the houses which they inhabit, or to introduce all the members of a family circle to each other, would be about as wise and necessary as to play the master of the ceremonies between the creations of the novelist [Dickens] and the public. The characters and scenes of this writer have become, to an extent undreamed of in all previous cases, part of our actual life. Their individualities, whether mental or external, are as familiar to us as those of our most intimate associates or our most frequent resorts."[46]

Both Forster and this reviewer typify a common response to serial fictions of all types: they are treated paradoxically as both fictions and realities, a syndrome that is partially responsible for criticism of (especially soap opera) fans as ignorant dupes of the media. In the case of Dickens's novels, this response takes visual shape in the many artists' images of Dickens with his characters (see figs. 1 and 2). Other authors also encouraged the slippage between fiction and real life. Thackeray is perhaps the most notorious, with his alter-ego narrators and his famous postscript to *The Newcomes* (1854–55), which opens by telling us that "Pendennis and Laura, and Ethel and Clive, fade away into Fable-land. I hardly know whether they are not true; whether they do not live near us somewhere. They were alive, and I heard their voices. . . . Is yonder line (———), which I drew with my own pen, a barrier between me and Hades, as it were, across which I can see those figures retreating and only dimly glimmering?" (926–27). Having leveled the distinction between author and audience by depicting both as engaged in the process of disengaging from characters who have been intimate friends for twenty-three months, Thackeray literally draws a line between fiction and reality to force our attention to the self-conscious process of inscription involved in the creation of these "friends." He then proceeds to use the just dismantled "reality" of his characters to evade charges of sloppy plotting and too many loose ends: he claims himself as a mere conduit for the narrative conveyed by Pendennis and joins the audience in complaining of the many questions left unanswered by the narrative.

Fig. 1.1: W.H. Beard, "Dickens Receiving His Characters" (1874). Reproduced by courtesy of the Dickens House Museum, London.

Speaking of fictional characters as members of our "family circle" is grounds for mockery at best when soap fans do it, but the practice actually meshes with the nexus of conventions Ian Watt terms "formal realism" in his theorization of the eighteenth-century British novel. These conventions include careful location of the novel's action at a specific point in place and time and an attempt to capture the "texture" of life at that point. Terry Lovell points out that "authenticity is, for him [Watt], the keynote of the realist novel" (8), which reached its apex in the nineteenth-century serial. Thus soap and other serial fans are simply honoring generic tradition when they pretend to see characters as real people. On the other hand, because of their narrative complexity most serials work to problematize "formal realism," just as most novels do. As Thackeray goes out of his way to emphasize, readers and viewers have long proved themselves capable of holding a double vision of their texts as at once realistic and fantastic, quotidian and otherworldly; it is only critics who at times manifest a need to reduce texts to fit pet theories. For example, Lovell rightly emphasizes the fact that Watt's "authenticity" is hardly an unproblematic term in itself. To support his thesis, Watt privileges (male) authors who manifest characteristics of his pre-

Fig. 1.2: J.R. Brown, "Dickens Surrounded by His Characters" (n.d.). Reproduced courtesy of the Dickens House Museum, London.

ferred narrative of novelistic development, the rise of formal realism. Therefore he virtually ignores texts that subvert that narrative, the so-called
"women's" novelistic forms such as the Gothic, Sterne's *Tristram Shandy*, and
so on. Similarly, reviewers stressed Dickens's depiction of "actual life" and at
times resisted his incorporation of fantasy, slapstick, melodrama, and other
narrative modes. Their response tells us much more about reviewers' desire
to categorize and thus control the baggy-monster fiction they assessed than
about either the novels themselves or "actual life."

There is also a class component to definitions of realism. The *Illustrated
London News*, for example, with its middle-class bias, seems to equate a simple,
"natural" style with good writing. As we have seen, the reviewer continually
berates the author's "clumsy delineations of West-end refinement" and
"strained and tedious sentiment" (June 4, 1864). These comments indicate
not only the paper's resistance to Dickens's satire of the upper classes, but
also a quality most reviewers value highly: Dickens's descriptive abilities.
The highest praise seems reserved for those moments when Dickens makes
us "see" his scenes or describes characters we already "know." For example,
number 5 is described as "an excellent number" because it "opens with one
of those river-side descriptions in which Mr. Dickens is so invariably successful. Nothing can be more vivid. We seem to hear the sullen lapse of the
thick water among piles and barges, to see the 'great grey hole' in the murki-
ness that announces the dawn, and to shudder at the blank uncomfortableness
it everywhere brings to light" (Sept. 10, 1864).

The *Sun* also praises Dickens's descriptive powers, especially his ability
to capture landscape: "The description of the toy Neighbourhood, by the
way, where his school stands, is inimitable—just one of those rapidly-pen-
cilled Boz vignettes that are marvels of realistic word-painting" (Oct. 3, 1864).
Indeed, the *Sun* places such high value on narrative authenticity that it uses
the word "realism" even to capture—and somehow to excuse—Dickens's
excesses. For example, we are told that a scene with Rogue Riderhood is
conveyed "in one of those strange grotesque sentences (wondrously realistic
in their way), that no one but Mr. Dickens would ever dream of writing"
(Aug. 3, 1865).

For its part, the *Weekly Times* emphasizes a different interpretation of
the "natural," one that invokes the sentimental: family interactions, romantic love, the figure of the dying child. In reviewing number 2, the *Times* says,
"We will not essay to 'paint the lily, or to gild the refined gold,' and, therefore, shall not attempt now to eulogise any production from the fertile genius and ready pen of Charles Dickens. The following touch of nature will
suffice to create an impression in favour of 'Our Mutual Friend.'" The "touch"

so described is Lizzie's interaction with her father and brother (July 3, 1864). Like the *Illustrated London News*, the *Weekly Times* loathes the Podsnaps on the basis that they are caricatures of the upper classes and therefore "absurd" and "extravagant" characters rather than "natural" ones (Nov. 20, 1864). However, the root cause of this loathing is very different for each paper. As we saw, the upwardly mobile *News* disapproves of Dickens's taking liberties with a class he does not understand. The more egalitarian *Times*, on the other hand, claims that Dickens's greatest achievement has been to reveal the working and middle classes as suitable heroes for fiction. Thus the reviewer quotes a description of upper-class life from number 4 and then adds, "This is not the sort of writing that won for Charles Dickens fame and fortune, and a pedestal; but, however, the obscuration of the literary planet is but for a moment, and in many of the subsequent pages we find 'Richard himself again'" (Aug. 14, 1864). And of the final double number, the same reviewer praises above all the author's realism in producing "photographs of classes" and makes its class sympathies quite clear by ending with the praise, "We know of no writer who has done more for the amelioration of the sufferings of the poor than Charles Dickens himself in his various contributions to the literature of the country during the last quarter of a century" (Nov. 26, 1865).

The *News of the World* concurs with the other papers in praising what seems "true to life" and condemning what seems staged. For example, "Mr. Bradley Headstone, the cheap schoolmaster, a patient drudge, and Miss Peecher, the schoolmistress, who cherishes a hopeless passion for that gentleman, are natural and effective sketches," while the Veneering electioneering chapter "is not equal to the other contents of the number. The figures are numerous, but they are mere wooden figures, moving as the wires are pulled" (Oct. 9, 1864). Later in the novel, this reviewer objects to the dearth of "correct" sentiment: "The present chapters are sentimental and humorous; but both humour and sentiment are open to criticism. The pickling of Mr Fledgeby, an impossible thing as far as Miss Jenny Wren is concerned, would make an amusing incident in a pantomime; and the bed-room scenes of Mr. Eugene Wrayburn, who is not dead at all, but alive to be married, give the idea rather of a sensational burlesque, in the manner of the 'Woman in Mauve,' than of a serious reality" (Oct. 8, 1865). This rejection of tropes appropriated from the popular stage is especially interesting considering that Dickens did in fact draw heavily and frequently on popular theater.

In these papers, then, we can see that reviewers placed high value on Dickens's construction of a "realism" that privileges familiar characters and settings, exactly that emphasis on the intersections between fiction and "real life" that so disturbed early critics of the serial form. In his discussion of the discourse of realism as applied to mid-nineteenth-century novels in general,

Andrew Blake also finds that readers and reviewers alike emphasize the "everydayness" of approved characters, dialogue, and incidents. He concludes: "By the 1850s, then, 'realism' largely meant the focusing of attention on the domestic lives of middle-class people. . . . But this did not mean the 'reflecting' of an already-given ordinary, but the *establishing* of the ordinary, the forming of the norms by which 'ordinary' people should live" (78; also see 69–78 passim). Blake's emphasis is a crucial one: *Our Mutual Friend* and the discourse that surrounded its appearance in print played an important role in establishing expectations of everyday life. The insistence of the reviewers cited above on the value of the natural or realistic in literature (Dickens's "photographs of classes," for example) as well as the range of associations reviewers make with those terms support Blake's argument here. Clearly, each newspaper had a slightly different agenda, and therefore each desired to normalize a different worldview as the "real" or "natural" one. Of course this negotiation of meaning took place not just within reviews but across the spectrum of a text's consumption in casual discussions, family readings, boardinghouse readings, comments to the author by friends or fans, and so on. In other words, readers negotiated definitions of "realism" in ways that affected authors in turn—and most of all the author of serial fiction, still in the process of constructing an ongoing fictional world.

"There was no such thing as I": The Narrative Preoccupations of Serial Fiction

We have seen reviewers attempting to shape the parameters of the "real" and "natural" and negotiating appropriate heroes and plot strategies. These issues combine in two interrelated subplots that have long been the foci of criticism of *Our Mutual Friend*, and that have much to teach us about the generic development of serial fiction: Noddy Boffin's radical character transformation, and John Harmon's triple identity and the necessity, finally, of a "Solo" chapter to explicate his history. Read as incidents of a conventional novel, both are indeed confusing. Read as episodes in a nineteen-month narrative experience, both have essential work to perform. The sheer length of the serial experience can make such shifts in identity seem far less arbitrary than they would in a conventional novel. In addition, as we have seen, radical transformations of identity reverberate both with the themes of this novel and with the serial reading experience.

A number of nineteenth-century serialized novels, by Dickens and others, have been criticized for exactly those elements most likely to have been encouraged by the practice of serialization. We have seen Dickens's contemporaries articulating their demand for increased authorial control over the novel's plotting, and some later critics attributed specific plot "flaws" to the book's serial publication. For example, both George Gissing and G.K. Chesterton believe that Dickens intended Mr. Boffin's conversion to miserliness to be "real," but retroactively made it altruistic (Boffin, we learn at the end of the novel, acted the miser to educate the charming but acquisitive Bella in the dangers of money-love) either because he changed his mind at the last minute and thus "patched up [a mistake] with another mistake" (Chesterton 215) or because his first principle was "[a]voidance of the disagreeable, as a topic uncongenial to art" (Gissing 89–90).

The decay of Boffin's once generous nature beneath the corrupting influence of his unexpected inheritance is so well-prepared and so gradually effected that readers are duped right along with Bella, a fact that may account for some of the annoyance underlying many critiques. The process begins when Bella hints to her father, in number 11, that Boffin's character seems to be changing for the worse (March 1865); is crystallized when we witness Boffin's obsession with the lives of misers in number 12 (April); and culminates in number 15 (July) when Boffin fires Rokesmith in a scene of high melodrama. This scene spurs Bella, whose sympathy for Rokesmith and revulsion for Boffin's greediness have grown gradually over the past five months, to take his side. Later readers, like Gissing and Chesterton, often find this subplot overly melodramatic and Boffin's reversal back into a nice guy at the end of the novel much too abrupt. But Dickens's contemporaries would have experienced the melodrama in its original context: as a narrative mode used to express dichotomous power relations and hence as signifying the class struggle between the now wealthy Boffin and his employee Rokesmith. Contemporary readers also had the advantage of reading a plot that meshed cleanly with current ideologies of the danger of excessive wealth and the superior moral character of the middle classes. And perhaps most important, contemporaries were drawn into this "sudden" personality change over half a year rather than in the few days of our reading of the text.

Therefore it is not surprising that the novel's original readers appreciated this plot much more than later critics. *News of the World* asserts of number 12—the part that introduces Boffin's transformation—that "the first chapter of this number is one of the best of the book. Therein we find a change coming over the felicity which the golden dustman has enjoyed since his sudden acquisition of a large fortune. He was a generous, kind-hearted man, but wealth has made him covetous, arrogant, and exacting" (April 8, 1865). Of the same number, the *Illustrated London News* says, "the present deserves to be ranked among the best numbers of this unequal serial. Mr. Boffin is introduced in a new light, and the effect of sudden wealth in perverting a generous character is shown with great psychologic [sic] truth" (April 9,

1865). And the *Sun* concurs in believing Boffin's performance: "Incredible though Bella's latest hint to Pa at the close of the March number appeared to us to be, it nevertheless turns out to have been only too true after all! The Golden Dustman (in chap. v. of vol. ii) falls into Bad Company, (in chap. vi. of vol. ii.) falls into Worse Company. Gets a hankering after details of the lives of those abject wretches—those exemplary persons—the Misers, whom he apparently meditates emulating. Has a kind of illegibility stealing over his face" (April 3, 1865). Perhaps even more tellingly, only one of these reviewers—from *News of the World*—asserts at the end of the novel that readers should not have been kept in the dark as to Rokesmith/Harmon's conspiracy with the Boffins. Even this criticism is mildly expressed, stating simply, "The discovery made that a considerable portion of the story is the issue of a plot between some of the characters, takes the reader by surprise, without inspiring any degree of pleasure. There was force in the exhibition of the golden dustman in the delirium of wealth committing certain excesses, and it is disappointing at the last to find this powerful incident is only a hoax" (Nov. 5, 1865). The *Weekly Times*, on the contrary, actually praises the denouement: "The description of Mrs. Boffin explaining the little deception that had been practised on Bella by herself, John, and Mr. Boffin is remarkably vivid and wonderfully graphic" (Nov. 26, 1865).

Boffin's transformation is paired with the John Harmon/John Rokesmith doubling. From the serial's beginning, Dickens intentionally arouses suspicion as to Harmon's identity. He points out this strategy in his postscript to the novel, and at least the *News of the World* picked up on it in its review of number 5 (Sept. 4, 1864), where it quotes a key description: there is an "unreadable something" in Harmon's face, we are told, when he looks at Mrs. Boffin. Thus Harmon becomes a text needing interpretation. The clue exists in his face (which retains traces of his childhood) and is finally "read" by Mrs. Boffin. Shortly thereafter, Mr. Boffin begins the mock transformation that is intended to teach Bella the dangers of her self-avowed mercenary leanings. From this point on, we are excluded from the secret shared by Rokesmith and the Boffins, an effect that Dickens only achieves by means of much manipulation of point of view, as his number plans make clear. For number 12, he notes that "Mr. Boffin and Rokesmith and Mrs. Boffin, having, unknown to the reader, arranged their plan, now strike in with it," and also notes his intention to "keep Bella watching and never suspecting" (Cotsell, 205). To achieve these goals, the narrative point of view shifts dramatically. Earlier, positioned with the near-omniscient narrator, we worked with the characters in trying to piece together a mystery. But suddenly this equality of reader and character disappears. Whereas hitherto the Boffins' private discussions took place in scenes we witnessed ("Mr. Boffin in Consultation,"

"Mr. and Mrs. Boffin in Consultation"), after John's proposal to Bella we almost invariably experience the Boffin household through the third-person-limited filter of Bella's eyes, a point of view in which the "limited" is particularly applicable since we as well as she experience a definite sense of exclusion. Dickens makes this choice explicit in his number plan for number 8 by noting the following sketch for Bella's character: in her "elopement" with her father, Bella "says she is mercenary and why. *But indicate better qualities. Interest the reader in her.*" We are, then, to be associated with Bella, who temporarily becomes the cultural dupe par excellence. She is first taken in by Mr. Boffin's Tartuffian stage-miser performance (readers, too, though often annoyed and puzzled by Boffin's overacting, usually admit to having had no idea as to the cause of it) and then agrees to marry a man who essentially wins her by a narrative combination of sympathy and suspense. She champions him in response to Boffin's bullying, which also confronts her with a mirror image of her own self-proclaimed consuming desire. She finally elopes with him, knowing that he has a secret, one that involves her being "tried"— a trial through which, Rokesmith tells her, she "will never pass quite triumphantly for me, unless you can put perfect faith in me" (815).

In other words, Rokesmith is testing Bella, forcing her to live in near poverty and absolute ignorance and to do so without question, putting her life in his hands until he should choose to reveal his secret. Like the ideal serial reader, then, Bella has learned to suspend judgment and to live with (perhaps even enjoy) suspense. But the serial reader also learns to predict, to look for clues, to compare notes with other readers in an attempt to unravel the mystery and predict the narrative outcome. In *Our Mutual Friend*, Dickens does what he can to make it impossible for the reader to predict Harmon's conspiracy with Boffin. Similarly, Bella is not allowed to question or guess, but must wait passively for Dickens/Harmon to make all clear to her. As we will see, despite their willingness to accept Boffin's character change, Dickens's contemporaries were not keen on the techniques he developed to convey Harmon's point of view.

In part 9 (January 1865) readers are given partial answers, in the form of Rokesmith's "Solo" or soliloquy detailing all he has done since returning to England. From the moment of his decision to "walk ashore . . . in disguise," we now learn, John Harmon attempted to keep his own subplot distinct from the narrative trajectory his father's will attempted to impose on him. He wanted to learn what he could about Bella (whom his father's will left him "like a dozen of spoons" as a condition of his inheritance) before deciding whether to claim her with his inheritance or to abandon both. This soliloquy has often been cited as a partial cause of the novel's failure. Critics see it as a tricky form of authorial intervention since it allows Dickens to convey information necessary to readers but inappropriate for conversation between characters: if Boffin's transformation is to remain convincing, readers must think Harmon's true identity unknown to all others within the world of the novel. That Dickens chooses to break the bounds of the conventional realist novel by introducing this soliloquy may seem awkward, but the technique is also indicative of the way he pressures the boundaries of the novel. Radical shifts in point of view become increasingly important within nineteenth-century literature as they achieve a central place within the serial genre; Esther Summerson's chapters in *Bleak House* are a key example, as is Wilkie Collins's *The Moonstone*, which unfolds through the contrasting first-person testimony of a wide range of characters. Moreover, the fact that Franklin Blake turns out, unbeknownst even to himself, to have been the criminal all along reverberates with Collins's theme of the impossibility of a truly "objective" narrative. Thus multiple voices produce a Bakhtinian polyphony complicating the "traditional" coherence and closure of the novel.

John Harmon's first-person, stream-of-consciousness narrative indicates the extent to which the self, with its menu of possible identities, has become a focus of the novel. In his soliloquy, Harmon seeks to consolidate an identity literally drowned in the flood of concerns—economic, social, romantic—surrounding him since his return to England. This point is emphasized when Harmon remembers himself drugged and all but unconscious: "I was trodden upon and fallen over. I heard a noise of blows. . . . I could not have said that my name was John Harmon—I could not have thought it—I didn't know it. . . . I cannot possibly express it to myself without using the word I. But it was not I. There was no such thing as I, within my knowledge" (369). Here Dickens renders explicit the novel's questioning of identity and the extent to which it has become dependent upon social context. Having dressed himself in the clothing of a different class, surrounded himself with strangers, and escaped his inheritance, Harmon finds himself annulled rather than liberated. Hence the necessary process of this "Solo," in which he reorients himself materially, geographically, and linguistically by recovering the pawned clothing he wore the day his true identity disappeared and by talking and walking himself through the events leading up to that "disappearance."

Having reclaimed a self who can propose marriage to Bella, he does so in the subsequent "Duett." Dickens intended John's proposal to Bella to produce this effect, as noted in his number plan: "Bella impatient and resentful. Bury John Harmon under mounds and mounds! Crush him! Cover him! Keep him down!" Harmon, scornfully refused by the girl who was willed to him but does not know his identity, first determines to bury himself under the dustheaps that separated him from "authentic" love before he met Bella and ironically work to prevent her love for him now that he has rejected them and is therefore poor. But the Boffins convince him to try another technique: the miser plan devised to push Bella into compassion for John.

This plot works, of course, as Bella falls in love with the man she thinks poor and abused. Dickens thus denies the economics of marriage as merger by first establishing the conventional trajectory of a marriage arranged by the Fathers and then explicitly rejecting it. In its place he substitutes the ideology of romantic love, which arises "spontaneously" and supposedly depends on the essential selves of the lovers, not at all on their material circumstances. In order to accomplish this feat of separating his hero and heroine from the economics in which they are so thoroughly enmeshed, Dickens—ever canny about the ways material conditions produce identity— must dissociate Harmon from the text that has produced him by giving him a supposedly unmediated voice. In other words, the contradictions reviewers resented in the novel's technique point to larger and unresolvable contradictions in its ideological foundations.

In response to complaints from some reviewers and readers about his high-handedness in keeping this secret from them, Dickens attempts to justify the technique in his postscript. In a move analogous to but more overt than Thackeray's postscript to *The Newcomes*, he reproaches readers who have failed to trust him by supposing "that I was at great pains to conceal exactly what I was at great pains to suggest: namely, that Mr. John Harmon was not slain." He then informs us that he intended to teach a lesson "in the interests of art" to his audience, who must learn "that an artist . . . may perhaps be trusted to know what he is about in his vocation, if they will concede him a little patience" (821). This statement is a little disingenuous on Dickens's part, since he made his living by encouraging audiences' active, rather than passive, consumption of texts.

One departure from the primarily negative commentary on this plot is Rosemary Mudhenk's relatively recent (1979) attempt to justify secrecy on the part of the author. She argues that Dickens positions us with the ignorant Bella in relation to both the Boffin and the Harmon subplots "to shock the reader with his own misjudgment, thereby to educate him [sic]. Dickens does for the reader, what Boffin does for Bella. The reader is forced to learn that his perception has been limited and his knowledge partial" (42). Though this didactic function does make sense given the moral weight assigned to the nineteenth-century novel, forcing the reader into the role of cultural dupe seems uncharacteristically condescending for Dickens. I would argue instead that *Our Mutual Friend*'s shifts mark developments in the contract, still in the process of negotiation, between serial audiences and creators, a contract that is very different from that between readers and authors of nonserialized texts. Serial readers learn to get all the facts before arriving at an interpretation; the genre teaches the impossibility of absolute interpretation before all voices have been heard. Hence serial's increased emphasis on tolerance of mystery, ambiguity, and doubt as well as a drive toward communal reading that allows a polyphony of interpretation paralleling the polyphony of the narrative itself. In this case, though, Dickens withholds too many facts and provides misleading "clues," thus denying his serial audience their expected role. Readers are placed in the position of the later Bella, urged to wait passively until all is revealed. As real rather than fantasy readers, reviewers proved unwilling to adopt the position of dupe.

The Boffin/Harmon secret also draws on a trope long common in literary history and now central to the serial: the use of doubles as a means of interrogating identity. The novel is constructed around (mostly male) pairs of characters who test, balance, or expose each other: John Harmon/John Rokesmith, Gaffer Hexam/Rogue Riderhood, Bradley Headstone/Eugene Wrayburn, Headstone/Rogue Riderhood, Bella Wilfer/Lizzie Hexam, and others. Of these, the most central are Bella and Lizzie and Eugene and Bradley.

Bella and Lizzie, together with other, minor female characters such as Georgiana Podsnap and Sophronia Lammle, demonstrate the consequences of the patriarchal refusal to allow women the right to choose a husband—or to choose *not* to marry at all. This pairing of young women also exposes the class and economic codings of marriage. Early in the novel, Bella rants about her peculiar relation to the missing John Harmon, whom she has never met but to whom she has been virtually engaged by his dead father's will: "How *could* I like him, left to him in a will, like a dozen of spoons" (37)—or, as she later puts it, "Willed away, like a horse, or a dog, or a bird. . . . Am I forever to be made the property of strangers?" (377). Lizzie, on the other hand, deprived of the luxury of such contempt, literally disappears from the novel in an attempt to escape the two men who have established her as the prize in their interlocked competition for status and masculinity. As Eve Sedgwick shows, this competition is a textbook illustration of René Girard's theory of triangular desire. Disturbingly but predictably (since Dickens generally succumbs to his penchant for "idealized," passive child-women by the end of a novel, if not earlier), Lizzie's passive renunciation of her own will is valued more highly, within the system of the novel, than Bella's active pursuit of her desires, to the extent that Bella must make a pilgrimage to Lizzie to learn humility.

Their interaction begins with an emphatic mirroring: "It's a pleasure to me," says Lizzie, "to look at you"; to which Bella replies, "I have nothing left to begin with. . . . because I was going to say that it was a pleasure to me to look at you, Lizzie" (523). The two then establish further parallels: that both have become pawns in the Harmon murder case, since as Bella puts it, "I was dragged into the subject without my consent, and you were dragged into it without your consent, and there is very little to choose between us" (523–24); that both have no female friends; and that both have love interests which they are (of course) too modest to discuss directly.

Then the differences—and the lesson for Bella—begin to emerge. Lizzie, with the "drooping head" and blush Dickens favors for his heroines, refuses Bella's suggestion that she forget her (silenced) love for Eugene since there is nothing to gain from it, asking, "Does a woman's heart that—that has that weakness in it which you have spoken of . . . seek to gain anything?" (527). And lest we have missed the cues pointing to Lizzie's role as moral model, Bella silently asks herself in response to this statement, "There, you little mercenary wretch! Do you hear that? Ain't you ashamed of yourself?" (527). On leaving Lizzie's cottage, Bella retains her lesson so well that she and John share their first romantic interlude in the train returning to London, complete with a cloyingly sentimental personification of the railway signals "knowingly shutting up their green eyes and opening their red ones when they prepared to let the boofer lady pass" (531). However, such effusions accorded well with the taste of the time, as can be seen in reviewers' comments. Lizzie in particular is unequivocally a favorite with contemporary critics, and her more sentimental passages receive especial praise. The *Weekly Times*, for example, says of number 5 that "there is, amidst much to excite mirth, one or two passages of deep pathos—especially that in page 132, where the daughter of Gaffer is supposed to apostrophize her absent father, whose death has occurred, and, as yet, is unknown to her" (Sept. 18, 1864). And the same paper declares of Betty Higden's death scene—which mobilizes some of the heaviest guns of Victorian sentimentality, including the Poor but Good Grandmother, the Young Girl as Angel, and the first-person apostrophe—that Betty and Lizzie together create "the occasional flashes of light scattered through the story" (Feb. 12, 1865).

Unlike the other doublings, Lizzie and Bella's is confined to this one scene; however, their didactic pairing must be seen in conjunction with the related pair of Lizzie's rival lovers, Eugene Wrayburn and Bradley Headstone. The contrast between the two—careless, charming, lazy Eugene on the one hand, impassioned, awkward, hardworking Bradley on the other—is painful to observe since we see the social context that has produced each. Both men are provided with biographical sketches that help us to understand the origin of their personality disorders. Eugene, the gentleman, was raised in an atmosphere of privilege that fostered his inability to exert himself; moreover, he had the handicap of a tyrannical father. In addition to the "excuses" provided for him by this background, Eugene gains sympathy by his sense of humor against all odds and his ironic running commentary on his own uselessness. However, he loses sympathy by wielding the easy, careless manners of a "gentleman" to devastating effect in his first confrontation with Headstone: "Passing him with his eyes as if there were nothing where he stood, Eugene looked on to Bradley Headstone. With consummate indolence, he turned to Mortimer, inquiring, 'And who may this other person be?'" (288). For the rest of the encounter Eugene insists upon calling Bradley "Schoolmaster," refusing to name him as an individual and emphasizing his class-bound identity.

This kind of treatment not surprisingly results in Bradley's obsessive defensiveness, and again we are given a thumbnail sketch that helps to explain this behavior. By means of extraordinary dedication to the facts of scholarship, he has dragged himself out of extreme poverty to the relatively exalted position of schoolmaster. But as Dickens had already argued in *Hard Times*, "Facts, Facts, Facts" do not alter basic human desires but merely rechannel them. What is more, Dickens's description of Bradley's education implicitly critiques the educational system. As Headstone himself asks Wrayburn, "Do you suppose that a man, in forming himself for the duties that I discharge, and in watching and repressing himself daily to discharge them well, dismisses a man's nature?" (291). This and similar statements help us to understand Headstone's desperate obsession with Lizzie: it is a consequence of the repression demanded by a class system that insists he transform himself quite literally into someone else if he wishes to escape poverty.

In a move typical of serial fiction, we may first be repelled by Headstone's less than charming personality but may learn to be ashamed of this snap rejection. Due to serials' characteristic subplot rotation, we see him at center stage occasionally and gradually learn more about the circumstances that produced him. As with Eugene, the emphasis on past history and the leisurely unfolding of character enables a layering of past cause and present effect, which teaches us that all behavior is more complicated than we might think, all characters deserve time at center stage, and all are worthy of sympathy.

The chasm between classes becomes clear in the first confrontation between the two men. In response to Eugene's cool avowal of the difference between Lizzie and "all the low obscure people about her," Bradley finally bursts out: "You reproach me with my origin . . . you cast insinuations at my bringing-up. But I tell you, sir, I have worked my way onward, out of both and in spite of both, and have a right to be considered a better man than you, with better reason for being proud" (293). Although Dickens's constant mockery of Wrayburn's languid uselessness has prepared us to realize the truth of Headstone's assertion, Wrayburn is unmoved: "How I can reproach you with what is not within my knowledge, or how I can cast stones that were never in my hand, is a problem for the ingenuity of a schoolmaster to prove" (293). On the most concrete level, of course, Eugene is absolutely right: he does not know much about Bradley's past history, although we readers do. But beneath this calm response to the *facts* of the situation is, as Bradley is well aware, a much more subtle assertion of class privilege. Eugene knows nothing about Bradley, still less about the conditions of the working class in England. He has no need to cast stones because he has simply removed himself from the struggle altogether. Or so he believes. For Eugene Wrayburn, the trajectory of the novel will work to teach him his inability to so remove himself: he is ineluctably entangled with Others of all classes. At the same time, the novel's gradual unfolding teaches us an equally gradual understanding of both sides of the story. Over nineteen months, we are eased into acknowledgment of the complexity and high cost of Victorian class relations.

As Eve Sedgwick points out, the triangular desire joining Lizzie, Eugene, and Bradley produces a violently erotic rivalry between the two men. This rivalry takes on the force of compulsion until Lizzie, vanishing upriver, removes herself from the equation (to which she seems to have become virtually extraneous in any case) as if to allow Eugene and Bradley's fixation on each other to reach its necessary, unmediated conclusion. Sedgwick also notes rightly that the homosocial "fantasy energies of compulsion, prohibition, and explosive violence . . . are mapped along the axes of social and political power; so that the revelation of intrapsychic structures is inextricable from the revelation of the mechanisms of class domination"(162). This mapping is clear in Dickens's depiction of Bradley's urgent erotic force, references to his "proud, moody, and sullen" attitude toward his childhood poverty, and constant invocations of his "origin," his "bringing-up." For his part, Eugene's wordless elision of Bradley's physical presence and insistence on the labels of "Schoolmaster" or "other person" (with its echoes of the put-her-in-her-place phrase "young person") combine to cancel Headstone's desire, class, and gender simultaneously.

Sedgwick argues that "the moral ugliness of Eugene's taunts against the schoolmaster is always less striking, in the novel's presentation, than the unloveliness of the schoolmaster's anxiety and frustration" (107), and Dickens doubtless did intend Eugene's easy, lazy grace to endear him to us on some level (thus helping to make palatable his eventual recuperation for the purpose of the novel's closure). However, these qualities more centrally symbolize the upper classes' easy, lazy refusal to acknowledge the suffering—and the rights—of the working classes. Lest we miss this message, Dickens drives it home by means of conversations between Eugene and Mortimer that strongly imply Eugene's intention of seducing Lizzie since he cannot possibly marry the daughter of a dredgerman. Within the moral universe of a nineteenth-century novel, this "gentleman's" intentions put him clearly in the wrong.

The intertwined doublings of Bella and Lizzie and Eugene and Bradley allow Dickens to interrogate the forces of gender, class, and erotic desire as these shape identity. Similar techniques have been expanded and even stylized in later serials. For example, the popular trope of identical twins, evil twins, and multiple personalities allow a single actor to expose dual facets of the "same" character as a result of shifted social and psychological circumstances. But Dickens's doublings were ultimately limited in scope by the necessity for satisfactory closure, a requirement already present in a novel's first number and constantly imposed throughout the serial run both by the pressure of that nineteenth double number and by the conventions and audience expectations of the nineteenth-century novel.

J. Hillis Miller was one of the first to recognize the novel's intentional departure from earlier tradition. Unlike, say, *Bleak House*, he explains that *"Our Mutual Friend* remains true to its rejection of the idea that there is an ideal unity of the world translating the differences between individual lives, and perceptible from the outside by Providence or by the omniscient eye of the narrator. . . . here there is no unifying center and no final scene which shows the chief protagonists looking forward to living happily ever after."[47] Miller sees the novel as anticipating twentieth-century modernist fiction in refusing the solution of a knowable, objective, unified world, thus revising early critiques of the novel's overcomplexity and juxtaposition of realism and surrealism.[48] And Edward Johnson joins the move away from criticism of the novel's too-ambiguous plot by praising the ending for its "realism" in avoiding conventional closure (1969).[49] From the 1940s on, in fact, Humphry House, Edmund Wilson, George Orwell, Arnold Kettle, Barbara Hardy, and others have contributed to this appreciation of the novel's complexities. In addition, the novel's surrealism begins to be lauded rather than condemned as unrealistic; in some ways its counterpoint of realism and fairy-tale or fantasy elements conforms much more to the modernist and postmodernist eras than to its own.

Thus much of the critical work on *Our Mutual Friend* has been intended to respond to early critiques that the novel's "flaws" are a result of sloppy plotting, insufficient authorial control, or reliance on sensational elements to catch an audience, all attributed to the novel's mode of publication. Of course, Dickens was not alone in receiving (and sometimes deserving) castigation. Thackeray seems almost to have cultivated his reputation for last-minute, sloppy writing, and as Edgar F. Harden has pointed out, this reputation was extended to damn serial fiction by association as "an artistically inferior medium that invited carelessness" (3). An infamous example of Thackeray's occasional lapses is his forgetting that he had killed off a minor character—Lady Glenlivet, Lord Farintosh's mother—in chapter 56 of *The Newcomes* and then blandly informing us that "Lord Farintosh's mother and sisters" were to visit Barnes Newcome in chapter 58. In the novel's postscript, Thackeray makes a good-humored, self-reflexive attempt to justify his mistake by blaming his alter ego and narrator: "By a most monstrous blunder," he tells us, "Mr. Pendennis killed Lord Farintosh's mother, at one page, and brought her to life again at another" (927). The pressures and duration of serialization do, of course, increase the risk of errors of continuity and characterization. On the other hand, while nonserialized novels may be less likely to revive killed-off characters or to abandon subplots, they are equally likely to include "typically" unbelievable plots. For example, in Wilkie Collins's *The Moonstone* (1868), the stone's mysterious disappearance turns out to have been effected, *without his own knowledge*, by the trusty Franklin Blake while under the influence of opium. This plot twist combines retroactive character reevaluation and a long-concealed secret with an aplomb worthy of any soap opera.

As a serial, *Our Mutual Friend* has, then, been accused of many failings, both in its own time and more recently. During its run, as we saw above, many reviewers complained repeatedly about its complexity, saying that the novel was too full of subplots, minor characters who persisted in taking center stage, and narrative strands not fully worked out. Serial audiences in 1864 had clearly developed distinct expectations, and these were forcefully articulated by reviewers as they attempted to guide readers' choices. Such expectations could be contradictory, as when reviewers praise Dickens's realism but also demand the comic relief derived from earlier traditions like farce and unrealistic characters like buffoons. But reviews demonstrate readers' ability to negotiate multiple narrative modes within serials. They also reveal an increasing sense that readers can and should participate in the process of shaping serial expectations in general, and still unfinished novels in particular, by making their likes, dislikes, and plot predictions known to serial creators. As representative of the discourse about novel reading during *Our Mutual Friend*'s run, these reviews provide crucial evidence of the kinds of activities engaged in by Dickens's readers and therefore of the factors influencing him during the writing process. They also shed light on the process by which serial techniques still in use today were developed. And finally, since we will see the same "flaws" critiqued in relation to both comic strips and soap operas, reviews help to reveal the genesis of long-standing resistance to the serial genre.

Early critics disparage too-complex plots and lack of closure; later critics began to recast the novel's ambiguities as strengths rather than weaknesses. However, in both the relationship between ambiguity and serialization is elided. If we see the novel as demonstrating Dickens's increasing development of serial techniques, such "flaws" as its multiplicity of subplots and narrative modes become explicable. Although *Our Mutual Friend*'s lack of traditional closure, dispersed plot strands, multiple points of view, and so on seem anomalous when compared with the "typical" three-decker Victorian novel, exactly these characteristics—and resistance to closure in particular—have become essential to serial fiction as a genre. So by the end of his career, Dickens had developed strategies that, although controversial at the time, would eventually harden into generic qualities. Plot devices like doublings and plot reversals merely extended techniques and tropes long used in literature. Dickens's response to readers, however, reconfigured the relationship between storyteller and audience for the industrial age; thus *Our Mutual Friend* develops strategies uniquely suited to serialization. In allowing space for alteration of planned events and expansion of popular characters, Dickens prepared the way for soap writers who put actors together on-screen for "tests" to determine "chemistry" before scripting story lines for them. By doing so, soap writers can be seen to privilege chance and contingency, forces that have replaced "fate" as perceived ruling factors in contemporary life and that, more importantly, play a major role in the production of a fiction that depends not on a single author but on a highly complex network of factors such as actors' chemistry, contract negotiations, producers' edicts, and ratings. Dickens, by contrast, privileged authorial control and narrative closure. After all, despite his eagerness for a personal relationship with his audience, he was solely responsible for shaping the novel published under his name; he knew the novel would ultimately be bound and sold as a complete text and that audiences expected some sort of narrative closure. But the expansive vision of *Our Mutual Friend* provided themes, tropes, and narrative techniques for serializers of the future, and Dickens's responsiveness to his audience increased their ability to have at least a partial voice in creating the fictions they consumed.

2

Terry's Expert Readers
The Rise of the Continuity Comic

> My task is to combine the pleasures of yesterday with the expectations
> of tomorrow and serve it up as the ten-cent black and white special
> available today.
>
> —Milton Caniff

"HIS WORKS ARE a sign of the times," a reviewer said as Charles Dickens's
Oliver Twist began its serial run; "their periodical return excites more interest
than that of Halley's comet."[1] Manufactured, mass-cultural time replacing
organic, celestial time: from Dickens's era through World War I, new technologies impelled new modes of thinking about and experiencing temporality. For thirty-odd years (1836 to the 1870s), serialization was the most popular method of nineteenth-century novel publication. Seen in the context of
generic development, this popularity indicates a remarkable process of cultural adjustment to the changed experience of time. Part-published novels
parallel transformations in cultural constructions of temporality, especially
in terms of the relations of an individual life and death to a larger historical
span. Meted out in small doses, awaited eagerly, consumed steadily, used as
a means of constructing leisure and a measure of passing time, serial novels
may seem interminable and chaotic. But there is always a drive toward narrative resolution, always a reweaving of plot strands, always the implicit
contract between writer and reader: all this, the nineteenth-century novel
promises, will eventually make sense.

In the early twentieth century, inventions such as the automobile, air-
plane, telephone, cinema, and x-ray all served as material foundations of
cultural reorientation as expressed in, for example, the theory of relativity,
psychoanalysis, cubism, and the stream-of-consciousness novel. With the
inventions of industrialization and after, Lewis Mumford (1934) theorizes
that "time took on the character of an enclosed space: it could be divided, it
could be filled up, it could even be expanded by the invention of labor-
saving machines" (17). A crucial manifestation of new modes of organizing

the workday was the time clock. Workers had to be *on time*; their lives were slotted into hours on the factory clock and blasts of the factory whistle, and "leisure" became the space marked out as separate from work. Artists attempting to depict shifting relations between time and space were haunted by Gotthold Lessing's eighteenth-century division of the arts into those capable of representing time (which include narrative and music) and those portraying space (the visual arts). Stephen Kern, in *The Culture of Time and Space 1880–1918*, cites early-twentieth-century artistic response to the situation: Joyce's fascination with the cinema led to his re-creation of filmmakers' montage techniques in *Ulysses*, for example, while Proust exploded narrative teleology by recapturing time through sensual memory impressions.

While writers experimented with traditional ways of representing time—and thus with conventional ways of thinking about it and about history, both national and personal—visual artists sought to represent temporality within a supposedly static medium. The impressionists (and Monet in particular) conveyed change over time by rendering sequences of the same visual space at different hours or seasons. The futurist Umberto Boccioni's sculptures twisted time and motion into a dynamic whole. Explicit representations of time out of joint invaded paintings of every school: Paul Cezanne's still life dominated by a massive black clock without hands, Juan Gris's mutated, broken *Watch*, Salvador Dali's *The Persistence of Memory*, crammed with melting timepieces (Kern, 21). But Kern argues that the project failed: "Aside from de Chirico, who placed readable clocks clearly in view, all the other painters deformed, obscured, or defaced these reminders that their genre is incapable of representing time. Lessing's iron law was challenged but never surmounted. The argument on behalf of the flux of time would be carried through more effectively by the philosophers and novelists who could give it an extended formulation" (23). Painters were, then, unable to surmount the challenge of incorporating temporality within a visual medium. But comic strips, which also developed during this era, could and did tackle the existential, technological, and mechanical aspects of altered temporality in a way no other art form was capable of doing (with the possible exception of the cinema).

Comics literalize Mumford's dictum that "time took on the character of an enclosed space" by using visual blocks to separate narrative into distinct segments. By taking a story and dividing it up into separate, isolated instants, comics annihilate the seamless "flow" of narrative, forcing viewers or readers to subjectively justify leaps from frame to frame across temporal or spatial gaps. The reinvention of text/reader relations is troubled by the additional requirement that these disjunctive little boxes can only appear four at a time. This requirement has two consequences: creators are forced to leave out large chunks of narrative as they compress their stories, and narrative flow must be continually interrupted, frame to frame as well as day to day. Because of the gap signified by the thin line separating one frame from the next, the genre gradually developed conventions to signal any transitions that had been made in time, space, or subject. By actively interpreting these relationships of cause and effect, time, and space, comic-strip readers virtually create the story. We make connections and fill in gaps for ourselves, and our conscious experience of doing so works to graphically alter perceptions of time: moments become both unique and disjunctive as the connection between time and space becomes subjective, based on perception and convention.

Before this active reading was possible, however, comic artists and their readers had to make the exigencies of the form manageable by developing these conventions. As Martin Barker argues, comic artists (like filmmakers) gradually accumulated methods of conveying a vast range of possible meanings within static, separate frames, and we, the readers, simultaneously acquired the cultural capital to interpret these conventions. Most of us now instantly comprehend comics' visual shorthand for an immense number of actions, effects, objects, even mental states: text-filled balloons within the strip signal spoken words, balloons connected by bubbles represent unspoken thought, parallel lines trailing behind objects or characters imply quick motion, sweat drops mean distress, stars equal pain, a jumble of symbols indicates profanity, and so on. In addition, the composition within individual frames conveys spatial or hierarchical relationships, mood, and tense, while the overall relation of frames to each other can indicate cause and effect, relative importance of actions, disjunction, simultaneity of two actions at different points in space, containment of one segment of action as a "close-up" within another, or even the fictional nature of the comic itself or of its characters. All these complex meanings are conveyed to readers through "simple" conventions developed by a process of negotiation between creators and readers or by subversions of these conventions once they have become fixed.[2]

David Kunzle (1990), in analyzing the development comic-strip conventions, demonstrates the development of a "grammar and syntax" of graphic language by Goethe's friend Rodolphe Töpffer as early as the 1830s, including montage to create a sense of narrative movement, with jump cuts or the occasional close-up for effect. A few decades later, Wilhelm Busch moved away from caricatured representation by experimenting with representation of internal realities as well as externals (thus anticipating the modernist movement). As Kunzle explains, "Busch realized that there were occasions when the posture did not match the intensity of feeling. How does one represent the essential *internality* of powerful sensations, the psychological component as well as the physiological. . . . He pioneered certain of the most basic conventions of representation of movement and emotion we now take for granted: air currents, impact lines, speed lines, patterns of oscillation" (351). Kunzle also discusses development of the aerial or bird's-eye view, which became so popular in the last quarter of the nineteenth century. As he notes, this panoramic view "expresses, graphically, intentions that only the most capacious novelists—a Balzac or Dickens—could actually fulfill. Yet both writer and caricaturist operate from the idea that by taking sufficient distance one might approximate a kind of scientific mapping of the social totality" (365). Also, as film theorists have noted, the aerial view works to give the spectator the illusion of control over the object of representation.

Both Kunzle and comic expert Thomas Inge claim Dickens as a forerunner of contemporary comic strips: Inge cites *Pickwick Papers* as a landmark production in entwining text and illustration within a single fiction (132). In fact, it is both sad and fascinating to see just how often apologists for mass serials in many media invoke the holy ghost of Dickens in order to acquire a bit of respectability by association—Dickens, who himself was hardly considered "respectable" in his own time. But other major comic-strip influences—Töpffer is a case in point—are rarely acknowledged by American comic fans and creators. As Kunzle ruefully admits in justifying his analysis of early comic strips, "By now I should have learned that to deny in the face of the U.S. media that the United States invented the comic strip is about as pointless as denying that the United States invented freedom and democracy" (xix). Kunzle's parallel between genre and ideology is not just a facile comparison. Shifts in the narrative form and appearance of the serial genre do reflect significant alterations in political and cultural climates and thus become closely associated with the milieu that produced them. Although all the elements of the adventure comic were already in place, it was indeed in the United States that a new kind of serial was invented in the first decades of the century by extending comic art to include continuing narratives based on the actions of a consistent cast of characters, with dialogue in speech bubbles. And over the next few decades, American artists further developed these narratives into adventure strips by adding multiple subplots, suspense, a succession of delayed climaxes, and a pro-American agenda to the comic serial. As we have already seen with Dickens and as we will continue to see with strips and soaps, the combination of the first three elements works as one of the biggest marketing pulls ever invented. But why was the adventure comic a specifically American invention? Two reasons stand out as most crucial: the rapid development and intense competition of the New York newspaper industry at the turn of the century, and the emphasis on optimum efficiency produced by the time-motion studies of Frederich Taylor, among other factors.

"Streamline your mind": Comic Strip Production in the Age of Ford and Taylor

Cave paintings, Egyptian art, Roman friezes, Middle Ages' stained glass, triptychs, illustrated manuscripts, Hogarth's graphic series: all can be seen as precursors to the comic since all tell stories through a sequence of visuals, sometimes with text added to increase the ability to convey narrative. According to comic expert Maurice Horne, all that is needed to satisfy the generic requirements of a comic strip is the addition of consistent characters and text to a series of pictures. A broad definition, certainly, and one that allows almost endless permutations. However, in *Comics: Ideology, Power, and the Critics,* Martin Barker collapses generic restrictions by pointing out that in fact "a comic is what has been produced under the definition of a 'comic.' There has been a historical process whereby public arguments about comics, and what is acceptable under that name, have become in their turn powerful determinants of what is produced" (8). This statement resonates with my earlier argument for serial fiction as a generic form developing over time and in response to public discourse. The horizon of expectations produced by such discourse helps define what is acceptable as well as what is popular, and these expectations in turn shape the narratives produced, a strong argument in support of the effectiveness of both audience response and cultural criticism.

The history of comic-strip development is inseparable from the transformations in technology and literacy that also impelled the rise of part-issued novels. Cheaper paper, improvements in printing technologies, and expanded distribution networks enabled Dickens to sell forty thousand copies of *Pickwick Papers* and also helped newspapers to create a market for themselves as increasingly affordable sources of information. James R. Beniger, in *The Control Revolution: Technological and Economic Origins of the Information Society*, dubs the newspapers produced by the combination of these factors the "first truly mass medium" since by 1827 presses could churn out twenty-five hundred pages per hour. Efficiency improved rapidly, and by 1893 the New York *World* printed ninety-six thousand eight-page copies per hour, a 300 percent increase. As competition stiffened, newspaper publishers realized that breaking up solid columns led to greater ease of reading and therefore to wider circulation. The popularity of illustrations proven to increase circulation of part-issued novels also helped popularize newspapers and journals: texts that combined print and pictures (Dickens's serials and the *London*

Illustrated Times, to name just two of the almost infinite examples) sold enormously. This obsession with visual aids was initially attributed to low literacy; but even after American and British literacy levels increased, the popularity of the ubiquitous illustrated newspapers and penny dreadfuls, spinoffs like "authorized" scenes from *Pickwick* or *The Old Curiosity Shop*, sketches of royalty or criminals, and other illustrated texts continued to rise. Publishers began to refine layout techniques, emphasizing graphics and illustration. In 1873, the invention of photoengraving enabled inexpensive newspaper illustration, which encouraged publishers to increase the percentage of graphics in their papers.

But a potentially huge market for newspapers had not yet been tapped: urban workers, who in many cases could not afford even the relatively modest additional daily expense of six cents for the cheapest journals. In 1833, the publisher Benjamin Day started the eponymous New York *Sun*, priced at one penny. As the new paper informed its readers in its first issue (Sept. 3, 1833), "The object of this paper is to lay before the public, at a price within the means of every one, all the news of the day, and at the same time afford an advantageous medium for advertising" (quoted in O'Brien, 6). The key word here is advertising. Although improved papermaking and production technologies did facilitate drastic reductions in price, advertising revenues enabled Day to lower prices even further. By 1919, nearly two-thirds of American newspaper revenue came from advertising, and by the time radio broadcasting appeared on the scene as a competitor, 48 percent of advertising expenditures went to papers (Beniger, 18, 361).

To attract big advertisers, papers had to keep up with the latest technologies. In the last decade of the nineteenth century, chromolithography and the trichromatic process were perfected. Papers needed a medium for this new, attention-grabbing technology. In 1893, Joseph Pulitzer bought a Hoe four-color rotary press for his New York *World*, planning to add reproductions of famous artworks to his highly successful Sunday supplement formula. Art did not reproduce well, so the Sunday editor persuaded Pulitzer to let him try the color press for the comic section. The infamous "Yellow Kid" of Richard Outcault's strip "Hogan's World" was born when the foreman of the press began experimenting with the most difficult color to reproduce, yellow (Robinson, 12–13).

Also in the 1890s, San Francisco's sensational newspaper baron William Randolph Hearst moved into the Manhattan market, buying the failing *Morning Journal* from Albert Pulitzer, Joseph's brother. He began a series of raids on the staff of the *World*—at one point pirating the entire Sunday supplement staff—and on October 18, 1896, he advertised:

NEW YORK JOURNAL'S COMIC WEEKLY—EIGHT FUN PAGES OF COLOR THAT MAKE THE
KALEIDOSCOPE PALE WITH ENVY . . . Bunco steerers may tempt your fancy with
a "color supplement" that is black and tan—four pages of weak, wishy-
washy color and four pages of desolate waste of black.

But the JOURNAL'S COLOR COMIC WEEKLY!

Ah! There's the diff!

EIGHT PAGES OF POLYCHROMATIC EFFULGENCE THAT MAKE THE RAINBOW LOOK
LIKE A LEAD PIPE.

That's the sort of color comic weekly the people want: and they shall
have it. [quoted in Robinson, 13]

Like the *Pickwick Papers* plug printed by Chapman and Hall to increase interest in the serial, again we see marketing genius at work: Hearst runs down
the competition, then pumps his own product in (literally) glowing terms.
Finally, he tells the people what they want and then proclaims his intention
of satisfying them. This last slippery stroke is his greatest. Eliding his own
highly profitable position as agent of their satisfaction, he presents the weekly
almost as a spontaneous manifestation of "the people's" autonomous desire.
With the inception of comic strips as tools to increase sales of newspapers,
we have the beginnings of institutionalized attention to the desires of serial
readers. But despite Hearst's belief, readers are not to be tricked by being *told*
that they are getting what they want. We will see concrete evidence of this in
the Letters to the Editor written by Caniff's fans.

Many critics laud the early comic-strip era, 1900–10, as the time of newspaper comics' greatest diversity, imagination, and originality, and these strips
were certainly remarkable. For example, George Herriman's *Krazy Kat* (begun in 1908) developed a unique iconography for exploring the slippage
between apparently solid constructs of gender, race, and language, while
Winsor McKay's *Little Nemo in Slumberland's* amazing visuals and dreamscapes
influenced later filmmakers with its experimental camera angles and creation of subjective perspective. In their ability to tell stories, however, these
early strips are limited, tending to feature animals or children and focusing
on humor. As a rule, they are series rather than true serials since they center
on the activities of a consistent cast of characters but do not usually involve
narrative continuity. Instead, each day's strip either rings changes on a set
plot or sets up a new "gag" whose punch line is delivered in the last strip.
These comics lost ground quickly once the serious strip was introduced in
1924. By the 1930s, gag strips had given way to the enormously popular
adventure comics, streamlined, action- and romance-packed narratives paralleling movie and magazine serials in providing ongoing topics of interest
and conversation and having the considerable advantage, in this age of in-

creased emphasis on efficiency, of requiring an investment of only a few cents and minutes a day.

In 1929, Antonio Gramsci speculated on the effects of the new "rationalized" modes of production on its practitioners, arguing in "Americanism and Fordism" that Fordist methods, especially the assembly line, were developing "a new type of man suited to the new type of work and productive process" (286). He saw one critical requirement for the development of this "new man" as a progressive destruction of "animality," claiming that the history of industrialization traces "an uninterrupted, often painful and bloody process of subjugating natural (i.e. animal and primitive) instincts to new, more complex and rigid norms and habits of order, exactitude and precision which can make possible the increasingly complex forms of collective life which are the necessary consequence of industrial development" (298). This analysis curiously echoes the comic-art transition from free-form, one-joke "animal and primitive" strips to tightly woven narratives. Indeed, continuity strips can be seen as meshing with Taylorist dictates of efficiency in being streamlined versions of Dickensian fiction, narrative subjected to a kind of time-motion study and broken into discrete moments and events, which comic creators then pack into four frames a day. All wasted movements are eliminated, all nonessential characters weeded out, all irrelevant actions unrepresented.

But these surface parallels between mode of production and formal qualities of the narrative produced are far less significant than the implied shifts in "human nature." Just as serialized novels became popular after changes in work schedules produced a new emphasis on leisure, comic strips developed concomitantly with transitions in attitudes toward work and economic and social organization. Chief among these was the Fordist concept of the large-scale, centralized manufacture of interchangeable parts.[3] But Gramsci's insight into the primary aim of rationalized production—to make workers over in the image of the new technologies or rather to make workers *into* technologies, machines for the production of labor—is actually closer to the tenets of Taylorism. It was Frederick Taylor who concentrated not on the machinery but on the *worker* as a cog in the rationalized production wheel, drawing on the newly developed capabilities of cinema (which held its first public showing in 1896) to institute, in 1913, the time-motion studies isolating workers' movements frame by frame so that any wasted motion could be eliminated. And these produced fears like Gramsci's about the dehumanization of labor.

Rationalized production soon trickled down into earnest American manifestos of efficiency. Pop psychology publications include James Mursell's *Streamline Your Mind* (1936), a get-ahead manual for self-teaching of maximized efficiency. In chapter 1, entitled "The Psychologist Looks You Over" (*frisson* of Big Brother), Mursell explains that his putative psychologist instantly perceives, in "you the average man of today," the sin of "*your toleration in yourself of needless personal inefficiency in an age which requires efficiency*" (his emphasis). And Mursell kindly provides a solution, couched in technological metaphor: "When the machine age was ushered in some two hundred years ago the great problem was to develop new sources of energy. . . . But now scientists . . . are showing us how to use more economically the power that we possess. A most important device which they apply for this end is *streamlining*" (9–10). These theories had strong effects on the nation's work force, especially since the Depression had done much to enforce both the physical and psychological need for efficiency. As part of America's culture industry and therefore inseparably entangled with ideologies of rationalization, comic strips were subjected to similar expectations of efficient and continuous manufacture, expectations difficult to uphold as increased newspaper circulation and syndication necessitated stepped-up and reliable production.

From the 1930s on, comics entered a new era. Increased demand necessitated changes in modes of production and even in the types of strips produced. Although new strips were often given trial runs in the Sunday color supplement—only once a week, in other words—until they either caught on or were canceled, once a serial had found its audience it had to be cranked out every day, six days a week. In addition, established comics generally included a full-color spread on Sundays (and just to complicate things, this Sunday strip generally had to follow its own storyline since many readers bought either Sunday or daily papers, but not both). The sudden proliferation of serial strips or "continuities" in the early 1930s reflects artists' response to increased demand. Writing the next installment of a continued storyline is in many ways easier than churning out a new joke day after day. At the same time, the continuities helped to increase audience loyalty, encouraging daily reading and increasing the popularity of a strip. Missing an isolated joke is one thing, missing a possibly crucial plot twist quite another.

Syndication required refinement of copyright laws. Early strips, bought outright by publishers, belonged entirely to individual papers. The 1912 Hearst-Dirk case created a precedent by confirming the employer's ownership rights to the strip, the title, and in most cases the characters as well. Early comic artists put up with this situation because they had no idea how valuable the strips would eventually become; initially comics were simply a gimmick to increase circulation. The industry began to shift, however, once reader demand made comics an integral part of newspaper format.[4] As artists became more aware of their economic power, so did editors, who realized the profit potential of organizing a sort of comic clearinghouse responsible for finding, producing, and selling cartoon reprint rights to papers nationwide. It was Hearst, not surprisingly, who organized the first great syndicate—the International News Service—in 1912, with his King Features following in 1915. Other major syndicate leaders included Joseph Patterson, who later commissioned *Little Orphan Annie*, *Terry and the Pirates*, and other now-famous strips. Smaller papers were the first to take advantage of syndicate services, which enabled them to avoid the costs of keeping their own "stable" of cartoonists (the actual term used at the time and one that signals the dubious status of early comic artists).

Early cartoonists worked in syndicate studios, where—since they were not given much space—they created their strips literally side by side with other artists also working to develop the vocabulary and expressive potential of comics.[5] This forced exchange was remarkably productive for many artists. At this early stage of the streamlining of comic production, for example, Milton Caniff used his friend, fellow artist, and Associated Press studio mate Noel Sickles, then developing *Scorchy Smith*, as an unofficial artistic consultant and collaborator, and Sickles had an enormous impact on Caniff's ground-breaking style. Caniff developed as an artist by fusing the cinematographic techniques of comic artists Hal Foster and Alex Raymond with Sickles's brilliant draftsmanship; later in this chapter I will enumerate the innovations these two collaborated to create. Once *Terry* became popular, Caniff increased his efficiency by employing a background assistant, a letterer, and a studio assistant.

By the 1930s, when surrealistic, atemporal strips like *Krazy Kat* ended and adventure and crime comics took off, most comic artists had shifted, like Caniff, from full control over the creation of each strip to a streamlined assembly process involving a breakdown of tasks. The stereotypical view would have it that such a production process unavoidably negates creativity and produces a sterile, conventional "product." However, this result did not follow in the case of comics, since adventure strips of the 1930s and 1940s (later dubbed the "Golden Age" of adventure comics) mark highly imaginative narrative and artistic experimentation with comic-strip themes and techniques—experimentation made possible, it can be argued, by the collaboration enforced by the requirements of a daily strip as well as by the enormous influx of talent that followed the profits and publicity of national syndication.

Caniff's narratives are, then, necessarily much tighter, more focused, and more condensed than Dickens's (or than the soap operas to follow). One of fiction's crucial functions in any age is to provide myths to live by, ways of organizing and assimilating existence. By affecting audience perceptions of narrative organization—focusing, for example, on one or two "heroes" at any one time, emphasizing action rather than reaction or emotion, or reducing that action to its most essential elements—efficient, pared-down comic strips may have reoriented readers' attitudes toward fiction by inflecting traditional ways of organizing "reality." On the most obvious level, narrative strips recall Fordist modes of production and Taylorized identities much more closely than do the rambling, digressive, multiplot novels of Dickens. Theorists of the links between Taylorization and American culture would also argue that cultural developments (including novels, advertisements, cinema, and comic strips) intersected with an increasing industrial obsession with optimum efficiency. Comic strips, for example, delivered the pleasures and satisfactions of narrative in three minutes a day. David Kunzle takes the comparison further: "It has been said that the cinema is the product of the railway experience and the demand for accelerated vision, a moving picture seen through a frame as it were through a train window; even the celluloid itself, running on little wheels and tracks, has been compared to the train on its great iron rail. Railway, movie, and comic strip accelerate but also abbreviate vision" (378). Although this metaphor has some validity, it cannot be pushed too far since it implies a reader "just along for the ride." In *Taylored Lives: Narrative Productions in the Age of Taylor, Veblen, and Ford*, Martha Banta carefully avoids this predictable social control approach by emphasizing the reciprocity of interactions between cultural and industrial production: "It is not merely that Taylor, in defining Taylorism, creates narratives of power relations and a mode of narratology for their analysis. It is that everyone caught up in the times had tales to tell that 'spoke' the times into being" (5).

This emphasis on the hegemonic process of cultural formation helps to demystify the ubiquitous metaphors of mass culture as junk food and audiences as passive consumers. The serial strip became popular because of a complex network of factors, not least of which is the fascination of audiences for serial narratives intersecting with political and social issues of relevance to them. The trajectory of the serial genre traced so far in this study has established that serialization proved compelling long before it formally reflected the production lines on which sectors of its audience labored. Nor can comic-strip narrative be reduced to a simple sequence of Taylorized text stations.

A more crucial connection between Taylorism and comic production may be the ways the rise of the continuity comic impelled readers to become critics, analysts, even creators of comic art themselves. As the evidence of their letters proves, Caniff's readers are not passive Taylorist cogs, waiting for the next segment of narrative to come down the line and streamline their minds. They articulate the elements of the strip they appreciate (favorite characters and plotlines, Caniff's artwork, his reflection of wartime "reality") and demand changes in elements they dislike or feel are manipulative. As a serial creator, Caniff was necessarily conscious of his debt to readers. He expressed this obligation most usefully by directly responding to fan requests and corrections in the strip itself as well as in statements like the following: "Reader editing of the comic strips is an unprecedented phenomenon of publication history. It is not the fan mail phenomenon, as the movies know it. A movie, or a play or a novel, is a completed product before the fan mail starts coming. But the course of events in a comic strip can be influenced, practically, sometimes even advantageously, by fan letters" (quoted in Morrison, 40).

In addition to interacting with the creation of the comic strip, readers play a much more active role in the production of meaning during the reading process than is often acknowledged. First there is the physical impact of the comic page itself: strips are juxtaposed against others of differing genres, so that the page in its entirety resembles a Dickensian melange of types, themes, genres, and characters. Then there are the strategies readers develop: they select certain strips and reject others, choose the order of reading as well as the time, place, and company in which the experience takes place. Finally there is the way that fiction packed in tiny, separate boxes elides connections so that readers must draw on a complex system of linguistic and visual conventions, signals, terms, and signs as they decode comic-strip meaning.

Case Study: Terry and the Pirates

At first glance, Milton Caniff's *Terry and the Pirates* seems to epitomize rationalized production of the mass media since it was intentionally "manufactured" as a virtual pastiche of preexisting plots and characters that had already proved their popularity. Since adventure strips had clearly become circulation leaders, Joseph Patterson, head of the New York/Chicago *News International* syndicate, decided to develop a new one with a particular configuration of demonstrably popular elements. Caniff, already working for the Associated Press, was put in contact with *News* syndicate editor Mollie Slott. The three collaborated on developing a basic plot and format. As Caniff put it in Martin Sheridan's *Comics and Their Creators*, "A strip that is to compete in the open market against the product of rival syndicates is not born full-blown from the brain of a single person. . . . Captain Patterson wants a strip that will have as universal an appeal as possible" (156). Captivating the newspaper's entire range of readership, Caniff adds, "means a youngster for juvenile interest, a big handsome chap to do the strong-arm stuff and handle the love interest. (The distaff side calls for a succession of pretty ladies. Marriage, with its slipper⌐ and fireside, hardly becomes an adventure tale.) For comedy there must be a personality who logically belongs with the man and boy. . . . the last outpost of adventure is the Orient, so why not a screwy Chinese who can act as valet, interpreter and purveyor of the bams and zowies?" (156–57). The strip's marginalization of women and ethnic characters (to be discussed later) is prefigured by these offhand quips about "the distaff side" and the "screwy Chinese." The statement also emphasizes the heterogeneity of the strips' target audience as well as the collaboration and compromise necessary between mass-cultural producers who often have separate agendas but a common goal: to catch, and keep, a mass audience.

In many ways Caniff's position within the mass-media world and his attitudes toward his art parallel Dickens's. Both created overwhelmingly popular texts at the behest of sales-minded publishers: at its peak, *Terry* appeared in more than three hundred papers, with a combined total of more than thirty million readers. Despite their streamlined production techniques, both were compelled to see their texts as much more than just commodities; both considered themselves craftspeople, worked hard to forge communication with their readers, and had enormous investment in the artistic value of their work. Nevertheless, both were committed to the race for ever-higher sales figures and profits. The purpose of *Terry and the Pirates,* Caniff emphasized, was "to force the customer to buy tomorrow's paper": "If a strip didn't sell papers for the publisher it was useless. . . . the late Heine Reiher, one-time managing editor of the *Dispatch,* said, 'Always draw your stuff for the guy who pays for the paper. Kids will never see it unless the old man likes it well enough to bring it home'" (quoted in Sheridan, 156). Therefore, all levels of the strip—narrative mode, pacing, balance of subplots, draftsmanship, dialogue, character choice—had to be planned with a multiple readership in mind (though readers were still presumed to be male, as the quote above reveals). The overwhelming success of *Terry* demonstrates that by the 1930s comic-strip producers had become expert at manipulating a historically proven formula for success: a little adventure, a little romance, a little difference, but not too much, not enough to turn off readers by undermining their stereotypes too violently. The idea of "China," the last outpost of adventure, worked beautifully for Caniff until his well-traveled readers combined with history (in the form of the Sino-Japanese conflict) to catch up with him. As we will see, he was then forced to ground the exotic stereotypes with a touch of reality. But first, a brief overview of the context of *Terry's* production is in order.

Caniff's most noted contribution to the development of comic art is his experimentation with the visual components of comic-strip storytelling. He

Fig. 2.1: The first strip. Terry and Pat land in China (Oct. 22, 1934). © Tribune Media Services, Inc. All rights reserved. Reprinted with permission.

repeatedly acknowledged the overwhelming influence of movies on his development as an artist, saying, for example: "The play is cast. The sets are up. Sounds like a movie. Why not? The movies have learned to appeal to the greatest number of people. Use motion picture technic [*sic*] in the execution. First panel: long shot with the speaking characters in the middle foreground. Second panel: medium shot with dialogue to move the plot along. Third panel: semi-closeup to set reader for significant last speech. Fourth panel: Full closeup of speaking character with socko line" (quoted in Sheridan, 157). He makes his approach sound essentially formulaic, and of course it is. However, just because Caniff sold millions of papers does not mean he did not also work creatively to explore and expand the existing formula. Even in early strips, Caniff, a child actor in silent movies shot in California in 1916, borrows film techniques: silhouettes against white light, close-ups of crucial objects like a gun or an enemy hand pulling shut a door. Apparently he and Sickles often skipped deadlines to go see films. Caniff's cinematic frames reveal his awareness of the dramatic impact of point of view in narrative as well as his willingness to test different shot angles, exposures, framing, shading, and contrast to find the best means of visually conveying mood and meaning. In fact, the very early strips are perhaps too film-derived: Richard Marschall points out that the cartoony, stereotyped appearance of Terry and his buddies "portends epics of a prepubescent Douglas Fairbanks cast" (212; also see fig. 2.1).

The influence of film was almost inescapable for comic artists of this era. Since both media were relatively new, artists in both were engaged in working through related problems of visual narrative. The interdependence of the two makes sense given their virtually simultaneous development and their remarkably similar imperatives: both tell stories using predominantly visual means though with a strong verbal component; both build stories by means of a succession of individual squares or "windows" of narrative, though of course the speed at which film is projected creates an illusion of continuity;

and both use a frame-to-frame construction enabling sudden cuts from one time or space to another.

Discussing the genesis of these effects, Sergei Eisenstein traces D.W. Griffith's development of montage to the influence of Dickens, as discussed in my last chapter. "What were the novels of Dickens for his contemporaries, for his readers?" Eisenstein asks, answering, "They bore the same relation to them that the film bears to the same strata in our time. They compelled the reader to live with the same passions" (206). He then analyzes the techniques Dickens created to enable readers to experience the world in both panoramic and detailed views. Like Griffith, Dickens experimented with innovations such as multiple points of view, cutting from scene to scene, close-ups combined with panoramas, and unusual camera angles and used these techniques to enhance his ability to situate individuals within a social context as well as to link multiple storylines by creating parallel action. Although Eisenstein does not discuss them in this context, movie serials such as *The Perils of Pauline* also draw on Dickensian strategies, cliff-hanging suspense and melodrama most obviously.

In the early twentieth century, comic artists began trying out similar techniques, often directly inspired by early film. Film had the advantage of live actors, movement, and extended narrative duration, which allowed development of character, mood, and tone. From film, therefore, comic creators appropriated a kind of narrative shorthand by borrowing tricks of suspense, point of view, framing, shadow and light, and so on to recall the relentless pacing of action movies or the suspense-saturated mystique of noir films and thus to effectively capture mood in a minimum of space.[6] Caniff also insisted that movie stars provided him not only with inspiration but with a kind of reference system or character shorthand: by appropriating the appearance, habits, or tricks of speech of a nationally known movie character, he instantly communicated personalities that would have taken weeks or months of four-panel strips to build up. He claimed that his character Big Stoop is a Karloff monster caricature; the Dragon Lady draws on Marlene Dietrich of Von Sternberg's *Shanghai Express*, Tony Sandhurst alludes to Charles Laughton, and Burma recalls a wide range of stars, including Jean Harlow, Carole Lombard, and Joan Crawford's Sadie Thompson character in *Rain* (Marschall, 216).

The influence was reciprocal, as filmmakers also derived inspiration from comic artists in their search for an adequate visual language. Comic artists had the inestimable advantage of being technically limited only by the extent of their imagination and artistic ability, so as new technologies developed, filmmakers borrowed special effects or action shots first invented in the fluid, easily manipulatable strips. An example of beginning visual experimentation is Winsor McKay's aerial photography in an early *Little Nemo* airship adventure. Nemo passes over the Statue of Liberty, and McKay "literally invents a place from which to view his adventures with the consistencies of an as yet nonexistent aerial camera shot."[7] The forms are still intertwined; as Thomas Inge explains, "At their best, comic book artists carry the visual narrative into areas of innovation that the restricted camera cannot enter . . . such as simultaneous continuities, or scenes that literally explode the strictures of the conventions of comic art. It is not surprising that student photographers and filmmakers now turn to comic books to learn the rudiments of their craft" (144). Among such students are Orson Welles, Alain Resnais, and Federico Fellini, all of whom have credited comic strips with influencing their work, while George Lucas and Steven Spielberg claim that their cinematic vision was largely inspired by an early love of comic books (Inge, 143). William Friedkin (producer of *The French Connection* and *The Exorcist*, among other films), in announcing his plan to remake Will Eisner's *The Spirit* for television, explains its visual effectiveness: "Look at the dramatic use of montage, of light and sound. See the dynamic framing that Eisner employs, and the deep vibrant colors. Many film directors have been influenced by *The Spirit*, myself included. . . . This [an Eisner cover of a man chased by an elevated train] is where I got ideas for the chase in *The French Connection*" (quoted in Inge, xx).

For the purposes of this study, the interchange of visual techniques is important chiefly for what it reveals about the explosion of visual media in the first part of this century. The serial narrative left the printed page in search of higher profits and found them in what had become the new mass media: newspapers, film, and television. With this proliferation of new technologies, competition for audiences increased drastically, and as usual the serial was exploited by producers of a range of media. Comic artists mobilized film techniques to increase the creative power of their strips, and filmmakers reciprocated. Even before the demand for realism necessitated increased attention to the visual dynamics of storytelling, artists pushed the limits of what could be "seen" and represented, concurrently working to develop visual narrative techniques to convey information traditionally provided by text. Serial strips had especially strong motivations for this practice since their narratives were necessarily much more enꞈangled than gag strips, with parallel subplots and a network of characters. The discontinuity imposed by a succession of "windows" into the narrative world may require the division of narrative into distinct blocks, then, but it also frees artists from restriction to a particular spatial or temporal context or fixed point of view. Once they had established sufficient generic vocabulary and codes, comic artists could achieve narrative effects that filmmakers envied.

Caniff drew the strip from 1934 to 1946. Over those twelve years, the strip changed in almost every conceivable way: artwork, narrative style, subject matter, theme, underlying purpose. As we will see, these changes reflect not only Caniff's own development as an artist but also larger shifts within the comic industry. When World War II ended, the purpose of *Terry* seems to have ended too, and Caniff accepted the Chicago Sun Syndicate's offer of two thousand dollars a week for five years—plus ownership of his new characters—to create a strip for them. The new strip became *Steve Canyon,* while *Terry* was handed over to new authorship (Goulart, 136). The war had a powerful influence on all strips of the time. On the home front, the demographics of both creators and audience shifted as younger men left; in addition, Pierre Couperie demonstrates that the war directly impelled large-scale shifts in comic-strip subject matter. From 1915 to 1920, war strips made up only 4 percent of overall comics, reflecting America's relative isolation during World War I. From 1940 to 1944, on the other hand, the proportion jumped to 18 percent. In the same era, only 17 percent of minority and foreign characters were positively portrayed (though we will see the limitations of these "positive" characterizations) while 36 percent were villains, with demonized Japanese and Germans leading the pack.

In this era also, many artists besides Caniff began creating extended narratives. Serial strips—with subgenres included quest, mystery, adventure, and romance—rose steadily in numbers from 1920 until 1949, then dropped (Couperie, 48, 155). Comic attitudes toward temporality shifted accordingly. The timeless fantasy of early animal and child strips like *Krazy Kat* or, more characteristic of its age, *Little Nemo in Slumberland* gave way to the concrete, historically specific sequence of events of *Terry,* *Miss Fury,* or *Little Orphan Annie.* To express this new content and ethos, artists had to develop new styles. Visual as well as narrative realism replaced the surrealistic fantasy of earlier artists such as Herriman and Winsor McKay. Changes—many of them pioneered by Caniff and Sickles—included harder-edged figures, narratively significant landscape, increased use of shadow and texture, experimentation with camera angles to reinforce narrative signals, "authentic" dialogue (including, or inventing, slang), and increased realism.

And finally, the construction of strips changed. In early strips, loose, floating borders between frames and an almost abstract composition of frames on the page created a blurring of cause and effect (a style beautifully illustrated by *Little Nemo* or *Krazy Kat*). Later, this surreal layout gave way to almost invariable use of a rectangle divided into distinct but connected frames that varied in length to convey the relative importance and/or duration of each narrative moment, but conformed in height. While standardizing their

Fig. 2.2: Seven months later: Caniff's developing artistry (May 13, 1935). © Tribune Media Services, Inc. All rights reserved. Reprinted with permission.

form, however, comics diversified their content, so that the comic supplement increasingly included a variety of strips intended to appeal to a range of readers. Although many comics did incorporate two or more subgenres—Caniff, for example, always ran romance and adventure storylines concurrently, with a little humor thrown in for good measure—serial strips just did not have the space that novelists such as Dickens had. While Dickens included a wide range of storylines to appeal to an equally wide variety of readers (male and female, child and adult, working and middle classes), comic syndicates essentially streamlined this process by creating a division of labor. The comic page as a whole provided all the variety of a serial novel but did so by means of juxtaposition rather than inclusion. *Terry and the Pirates* appeared side by side with *Little Orphan Annie*, *The Katzenjammer Kids*, *Superman*, and many others.

Caniff's artistic developments paralleled those of other comic artists of his time, but he is also uniquely noted for considerably refining his artistic storytelling skills during the run of *Terry*. In the mid-1930s the strip focused on its original goal of providing fast-paced escapist fantasy. Early strips show Caniff working with the bare bones: a strong story idea and an underdeveloped artistic style. The strip is predominantly white, with characters standing out in sharp relief from grayish, amorphous backgrounds, which gives the strip a blank, cartoony look as well as a flat two-dimensionality without much detail, perspective, shading or background (figs. 2.1 and 2.2). Caniff relied heavily on text to carry the narrative weight of the strip; virtually every strip contains dialogue, and many include text in the form of explanatory notes that occasionally occupy an entire frame. These techniques were much reduced once he had his visual storytelling conventions well in hand: less than a year from its inception, *Terry* made an astonishing transformation from cartoon stereotype to vivid realism darkened by what have been termed *film noir* effects. A comparison of the first 1934 strip (fig. 2.1) with a sequence

Fig. 2.3: Hu Shee rescues Terry: storytelling through shadow, perspective, and drama (Nov. 30, 1940). © Tribune Media Services, Inc. All rights reserved. Reprinted with permission.

created less than a year later (fig. 2.2) shows the difference in every element, including angle manipulation, sensation of movement and action, balance of successive frames, depth of background, serial plotting, and suspense.

As discussed earlier in this chapter, much of this development has been ascribed to Sickles's influence. Marschall claims that the two artists worked symbiotically, with Caniff responsible for much of the narrative and dialogue while Sickles focused on artwork (212). Whether the interaction was this extensive or not, it is clear that Sickles helped with *Terry* until well into 1941. His trademark brushwork, impressionistic shading, and constantly moving "camera" leave clear traces in the strip from the first year on, and the collaboration forged a style that had an immense influence on the next generation of comic artists. Among the strip's innovations were extensive use of shadows, silhouettes, and chiaroscuro; experimentation with unusual camera angles and light sources; reliance on large areas of black to increase the effectiveness of a frame by strong contrast; construction of highly detailed, visually striking backgrounds; and exploration of the narrative potential of silent (dialogueless) frames in creating both mood and meaning. Perhaps most revolutionary was Caniff's development of an effective realism (especially in drawing the human face and form) achieved by means of impressionism. As Marschall explains, "Their [Caniff's and Sickle's] brushwork and chiaroscuro were actually used as time-saving devices. When they depicted shadows and wrinkles and textures, they used an impressionistic approach that, when reduced on the newspaper page, created the effect of photographic realism" (219). This "impressionism" was created by laying in lines and folds in characters' skin and clothing after the basic drawing was complete, using a wet brush instead of the standard thin-line method.

Along with Foster and Raymond, Caniff was one of the first comic artists to adapt a unified narrative technique, with all elements working toward the same goal. In discussions of his art, Caniff stresses that layout acts as single unit, with each frame marking progress toward dramatic significance and acquiring its full value and meaning only in relation to adjacent frames. In its middle and later phases, *Terry* beautifully manifests Caniff's developing realization that comic rhythm and layout are necessarily closely linked. For example, figure 2.3 shows how shot angles, distance, perspective, and background work together to convey mood and perspective while simultaneously furthering storylines. The first frame situates us in relation to the landscape; it also provides a touch of suspense by rendering the speaking characters invisible while adding movement and action to an otherwise purely informational panel. Next we see the speakers, but with a tilt to enhance suspense and mood. In the third panel a slight angle from the ground up increases the off-kilter feel of the strip, placing us in sympathy with Terry's clearly off-balance physical condition. Finally, a severe ground-angle shot enforces the bleakness of Terry and Hu Shee's plight: the background cues of cold black ground, rivulets of water, sparse tree, and ramshackle building, as well as the empty sky and small, isolated figures, combine to set the mood for the strip's end. This final frame works to enforce interest in what will happen to the characters, thus satisfying serial requirements; however, the suspense here is subtle and overshadowed by desolation. The strip's overall structure works to enforce an impression of entrapment within an excess of empty space by means of its narrow central close-ups enclosed by wide, sparse distance shots. Finally, the strip shows the extent to which Caniff had moved past earlier stereotypes of women as invariably helpless and passive: Hu Shee actively rescues Terry in this sequence.

Over the twelve years of Caniff's authorship, he also advanced his skill in both narrative technique and characterization. In fact, the strong serial pull exerted by the strip makes it pleasurable to read even today, in spite of its stereotypical characters. Together with his ground-breaking artwork, Caniff's skill in constructing a compelling, suspenseful narrative may well account for the recent reissue of the complete run of *Terry*. When the strip started in 1934, it followed a fairly rigid narrative formula. Every episode focused on Pat Ryan, a handsome bachelor in his twenties or thirties, and Terry Lee, a preadolescent boy searching for legendary buried treasure. These two were quickly balanced by a "comic" Chinese caricature who serves as stooge, servant, and translator of Chinese language and customs, and who— at least in early strips—seems thrilled to be ordered about by a young boy. Terry, Pat, and Connie invariably start out on a mission (to hunt for treasure, rendezvous with a new employer, and so on), run into or rescue an attractive woman (the daughter of the boat captain they hire, the niece of a millionaire who hires them), and are then swept into a whirl of danger (kidnapping, double-dealing, enemies passing as friends). The possible permutations of this basic formula are endless, as they must be in a serial.

Over the years, Caniff became more adventurous in his serial techniques. As they develop over time, these methods come to resemble Dickens's, though necessarily pared down and streamlined because of space constraints and for maximum clarity and effect. For example, Caniff expands the strip's appeal by introducing a succession of foreign villains (the "half-breed" Poppy Joe, Klang the warlord, the Nazi Kiel), all-American heroines (Dale, Normandie Drake, and April Kane), and sirens, often Chinese or part-Chinese, who are sometimes redeemed as heroines. These include the Eurasian Dragon Lady most notoriously but also the guerrilla Hu Shee, the shady Burma, and the mysterious gangster Sanjak, who develops an obsession with young April. While Dickens dealt with large casts of characters and at least three or four subplots, however, Caniff tended to stick to a single adventure plot or at most two closely intersecting narratives. A quest such as the search for a lost treasure mine or the rescue of friends from the Dragon Lady's pirates or of allies from Japanese forces runs as a connecting thread beneath a succession of minor subplots involving character interrelations. As a general rule, these secondary plots involve a romance, sometimes two competing romances: Caniff often switched between the adventurer Pat Ryan's tragic passion for Normandie Sandhurst or ongoing love/hate relationship with the Dragon Lady and young Terry's comic puppy love of the moment.

By way of variety, he occasionally separated the strip's heroes as well, with one or both shanghaied, double-crossed, or otherwise exposed to danger. This technique effectively increased narrative suspense since each strip could include not just one but two cliff-hangers, and the cost of missing even a day's episode was thus heightened. In 1936, for example, Terry and Pat part ways for an extended period of time, as the Dragon Lady kidnaps Pat, leaving Terry and Connie to search for him—and get into troubles of their own—while she and Pat pursue their ambivalent romance. Caniff was to use this technique more often as the strip progressed, since it enabled Terry to take an increasingly adult part in the action as he got older while adding suspense by leaving our other hero dangling, which happens, for example, for two months of a 1941 subplot featuring Burma and Terry as its central characters. On April 14, Burma watches as Terry is taken by the evil Nazi Kiel to serve as a decoy on a false "raft," really a submarine designed to lure British ships to the rescue and then torpedo them. Not until June 14 are the two plus a "good" (in other words, democracy-loving) Nazi reunited. In the intervening month, Burma is held captive by the Nazi secret police and successfully outwits them, while Terry escapes German captivity to join a group of British spies in an ultimately successful attempt to locate Burma.

Caniff's treatment of this quite complicated narrative shows his skill in intertwining subplots without losing his readers. For clarity, the strip tends to follow one subplot for two or three days, then signals a shift to the other with a "Meanwhile . . ." at the top left of a frame. On the other hand, the much longer Sunday strips (four rows of frames as opposed to one) generally focus on one subplot but give at least a glimpse of the other. For example, Burma spots Terry, in disguise, from a train window as she is taken away to the Nazi camp.

In addition to developing serial techniques suited to the constraints of the comic form, Caniff drew on proven sensational devices for capturing readers (especially cliff-hanging endings, popularized by serialized movie sequences like *The Perils of Pauline,* which ran weekly at movie theaters during the 1920s), then moved beyond sensationalism once his strip had acquired a loyal following. As he explains, "It takes a good year to get the average reader really to become vitally interested in a new strip, to read it every day and talk about it to his friends. In order to try and cut that time down it seems necessary to startle the public in some way right off the bat" (quoted in Sheridan 157–58). Again we see the importance of communities of readers talking about their serials. Once a critical mass has been achieved, elements such as the ritual of serial consumption, the depth and development of characters, and a compelling narrative become more important than suspense. After the initial shock effect necessary to accumulate a readership, then, Caniff developed other techniques for holding audiences. Although character creation was perhaps his greatest strength as a storyteller, he also remains justifiably famous for dialogue and plotting. He perfected the ability to control narrative pacing by means of the type of dialogue spoken and learned to use silent panels to great effect, creating the impression of frantic action by means of crowded frames and angle shots or slowing action down by means of static close-ups or two-shots. And his audience repaid this creativity by writing over 100,000 letters to thank him for the strip, to request drawings of favorite characters, to berate him for errors in fact or continuity, and to offer advice.

Active Readers and Comic Agendas

Caniff had a reputation for being immensely responsive to fans, and his correspondence files certainly support that reputation. Devoting enormous amounts of time to reading and responding to audience suggestions, Caniff tended to belittle his efforts, claiming that he was simply fulfilling his duty as a serial artist. Late in his career, he explains that "in a real sense we involve the reader as much as an audience participation show in the theater or on television. Our reader loyalty is less overt, but has a longer life expectancy."

In keeping with the close associations between movies, television, the stage, and comics, Caniff advises aspiring cartoonists to study other popular media in order to learn what kinds of stories the public wants to hear and what methods effectively communicate these stories: "When people flock into a movie or rave about last night's television show you should know *why* and be ready to work some of that surefire entertainment appeal into your feature" (Couperie 133). Translated into streamlined comic-strip narratives, this method was highly effective, and the popularity of *Terry* indicates that its audiences felt themselves to have a voice in determining its storylines. In addition to the common fan letter topics listed above, Caniff's correspondents predict or suggest future plotlines or characters, demand specific plots (the return of a favorite character, a particular romance, and so on), complain about the strip's depiction of China or of the military, and provide Caniff with up-to-date, firsthand information to make his strip more accurate. After the strip began focusing on the war, most of Caniff's regular fan correspondents became members of the military, the Red Cross, or other groups directly involved in the conflict, and we can trace Caniff's response to their suggestions in the strip itself. In spite of the existence of such evidence of reader involvement, however, comic-strip investigations suffer from the same difficulty as the other media discussed in this study: a dearth of analysis of audience attitudes toward the text. There have been any number of effects studies, from the 1920s to the present. But while these may produce interesting statistics, they fail to provide answers to questions of increasing importance to cultural studies and central to this book: how do actual audiences use mass-cultural texts, under what circumstances, for what purposes, and with what response and results?

These questions are equally crucial for producers and advertisers needing to chart the popularity or effectiveness of their products. In 1955—a prime year for comics as the target of critique—*Puck, the Comic Weekly* sponsored a uses-and-gratifications study of newspaper comic strips, carried out by Science Research Associates. The result, published as a monograph under the title *The Sunday Comics: A Socio-Psychological Study with Attendant Advertising Implications*, attempts to survey the variety of ways comics are consumed. Its purpose is twofold: to provide advertisers with a map of potential consumers' habits and thus of effective advertising strategies; and to increase comics' status as a viable narrative form. In the introduction readers are urged "to remember that Sunday Comics, as they are read on a typical Sunday, are a very unusual media activity. They are assimilated in an environment of relaxation, sometimes privacy or withdrawal, and reflect a feeling of communion with the printed word and colored pictorial episode that offer [sic] unparalleled opportunities for exploration by the advertiser."

But while constructing the comic reader as the ideal target of advertising, the authors emphatically refute the standard contemptuous view of readers as passive victims of the text. "Comic reading might be guessed as being a stereotyped experience for the reader," they explain, who "would, presumably, read the strips as the creators wish, and feel as they wish him to feel. This view is far from the truth. . . . our study shows that for the consumer and reader, the Comic experience tends to be personal, private, and even secret, not visible to others. . . . Most of the people we studied appeared to be *active* readers of the Comics. . . . They selected and chose, manipulated and interpreted, in order to obtain the experience they desired from the Comics."

The study also quotes readers themselves, and their voices support the claim that they are active readers. In 1955, then, comic-strip producers were already aware of the complex patterns of desire, choice, use, and response exercised by consumers, issues that have only recently begun to be acknowledged and explored in academic circles. The study asserts that comic readers negotiate an apparently satisfactory compromise between individual desire and marketplace reality. It describes comic reading in terms of activity, selection, and manipulation, terms generally used to describe producers of texts rather than consumers, and points out that comics are used in the service of secrecy, privacy, and individuality rather than swallowed wholesale by a mass, undifferentiated audience. (Of course, this insistence on active rather than passive comic readers served the needs of comic producers, who had to counter attacks on comics as having dangerous insidious effects on their "helpless" readers.) The *Puck* study thus implies that in order to satisfy real needs and desires, media consumers reconcile public and private modes by means of a complex process of negotiation .

According to the evidence of this study, one crucial aspect of comic satisfaction lies in the ritualization of reading. Many of the interviewees attest to the fixity of their consumption patterns: they read the Sunday page in the same time, place, and circumstances every week. As with Dickens's readers and soap opera viewers, familiarity and recognition feature largely in readers' descriptions of serial satisfactions. For example, many cite the importance of continued characters in strips they have followed for years, often from childhood. At the same time, though, readers balance this reliance on tradition and predictability by naming suspense and delayed gratification as crucial pleasures. "What I like about Brenda Starr," explained a male reader, George, "is that it always ends up in the air. . . . You wait and wait." Waiting and waiting, endlessly postponed gratification, seems to be so satisfying partly because the deferred desire and eternal unpredictability is contained within such a predictable form. Like soap opera viewers, comic readers know the parameters of their texts so well that pleasure lies in experiencing the small, limited, but endless variations possible within the safe boundaries of a textual frame and a ritualized reading practice.

What does the desire for this particular configuration of fictional pleasure say about the needs of its audience? In case we have missed the parallelism between the goals and pressures of capitalist consumption on the one hand and the individual need for textual gratification on the other, George spells it out. In his words, the satisfactions experienced by readers of strips, who never get to the end of the story, resemble those of "the man who works and works all his life, always wishing someday he'll retire and have those things [house and car]. That wish will probably never come true, but it's what makes life worth living." This reader, then, sees an explicit connection between the endlessly deferred desire of the strips and the apparently hopeless but paradoxically renewable economic optimism of the worker trying to save enough to own his or her home and car. In summarizing the suitability of comic strips to the industrial age, David Kunzle echoes George in explicitly connecting class and economic status with the new narrative experience provided by the "accelerat[ed] but abbreviat[ed] vision" of comic strips: "Such changeability and discontinuity were the physical experiences of lower classes with diffuse, unclear, distant, and ever-receding social goals" (378). This analysis also echoes, in reverse, the upper-class *Barnaby Rudge* reader Henry Crabb Robinson, who refused to finish the novel until it came out in volumes because "I will not expose myself to further anxieties" (578). Although it is too simplistic to claim that class determines the type of fiction enjoyed, the intuitive connection between the serial form, consumerism, and deferred gratification recurs again and again in readers' accounts of the drive for *more* narrative, the perpetual deferral of final satisfaction, and some readers' refusal to be subjected to that deferral.

On the other hand, my research into the readers of *Terry* implies a quite different lure of the serial strip, one not dependent on level of income or cultural capital: the community of readers created by long-term consumption of a narrative. A marked characteristic of the fan letters to Caniff preserved in the Caniff archive is that many are written by groups of readers or discuss the existence of such groups. Like both nineteenth-century serial consumers and later soap opera viewers, comic-strip audiences find that a large part of their pleasure comes from collaborative readings, interpretations and predictions and from generally sharing "gossip" about characters and situations. Readers of *Terry* also attest to the importance of the strip in fueling everyday conversations. For example, one fan says, "Every time a group of my friends gets together the question 'Have you read Burma [a popular *Terry* heroine] today?' is almost sure to arise" (June 1936).[8] In her thesis on Caniff's correspondence during the war years, Miriam E. Morrison draws on Caniff's papers to cite numerous letters from fans thanking Caniff for providing them with a new topic of conversation for awkward social situations. Among the letter writers Morrison quotes are carpooling adults, businessmen, cruise-goers, and a woman who says, "You probably don't realize that 'Terry and the Pirates' is to be recommended as the best conversational piece one can introduce. We've been able to strike up acquaintances every place we've been with the simple matter of asking—'Say, did you see "Terry and the Pirates" today?' It's a regular 'Open Sesame.' From then on we have something in common and we've never had to fall back on the old standby of the weather" (Jan. 14, 1943; quoted in Morrison 51).

These letters show that like Dickens's novels, *Terry* served as a bridge for 1930s audiences by providing a circle of ready-made "friends" about whom to gossip with new acquaintances, which in turn enabled the crucial bonding function of gossip. In addition to the evidence above, the Caniff archive contains many letters from college reading groups who, like contemporary college students, became strongly reliant on serial fictions that they, their families, or their friends had followed in high school. One *Terry* group, the "Winthrop House Burma Club" from Harvard University, wrote steadily during their college careers. At first, members simply requested pictures, mentioning the group only in passing. Then they began to write in praise of the pictures others in the group had received from Caniff. Finally, the self-described "one lone girl" in the reading group wrote to praise the strip's creator: "Religiously we all follow your strip. . . . you have that rare thing, an interesting plot that actually has continuity," she says, but adds, "I'm getting just a bit fed up with having that Burma drawing flaunted in front of my eyes all the time. So, could you possibly go to all the trouble of donating a picture of Pat, complete with shoulders and biceps?" (Jan. 27, 1937). Tired of listening to her male friends objectify a comic-strip pinup, this woman seems to have decided to play the same game by herself objectifying Pat Ryan.

Another writer, also from Harvard but with no apparent connection to the "Burma Club," says: "I'll bet I've been involved in about three hundred discussions about what 'Papa' or the 'dragon Lady' will do next—the discussions may be half humorous but they are equally serious. . . . If you ever run out of ideas, write us—we are lousy with them. In fact about all this place does is develop your imagination" (Jan. 1937). Later, during wartime, *Terry* became even more crucial in providing continuity and community in a world a bit more threatening than a college dorm. A representative of a group of soldiers wrote in 1942: "There are five other fellows in my tent beside myself, and we have kind of formed a little group to read 'Terry' after the duty hours. Right now with our training and preparations for a long trip . . .

'Terry' has become more enjoyable than ever" (May 26; quoted in Morrison, 158). Numerous other letters from troops both at home and abroad attest to the strip's inestimable value in providing a "morale booster," as many letter writers put it, for groups of readers.

This and many other letters attesting to the existence of *Terry* groups emphasize serial fiction's ability to fuel conversation that serves in place of gossip as a means of exchanging ideas. The letter also affirms the pleasure readers derive from interacting creatively with serials. Many letter writers offered suggestions—or commands—for future plots and seemed assured that their ideas would receive consideration. Caniff certainly had a reputation for his responsiveness to readers; so important was audience opinion that he kept all letters. Readers wrote to give him the latest slang, to correct the wing shape of a fighter plane, to request more coverage of a favorite character. His answer can often be traced in the strip within a few days of receiving the letter (Sheridan 158). In fact, it is fair to say that Caniff was obsessed with accuracy.

And readers seem to have felt it no more than his job as a media artist to respond to their desires. For example, a letter threatens, "I swear, here and now, if Milton Caniff takes his big hero off that island, where he is staying with that gujuss [sic] blonde, I will quit reading 'Terry and the Pirates'" (March 6, 1936). Conversely, another from the same time period (March 21) demands: "Hey Milton Caniff, quit that 'Oh Darling!' love scenes in your comic strip . . . and give us some real action. Right boys!" Also in the "suggestion" category, letters often asked for the return of favorite characters, an option Caniff (like future soap writers) left open, as we have seen, by simply sending extraneous characters off on their own until their return seemed desirable. Most of these "extraneous" people were women, and so readers demand the return of favorite heroines: "What happened to Dale of the Terry and the Pirates strip? Pat used to fight many a Chinese over her. Now he only has eyes for Burma. I want Dale. . . . Down with Normandie and Burma—" (March 21, 1936). Or, from another reader whose desire for more Normandie had just been satisfied: "A couple of days ago I wrote a goofy letter to the 'Voice of the People' care of the 'Daily News.' My idea in writing the letter was to make you and your readers 'Normandie conscious' and whether this letter found it's [sic] way to the waste-basket or your desk is immaterial since you have brought Normandie back into existence in this morning's issue" (August 28, 1936).

Many readers include with their suggestions the ultimate threat, the one they know publishers will listen to: "If the Dragon Lady in the strip 'Terry and the Pirates' dies I'll never read the News again. I know plenty more who won't read it either. Disgusted Reader" (Jan. 23, 1937). And again: "In reference to 'Terry and the Pirates,' we the 'Boys of James St,' object to the murder of the Dragon Lady. We demand the electrocution of the assassin. P.S. We quit buying the News" (Jan. 24, 1937). There are hundreds more along these lines. Such letters show comic-strip audiences as quite conscious that they wield the power of the consumer over this text that has become so much a part of their daily lives. Their power is seemingly acknowledged in the text itself: in response to the high volume of requests, Caniff brings the Dragon Lady "back from the dead" in January 1938, as so many soap writers do today for popular characters.

In addition to the threats, thanks, praise, and requests for drawings, Caniff's files are full of detailed critiques of the strip's errors. Readers offer substantial suggestions, based on their knowledge of the power of reader response: they write to point out errors, either trivial or serious. First, an example of the trivial:

> Dear Editor:
> Here I am, still complaining on your comic strips and will not be satisfied until they are immaculate, I mean right.
> I noticed another error yesterday and unless you correct it I will stop buying the "Newsy" with much regret. . . . [Here the letter writer points out that when Terry et al. are trapped in the temple, the idol holds his sword in his left hand in one day's strip, then switches to the right in the next.] Why? Did the idol get tired and changed position while we were not looking? Or perhaps Mr. Caniff has been reading the Skolsky's movie boners column too much and got jealous? (Dec. 15, 1934)

And again, concerning a more substantial error: "When Terry and Pat were arrested, he [Caniff] had them taken before a Chinese magistrate. However, in China foreigners enjoy Extra-Territoriality rights. That is: they are tried before a judge of their own nationality, usually the consul of their respective nation, not before a native Chinese judge" (Jan. 23, 1935).

These letters redressing Caniff's errors of detail are matched by more substantial critiques. For example, readers were often better informed about China than Caniff was. In creating the setting for his picaresque, Caniff clearly understood that right from the beginning "realism" is in the eye of the beholder, depending much more heavily on cultural construction than on facts. He had never been to China and therefore went to "the next best place"—the New York Public Library. After collecting visual data from picture files, encyclopedias, and travel books, he tackled speech: "For authentic speech mannerisms I plow through a pile of books from traveled people from Pearl Buck to Noel Coward" (not, perhaps, the authorities the Chinese would have chosen).[9] Caniff's doubly mediated representation of China, compiled from sources that had already adjusted their depictions for an American audience, echoed what readers already had heard and thus struck some as impressively authentic.

Praise of Caniff's authenticity did not last, however, and was balanced right from the start by critiques of his racism and factual errors. Caniff received feedback, first from people more familiar with China or Chinese culture than he and later from soldiers, pilots, and civilians involved in the early Sino-Japanese conflict and then in World War II itself. In clear reference to these letters, which he carefully filed and preserved, Caniff cites

> the period when, in my opinion, my strip passed over from pseudo-reality to straight realism. Pretty cheerfully, I had been putting Terry and pal Pat through their unchallenged paces on a comfortably remote Yellow Sea littoral, when history caught up with me. I soon learned the bitter lesson which all strip artists must eventually absorb: there are more people from Wichita, who have been to more places than you or I or Wichita would suspect. My characters were floating east on streams which course west. They were holding up Chinese pants with buttons sold exclusively by an Ohio dime-store chain, and anyway it is the general Chinese rule that the ladies wear the pants. . . . I was forced into realism. I didn't sell comic-strip realism to my readers. My readers sold realism to me. [Adams, Marschall, and Nantier, 39–40]

From his files, it is easy to see that Caniff tells no more than the truth. As the artist became educated by his readers, he gradually incorporated new information and attitudes into his work, although improved representation of the Chinese was unfortunately accompanied by creation of a new scapegoat, the Japanese. In 1938 and 1939, Caniff introduced "Klang the Warlord" to dramatize the plight of bombed Chinese cities and starving citizens. Because the United States was still officially neutral, syndicate owner Joseph Patterson forbade Caniff to explicitly name his villains as the Japanese (this policy was dropped after Pearl Harbor). Caniff, ever obligatory, carefully refrained from naming them but provided subtle clues like caricature Japanese eyes and teeth and prominently placed rising sun flags.

Despite the obvious limitations, over the years Pat, Terry, *and readers* shifted their vision of China, first to incorporate more realistic and individualized portrayals of the Chinese and later to follow the Sino-Japanese conflict while it was still virtually ignored in the American press. In fact, because of Caniff's respect for the authority of his readers, the audience of this comic strip received arguably more authentic—and certainly earlier—information about the conflict in China than did audiences of another cultural construct of the war, American news reports. As one reader wrote Caniff in 1944, "You've brought the war with Japan closer and clearer to me than all the movies, editorials, and radio commentators. You bring it to us in ALL its phases" (Aug. 27; quoted in Morrison, 135). Although the strip, with its focus on the adventures of two rugged American individualists working to combat the teeming hordes of Japanese villains and Chinese victims, obviously presented a very skewed perspective on the events, it could usefully be set over against the stories contained in newspapers as a kind of alternate narrative that worked to remind readers of the essential narrativization of all experience. This use of the strip as a foil for more "factual" reportage is exposed in another fan letter from 1944 explaining that "since our entry into World War No. 2, it [*Terry*] has become first class enjoyable instruction in the activities of our Air Force in China. To me your strip is so appealing and authentic that I peruse it on par with the headlines of the front page for the latest in what's going on" (Nov. 13; quoted in Morrison, 135).

Other readers, familiar with Chinese culture, were much more critical of Caniff's representations. One typed a three-page missive enumerating the factual errors Caniff had made in his depiction of China, noting that although *Terry and the Pirates* is "an excellent tale indeed," nevertheless there are a few problems

> which the kids in this neighborhood have noticed and which impair its authority. These occur in the dialog, the drawings, and the episodes. . . . For instance, throughout, the artist draws all roof-tops in straight lines . . . in the Orient all ridge-poles sag from the weight of the roofing. . . . The Pidgin English dialog, also, is faulty. This is'nt [sic] Pidgin. No China boy, such as Terry, speaks that way, nor do the coolies, enginemen, mariners, and other natives, when they can speak English of any sort, use the diction in exactly that way [examples follow]. . . . There are a number of factual rough spots. As an example of one or two of these: (1) there are very few if any tank vessels in the Orient, and those that are there are not of American registry. There seems to be no reason why the pirate rendezvous ship should be a tanker. . . . Miss Singapore Burma should have been under suspicion by the Wingates from the first. There is no place like the Far East for social classification, contrary to script, and the Wingates were British which would make it all the more difficult for the boys to be taken into the Wingate menage with open arms, as they were. [Jan. 20, 1939]

And so on. This letter is longer and nitpicks more than most others seeking to alert Caniff to his failings, but the motivation behind the attention to detail becomes clear when at the end of the letter the writer advises earnestly that "when you run one of these excellent orientals [storylines, apparently], you engage a good all around man to polish off the details and make the thing authentic. . . . there is myself, for instance."

A more critical letter is the following, explicating Caniff's misrepresentation of the Chinese and proving that at least some Americans were well aware of the possible repercussions of the stereotypes Caniff perpetuated. After assuring the artist that he loves the strips, the writer continues:

> You stress the "wickedness" of the Chinese a bit too much, and I wouldn't be surprised if you've received some complaints from that quarter. The average person's knowledge of this race is limited to chinese laundrymen and Fu Manchu in books and movies and a strip in a newspaper showing only villains doesn't help much. . . . I, too, am an artist and the only difference between you and me, is that you're good. However, I hang around New York's Chinatown sketching and that gives me the opportunity to be near to them and make friends. [The letter goes on to list specific errors in Caniff's depiction.] [undated; labelled Jan. 1935 in Caniff's files]

This reader demonstrates a number of typical fan letter qualities: appreciation of Caniff's art (in opening comments not quoted here); desire to make personal contact on some level ("I, too, am an artist") and to reveal oneself as more than just the stereotypical ignorant "fan"; and acknowledgment of the potential influence, for better or worse, of the text under discussion ("a strip . . . showing only villains doesn't help much"). Most important, this letter demonstrates a belief shared by many fans: that their voices are important and that they will be heard.

In return, Caniff clearly manifests the greatest respect for his audience, as well as a relationship with readers that Dickens would have envied. He does so in published comments like the one quoted above that publicly bows to the superior knowledge of his fans. More important, he does so by transforming the strip itself in response to that knowledge. By his own account as well as by the proof of his preserved correspondence, he paid close attention to his fan mail. These claims are borne out not only by his carefully organized files of letters but also by the evidence of many cases of multiple letters from the same person, with the subsequent ones thanking Caniff for responding to the first, for advice given, for the chance to come watch him work in his studio, and so on. We also know that he carefully read readers' letters, especially when they came from people actually overseas or in the forces he depicted, since some of these casual correspondents turned into steady sources of information when he felt uncertain about particular details of which they had demonstrated knowledge.

Caniff did not hire the job-seeking critic quoted above. However, he did make unofficial experts of many who started by writing fan-letters and ended by entering into lifelong correspondence. For example, two nurses, Ruth White and Florence Hunter, became regular correspondents and friends after he responded to White's suggestion that he add a Red Cross nurse to his cast of characters; he created Taffy Tucker in response. In August 1939, White wrote:

Dear Milt:

I know you think I am the most ungrateful cuss in the world not to have written to you earlier to tell you how swell Terry and the Pirates is with its Taffy as a character. . . . [She describes the travel itinerary of the Army War Show, which she accompanies for the purpose of recruiting nurses; along the way, she has chided editors of various Midwest newspapers for not running *Terry*, and tells Caniff that in Des Moines] I was reminded forcibly of the fact that I did, indeed, owe you a letter. I was at a Red Cross gathering and was asked idly, 'What do you do?' I answered 'I am in the public information service.' They all still looked blank and I went on, 'I do things like getting a Red Cross nurse in Terry and the Pirates.' They all sat up as if they had been shot. [Technical Experts Correspondence folder, Caniff archive Aug. 22, 1939]

Besides thanking him for what she clearly sees as an act of public service as well as publicity for the nursing profession, White also sent Caniff regular updates to ensure the authenticity of his depiction. He acquired another expert when Florence Henderson wrote to thank him for including a nurse in the strip and to ask for his autograph. In reply, he asked her to send any information she thought he should know about army nurses, and she too became an important source.

Taffy's dialogue sometimes becomes mechanical when Caniff too obviously tries to compress what he has learned from White about the inferior status of Red Cross nurses. In 1942, for example, Taffy informs us: "Those receiving room romeos give a gal no peace! . . . I joined the Red Cross Nursing Service to help save humanity—and I end up having to save myself. . . . It's because I haven't been inducted into the Army Nurse Corps! . . . Just wait until I get that lieutenant's bar" (July 18, 1942). And after Taffy was inducted into the Army Nurse Corps, White sent a letter "to tell you that the ban on married nurses has been lifted by the Army. . . . Furthermore, married nurses may join the Corps. In view of the fact that Flip and Taffy are having a romance, I though you might like to know this" (Technical Experts correspondence folder, March 8, 1943).

Once his characters officially joined the war, the strip drew so much notice in high places that Caniff no longer had to depend on friends and readers; he was involuntarily provided with outside experts. Since at this point the strip begins to lose spontaneity, it is interesting to speculate as to how much this official "help" contributed to the decline in creativity and the increase in propaganda. Caniff began getting his information from people with a definite agenda. For example, General H.H. Arnold of the Air Force was so impressed with the strip's devoted following among pilots that he detailed an officer to assist Caniff with technical details about fighter jet fuselage, technological capabilities, flight patterns, and so on to increase the accuracy of the strip's depictions (Adams, Marschall, and Nantier, 35). On the other hand, his lucky hits on military strategies were not so cheerfully received. Caniff was repeatedly questioned by the military during the war because his "fictional" espionage and counterespionage tended to veer too close to strategic reality.

Comic Ideologies: Pinup Girls and "Screwy Chinese"

In response to fan letters like those quoted above, Caniff deepened his perceptions of women and of race. First, we will analyze developments in his depiction of female characters. Of course, his growth as an artist parallels larger cultural changes: the period of the strip's run, 1934–46, is one of great change in the social and legal construction of American women. Trina Robbins and Catherine Yronwode, in their ground-breaking study *Women and the Comics*, explain that at their inception in the 1930s comic books were produced almost exclusively by men in their late teens and early twenties. Conscription and the war decimated these creators, and as a consequence the number of female cartoonists had tripled by 1942.[10]

Despite the persistence of masculine themes and barely dressed women in many comic strips, the increased penetration of women into the workforce did have its effect even on strips like *Terry* that were produced by men, since women (often using androgynous pseudonyms) created some very popular strips during this era and thus proved that complex, adventurous heroines drew high numbers of readers. At the same time, women often became primary wage earners and heads of households, in charge of the multiple economic decisions made by the family—including which newspaper to buy. This shift altered the attitude of commodity producers toward women. The female audience became sought after, and products were marketed specifically with female consumers in mind, a transition reflected in the rise of radio soaps to be discussed in the next chapter as well as in women-authored comics such as Dale Messick's *Brenda Starr, Reporter* and Tarpe Mills's *Miss Fury*. These strips feature strong, resourceful, professional heroines, reverberating with the energy and independence enabled by the new career possibilities open to their creators. And conversely, the heroines served as role models for female readers, providing narrative and visual representations of career women—in glamorous clothes, of course—who were at least as smart and strong as men. At the same time, however, even these female-centered strips draw on visual techniques that parallel the cinematic structuring of the male gaze, possessing and objectifying a woman who poses for the viewer's pleasure.

Some of Caniff's heroines deserve notice, appearing as they did in an era offering unprecedented opportunities for women. By creating independent, forceful, female characters, Caniff may have helped ease a difficult historical transition. The Dragon Lady, for example, is a powerful but still glamorous Eurasian villainess based on an actual female pirate along the China coast named Lai Choi San, which translates as "Mountain of Wealth." She is portrayed as courageous, beautiful, respected, overwhelmingly charismatic, impassively ironic, and—most crucially—capable both of rescuing Pat and Terry from death and of transforming her pirates into guerrilla fighters when China is threatened.

Other female characters include Hu Shee, a tough, down-to-earth, but initially mysterious Chinese guerrilla (hence the name—who she?—which provided fuel for bad puns) who singlehandedly rescues Terry after a bomb attack and after that drifts in and out of the strip, rekindling poor Terry's undying love and then, with utter reliability, disappointing him. Normandie Drake, a spoiled-heiress-turned-self-sacrificing-heroine, trades torches with Pat Ryan for years, even after she marries American traitor Tony Sandhurst, whose repulsive selfishness even the "evil" Japanese despise. Significantly, though, the American Normandie is unlike the Eurasian Dragon Lady or the Chinese Hu Shee in that her storylines generally emphasize her helplessness and passivity—her loyalty to Sandhurst, for example, defies all reason even while being presented as evidence of her "courage" and good values—and time after time she is rescued by Ryan. In fact, Burma, a beautiful, wanted woman on the run, is practically unique among the American women in being independent and self-reliant. Even she, however, is usually attached to a man (often an evil one) who is the source of her power. Fan letters often praised Caniff's creation of strong, independent female characters like Burma, occasionally by means of rather farfetched literary comparisons, as in this letter from a woman: "We indulge in lengthy arguments as to the fate of our old siren, Burma, who fled to a watery escape and has never been heard from since. . . . And did you get the idea of the triumph of feminine charm from Lysistrata and her women. The analogy seems rather obvious to me, but I may be wrong" (Jan. 20, 1937).

Despite their individuality and occasional autonomy, these women never control the narrative. Indeed, in the first years of the strip they seem entirely interchangeable, which becomes clear from the fact that one replaces the other in a kind of relay team of contrasting tokenism. Only the first Sunday strip is womanless; the Dragon Lady jumps into the second ("Luvva Pete!" says Terry, "we're captured by a WOMAN!"), and does not depart until the fourteenth. And when she is gone, Caniff does not waste any time introducing a new female figure: the very next Sunday he initiates a new "love interest," Sherry Granger. Sherry stays with us only until the twenty-second Sunday strip, when (maybe because she never quite came to life) we experience another changing of the guard; the Dragon Lady returns, and Sherry is sent back to America without a second glance.

In the daily strips (the continuity was separate until August 1936), Pat and Terry go solo for the first week, hooking up only with the feminized Connie. On Nov. 27, 1934, Dale Scott enters the picture as the daughter of the boat captain who the treasure seekers hire to take them upriver. On Jan. 25, 1935, Pat and Terry watch Dale's ship sail away, "each with his own thoughts about this girl whom they never expect to see again." This comment seems to be a hint that she will reappear, but fortunately she does not since Caniff soon developed much more interesting and popular female characters. With Dale safely out of the way, the coast is clear for Normandie Drake, who appears the next day (Jan. 26) when Pat and Terry recover her stolen purse. After Normandie has been cured of snobbism by shipwreck on a desert island (a storyline strongly reminiscent of Bella's "cure" by Boffin and Harmon, especially since Normandie also falls in love with her "teacher" Pat, the beginning of a mutual but blocked affair that will continue for years to come), she also sails off into the distance with implications of her eventual return, which in Normandie's case does indeed happen.

This pattern of relay-teaming women characters clearly worked well, for Caniff, and he continued it, with variations, throughout the life of the strip. Later, once these women characters had acquired personalities and followings of their own, Caniff occasionally allowed two at once—as in the series entitled, for reprint, "The Return of Normandie" (1942), when the Dragon Lady and Normandie share both strip space and the attentions of its hero, a convergence that ends in a stereotypical cat fight. The similarly inconclusive endings of the Dale/Normandie subplots indicate the move toward refusal of closure that the form underwent as temporal extension rather than ideological resolution became a central goal of serial fiction. And since adventure comics were perceived as a primarily masculine form, the fact that eternally deferred narrative conclusions develop early in the strip's run indicates that such open-endedness is characteristic of the form itself rather than being an essentially feminine narrative quality as some theorists of soap opera (Modleski 1979 and 1982 and Nochimson, for example) have argued.

Caniff's depiction of women shifted, then, in response to the cultural climate. Like the female-authored heroines Brenda Starr and Miss Fury, Caniff's hero Pat Ryan was denied the "fireside and slippers" that would be perceived as cramping his adventures; however, his replaceable early heroines generally either disappeared or got married. Later, however, Caniff began recycling strong and independent women (the Dragon Lady in particular) who rejected a succession of marriage proposals to keep themselves free for ca-

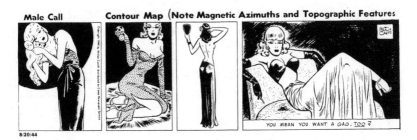

Fig. 2.4: Giving the troops what they're supposed to want (Aug. 20, 1944). From *Male Call* by Milton Caniff. © 1944 by Milton Caniff, used by permission of Milton Caniff Estate, © 1996.

reer and adventure, not to mention further strips. Thus what feminists would perceive as a move forward in mass fiction's representation of women was directly impelled not by the social conscience of an individual artist but by social and economic factors exerting pressure on that artist. Again we see the benefits of serial fiction's near compulsion to respond to both cultural climate and the demands of its readers (of course, this compulsion can have a regressive effect as well).

Besides adding to the alarmingly limited positive portrayals of strong women in comic strips, *Terry* is one of the first strips to have made the serial form and sexuality inextricable, a pattern also followed later by soap opera. Caniff used models as well as the inspiration of film stars to create his female characters, dressing them in skintight, glamorous evening gowns that often seem a bit farfetched given the setting, as when the Dragon Lady appears on the eve of battle in formal attire. Fan letters attest to the success of his techniques: his characters, both male and female, acquired the status of matinee idols for many readers. But since comics reached readers of all ages and both sexes, both syndicates and newspapers imposed stringent censorship guidelines on artists, guidelines that varied according to the particular paranoias of the morality watchdogs of successive ages. Early in comic history, the archenemy was sex: Dale Messick, creator of *Brenda Starr* in the 1940s, remembers editors airbrushing navels out of her women (interview with author, Jan. 1991). And any kind of explicit sex was of course utterly taboo, a repression that made strips in the hands of masters like Milton Caniff and Tarpe Mills into literal stripteases (see fig. 2.4) since in narrative terms it produced long-term deferred desire, always a strong pull for serials. Affairs smoldered for months or even years without being consummated. Both artists created extraordinarily erotic narratives as a result, frames or entire sequences in which situations were manipulated to expose passion, or at least reduce clothing. Characters' dialogue or silence, positioning, shading, motion or stillness reverberated with just barely repressed sexuality. As Ron Goulart understates the case of *Miss Fury*: "Tarpe Mills also seems to have been influenced by some under-the-counter literature. There are quite a few of the traditional bondage elements in the feature—whips, branding irons, spike heel shoes, men beating women, women tearing each other's clothes off, and a handsome selection of frilly lingerie" (180). *Terry*—and even more obviously Caniff's military striptease, *Male Call*—served the same purpose. Over the strip's early years, then, Caniff's female characters shifted from stereotyped and interchangeable objects to complex and active subjects in their own right. On the other hand, in the 1940s many women spent at least part of their strip time literally stripping as Caniff became increasingly obsessed with "satisfying" the troops fighting overseas.

In representing ethnicity, Caniff was, as we have seen, both more limited and more willing to learn from his readers and from history. Initially offering only stereotypes, he ended by providing readers with some of the most accurate information on wartime conditions in China available to the mass public at the time. In addition, his construction of nonwhite characters changed demonstrably in both visual and narrative terms. As Carla Zimmerman points out in discussing a parallel transition (that of a *Blackhawk* comic character from the dehumanized and entirely subservient Chop-Chop [1941–55] to a more human, less stereotyped Chop-Chop and finally to the realistic, self-aware We Cheng, who demands respect and equal treatment from other team members [1982–84]), the Chinese had a long history of denigration and oppression in the American legal system as well as in popular culture. Caniff seems well aware of comics' institutional racism, even in the early years. Describing his childhood comic-strip inventions as following "whatever the plotline of the Saturday and Sunday story called for," he explains that "my hero was a bold adventurer named Tom Martin (nonethnic label—editorial caution came early!)." The newspaper formula dictated that ethnic sidekicks were all right; identifiably ethnic main characters were not.[11]

In response to readers who encouraged Caniff to dismantle his own stereotypes in letters like those cited above, he created long-term sympathetic characters such as Connie who challenged myths of the stupid Chinese lackey. When we first meet Connie he dismisses his own culture, replying when asked his name, "Chinese name—nobody can say! —got plofessional name like movum pitcher actor velly swell. . . . Name is called George Webster Confucius! —George Washington velly honest fellah! —Webster speak good! —Confucius velly wise! —Me—all three in one! Hot stuff, huh?" (Oct. 24, 1934). This character neatly reduces all Chinese speakers to a collective "nobody." In addition, his speech, whether Caniff intended this effect

Fig. 2.5: Pat, Connie, and Big Stoop: shifting stereotypes (Dec. 28, 1941). © Tribune Media Services, Inc. All rights reserved. Reprinted with permission.

or not, implies the extent to which he literally acts a role in interacting with Westerners, adopting not only an inauthentic language but also a stage name and hence a stage persona. In keeping with Western stereotypes of sexually ambiguous Eastern men, Pat instantly feminizes this caricature by dubbing him "Connie," and Caniff reinforces this stereotype by depicting him in a long, frilly apron in most of the early episodes. Over the years, the caricatured Connie gives way to a character who—though still drawn with ludicrous ears and teeth—no longer ruins plans but aids and even conceives them. He also becomes capable of handling a gun and of working with speed and intelligence to rescue his friends when they are in trouble. In short, Connie becomes more ally than servant. Similarly, when we first meet the Dragon Lady (in the second Sunday strip, Dec. 16, 1934), she is a Chinese caricature, speaking Pidgin English: "So! It is the Amelican gentleman who resists so brashly—I am not su'plised!" Three Sundays later, she speaks perfect if overly formal English, and there is no mention of the shift in her diction. It is as if once Caniff had decided to make her a "real"—that is to say, central and serious—character, he had to move past his original stereotypical conception. Later, Caniff would become more sophisticated in his treatment of language. On several occasions, for example, he introduces Chinese characters who use Pidgin English as a kind of self-protection, though eventually we learn that in fact they speak perfect English.

From 1941 on, Connie begins to disappear from the strip for long stretches, and his place is eventually filled by an equal rather than a servant. The war hero Captain Bucky Wing appears on the scene, making Terry feel inferior since as a member of a neutral country he cannot see "real action." Wing is not only intelligent and brave, he is also handsome—and he eventually wins Terry's latest love, Hu Shee (of course, despite the rounded portrayal of both Wing and Hu Shee, Wing's arrival on the scene does seem conveniently timed in that it "saves" Terry from an interracial romance that would no doubt have offended many readers).

By the later years of the strip, readers are able to laugh while the heroes foolishly perpetuate stereotypes, only to be taught a lesson in respect. In figure 2.5, for example, Connie and Big Stoop together disarm one of Pat's most villainous enemies while Pat chides them, like children, for making so much noise. Later, he realizes that their "commotion" saved him from a bullet. And by the time America officially entered the war, we see heroes such as Flip Corkin working side by side with Chinese military commanders depicted as perfectly normal human beings who are highly intelligent and who lack earlier derogatory stereotypes like huge ears, 0–shaped mouths crammed with teeth, and the inability to speak anything but Pidgin English.

Over the twelve years of the strip, then, depiction of Chinese characters

Fig. 2.6: The Dragon Lady with a Japanese imposter (May 15, 1942). © Tribune Media Services, Inc. All rights reserved. Reprinted with permission.

Fig. 2.7: Exposing the imposter (May 16, 1942). © Tribune Media Services, Inc. All rights reserved.

changed considerably in response to readers' complaints and probably also in response to the Sino-Japanese conflict and the consequent need to humanize the Chinese in recasting them as allies set over against the new enemy, the Japanese. On the other hand, this humanization tended to be more true of male than of female characters. As we have seen, the infamous Dragon Lady persistently reinforces visions of the exotic, alluring, sometimes powerful and helpful but eternally treacherous Asian woman; indeed, her name has entered popular discourse as a label for that vision. Counterbalancing the increased respect for the Chinese is the rise of the Japanese as Other—and of the letters I have read, none berated Caniff for his stereotyping of the strip's new villain race. This blindness to Caniff's inaccuracy from readers usually only too ready to correct him reflects the extensive anti-Japanese spirit in the U.S. at the time. Chinese immigration was sharply reduced by the Exclusion Act of 1882. However, Japanese immigration increased at the turn of the century, setting off demands for further legislation to exclude this new "threat" as well. In 1900, San Francisco mayor James Duval Phelan made his racist agenda clear in complaining that "the Japanese are starting the same tide of immigration which we thought we had checked twenty years ago. . . . They are not the stuff of which American citizens can be made" (quoted in Cohen, 126). The 1924 Immigration Act forbade Japanese immigration to the United States. Tensions mounted, coming to a climax after Pearl Harbor. The Chinese Exclusion Act of 1882 was finally repealed in 1943, after America and China became allies against the Japanese. In other words, it was not a reevaluation of racist stereotypes but rather the existence of a common enemy and new scapegoat that enabled a revision of U.S. policies toward China and the Chinese (Hardy and Stern, 38), the same force that enabled Caniff's revision of the stereotyped Chinese characters in his strip. The repeal of this act symbolized a very partial shift in attitudes toward the Chinese for obvious psychological reasons: the role of demonized Other was more than adequately filled by the new American enemies, the Japanese and Germans.

While he may have helped ameliorate American suspicions of the Chinese, then, Caniff probably contributed to xenophobic persecution of the Japanese, who became the collective villain of the strips. Caniff's representations of the Japanese invaders of China were just as visually and linguistically stereotyped as his early Chinese characters, but while the Chinese were allowed to develop over time into more complex characters capable of performing heroic actions in the strip, the Japanese remained unmitigatedly evil for its duration. In fact, Caniff seems to seek justification for his new admiration of the Chinese and demonization of the Japanese in that he spends a good deal of time rehearsing ways of telling the two groups apart—a clear consequence of the ugly American "they all look alike to me" attitude (see, for example, figs. 2.6 and 2.7; there are many other examples).

Ironically obsessed with realistic representation of history if not of individuals, Caniff plunged Terry and the rest into the Sino-Japanese conflict with a vengeance. As Ron Goulart explains, "his dedication to authenticity got Caniff into the war against Japan several years ahead of anyone else in the United States" (135). The Chinese began fighting a Japanese invasion in 1937, with one million Japanese troops in China by 1939. Caniff first covered the invasion in the spring of 1938—long before the conflict had received much attention in the American press—and began focusing exclusively on the conflict by the end of 1939. Terry and Pat, who had been innocently pursuing mythical pirates and buried treasure on the China coast, suddenly found themselves immersed in guerrilla action. Especially early on, before other media were paying much attention to the Sino-Japanese conflict, *Terry* played a role in influencing American attitudes toward the war—to such an extent, according to Goulart, that syndicate editor Patterson "indicated that such unpleasant elements as war did not properly belong in a comic strip. Caniff disagreed. Patterson kept grumbling until Pearl Harbor, but he never directly ordered a change" (136). Later, the military became so aware of the potential influence of the comics that they sometimes attempted

Figs. 2.8 & 2.9: Milton Caniff as propagandist, 1941 and 1944. Used by permission of the Milton Caniff Estate.

Fig. 2.10: The rise of the pro-American agenda (Nov. 17, 1944). © Tribune Media Services, Inc. All rights reserved. Reprinted with permission.

Figs. 2.11 & 2.12: Wolff lectures Burma on the glories of American democracy (June 6 and 7, 1941). © Tribune Media Services, Inc. All rights reserved. Reprinted with permission.

to suppress political content by rejecting certain geographical settings and adventure plots, especially during "sensitive" times. War-comic writers including Caniff were occasionally rebuked for inventing comic military realities too close to actual projected strategy. According to Adams, Marschall, and Nantier, Chinese officials acknowledged the power of the strips as well, "publicly thank[ing] Caniff for keeping the menace of Japan and China's brave fight against it in the spotlight during the first years of World War II, when all eyes were on the Nazis" (40).

Publishers and syndicate editors were well aware of the power of comic strips in reflecting and influencing American attitudes. Comics were often seen and used as propaganda weapons and sometimes even prompted immediate enemy retaliation. Superheroes mobilized to join the war effort, becoming the favorite reading material of soldiers at the front. In 1940 Captain Marvel fought both Nazis and Japanese, and Captain America was created in 1941 to fight Nazis as well. In 1942 Superman demolished the Atlantic wall in preparation for the Allied invasion, reportedly causing a comic-strip reaction in impelling "a fuming Goebbels to scream in the middle of a Reichstag meeting, 'Superman is a Jew!'" (Couperie et al. 83).

Through the postwar era, stereotyped minority characters were the norm. But racial issues finally forced themselves on American consciousness when syndicate editors cracked down on stereotyping as a result of vehement protests by readers and others (protests that coincided with the early years of the civil rights movement). Minority characters were no longer portrayed according to racist ideologies. Instead, they were completely repressed. During the 1950s, nonwhite characters virtually disappeared from one of the central mass-media depictions of American life and did not reappear in significant numbers until the 1970s. Comic-strip representation of women and nonwhites is important in that mass-media texts such as *Terry* probably affected American attitudes more than, say, books such as Theodore Lothrop Stoddard's *The Rising Tide of Color Against White World Supremacy*. Since anti-Japanese sentiment resulted in the mass incarceration of Japanese Americans that still scars America today, it is clear that *Terry* packs essential lessons about the ideological responsibility of mass serials, which due to their longevity and their tendency to become intertwined with audience lives may reflect and help to shape audience attitudes more than other mass texts.

While *Terry* was running, in fact, the U.S. government acknowledged the power of comic strips when the Defense Department asked Caniff to design a poster educating citizens about the consequences of bomb attacks. As Caniff puts it, "At that point, any means were used to inform, recruit and raise morale" (*Male Call*, 9). The strip shows the consequences of his increasingly didactic and pro-American goals: he was very reluctantly 4–F and became defensively patriotic as World War II progressed. His contribution to the war effort centered on providing the troops with anti-Japanese propaganda as well as with whatever they wanted in terms of substitute sex objects in his strip *Male Call*, distributed only to military bases (fig. 2.4); he also volunteered his services to the military for recruitment and information posters (figs. 2.8, 2.9). Interestingly enough, once Caniff felt the weight of this responsibility he undid much of his progress in representation of female and Chinese characters. After 1940, *Terry* became less creative and adventurous and more rigidly ideological; three 1940s strips (figs. 2.10, 2.11 and 2.12) illustrate Caniff's increasingly explicit political agenda. On the other hand, his respect for the Chinese continued to increase. For example, in 1943 Terry joins the Chinese Flying Cadet school, and lest we miss the significance of this event, Caniff has the character Flip Corkin tell us explicitly that the decision "shows how we respect [Chinese] advances in aviation" (March 2, 1943).

The Decline of the Serial Strip

Earlier discussion included David Kunzle's evaluation of the nineteenth-century transition to humor as the primary function of comic art. With the Depression and the onset of World War II, Kunzle rightly argues that "the contemporary American strip has, in a sense, reverted to source; being only

Fig. 2.13: Terry has a sense of irony still—at least when it comes to the "Evil Nazi," Kiel (March 14, 1941). © Tribune Media Services, Inc. All rights reserved. Reprinted with permission.

partially comic, its appeal has widened, and in ideological content it has resumed somewhat its original role of providing people with moral and political propaganda" (1). After 1942, *Terry* shifted focus. Losing its overt romance and adventurism, it became much more concerned with explicit Americanism. Couperie opines tactfully that Caniff's post-1942 boosterism reflected post-Pearl Harbor American attitudes all too closely: "Without completely abandoning its romantic character, 'Terry' became a different type of strip, in which the individual deeds were muted before collective heroism" (83). Richard Marschall, on the other hand, is much more blunt. Unable to reconcile himself to changes in the strip's structure and themes, he argues that *Terry* went sharply downhill after mythic quests ceded to ideological battles against (equally mythic) evil Japanese invaders: "The magic element in *Terry* . . . .was the release valve represented by romantic, otherworldly, even picaresque (to recall one of Caniff's cherished self-representations) aspects. . . . Caniff, for the rest of his career, seemed more wedded to promoting military themes, loyalties, and causes" (221). And with Caniff's next strip, *Steve Canyon*, this trait had solidified: "To many readers it seemed, at best, that Canyon was a seven-day-a-week recruiting poster and, at worst, that his creator had lost the magic formula for mixing plot, character, dialogue, and art as he has so supremely in *Terry and the Pirates*" (221).

Marschall has a point. Although earlier Caniff strips show his ironic awareness of military delusions of grandeur (see fig. 2.13), later strips lost this distance. Caniff's ideological reorganization can be traced in part to his 4–F guilt complex and perhaps also to the military "experts" he began to rely on for information and ideas. Changes in the comic-strip industry played a major role as well. Comics securely established themselves in a very short period of time, and by World War II, the heyday of *Terry*, they had become an integral part of the newspaper trade. After this time, however, industry streamlining in the form of increasing technical restrictions began to take effect.

In the late 1940s and 1950s, syndicates reduced the size of strips so they could pack more variety into each paper, providing the "something for everyone" necessary for wide demographics (just as both Dickens's novels and soap operas cram a diversity of subplots and characters into each episode). In addition to these reductions of visual possibilities, layout editors often required artists to add "throwaway" panels, which could be printed or deleted as layout required. Transformations such as these tended to lead to "gag" or nonnarrative strips. The shrunken strips blurred the detail that a mood- and narrative-saturated strip requires, and narratives that worked by making every panel pack its full share of meaning now had to face the possible—and unpredictable—loss of one-fourth of their narrative space, thus imposing essential triviality on at least one panel.

Marschall, expressing a prevalent comic-world nostalgia that recalls Benjamin's mourning for the days of the Storyteller, insists that we should "curse the times, for in the 30s the whole world lived and breathed, it seems, for the adventures on comic pages, on radio and in the movies. Today, the work of Caniff and other victims of time and circumstance find their spaces shrinking, their editors restive, their skills insulted by an 'improving' technology that delivers constantly inferior reproduction. TV laugh machines roar at vulgarity, and gag strips last three months as they crowd worthwhile features out. Gags. Many of us *do* gag these days" (13). Because of these changes, experimentation in visual impact and narrative drive was progressively displaced from strips to the comic books that were fast becoming not just an offshoot of the strips but an increasingly creative (and profitable) form in their own right. *Terry* may provide an object lesson in optimal conditions for the production of responsive and responsible serial fiction. (By "responsible," I do not mean that creators should follow the agenda of academics, critics, or other "authorities"; I mean, rather, that creators should be impelled by their own creativity and by audiences rather than by producers, advertisers, or other interest groups.) Early in Caniff's career, he had the time and freedom to work creatively with his audience to produce a fair, progressive, imaginative strip. Later, time constraints and the ideological agendas of "experts" combined to stultify creativity and increase stereotypes. At the same time, of course, the primary function of strips like *Terry*—to provide serial narratives, including multiple subplots to appeal to a wide audience—was fast being taken over by serials in a newer media, radio. Not just radio soaps but also adventure serials such as *Tom Mix* and comedy series such as *Amos 'n' Andy* provided what *Terry* did—and in a more "lifelike" format since audiences could actually hear the voices of the characters whose lives they followed. In addition to the technological and profit-making shifts, then, strips such as *Terry* may well have been simply displaced by a new media seeking to popularize itself by using the serial format.

Another important factor in the decline of the serial strip was a sudden surge of attention to sex and violence in the comics. The real crackdown was on an offshoot of newspaper strips, comic books, which began during the 1930s as reprints of popular strips and soon attracted a huge market. In all fairness to their critics, comic books of the 1940s and 1950s were horrifically violent, but the increased censorship that resulted from the campaign against them also trickled down to affect their much milder cousins, newspaper strips. During this period, Dr. Fredric Wertham, a psychiatrist, published a series of manifestos against comics. These monographs and articles combined with other pressures to impel the appointment in 1948 of a Code Authority and Advisory Board over comic books. Wertham's writing culminated in the sensationally titled *Seduction of the Innocent* in 1954, and a brief analysis of his critique will usefully underscore its similarity to that leveled against serial novels in their early years.

All Wertham's publications delivered anecdotal "proof" of the detrimental effects of comics on children. Reading comics, he claimed, led ineluctably to violence, racism, sadism, and the inability to appreciate canonical literature. At times, Wertham seems unclear as to which of these evils is the most heinous. For example, the doctor relays this advice to "a ten-year-old girl from a cultivated and literate home": "If later on you want to read a good novel it may describe how a young boy and girl sit together and watch the rain falling. They talk about themselves and the pages of the book describe what their innermost little thoughts are. This is what is called literature. But you will never be able to appreciate that if in comic-book fashion you expect that at any moment someone will appear and pitch both of them out of the window" (64–65). After slogging through pages of rain and innermost little thoughts, I would think many readers—and not just comics junkies—would welcome the change of pace provided by a quick pitch out the window.

Wertham espouses an odd idea of literature here. Fear of a comic-book planet leads him to ignore the fact that even "literature" packs its punches of horror, violence, and social relevance. For example, his description of a novel recounting the innermost thoughts of a young girl watching the rain strongly recalls the opening passage of *Jane Eyre*, in which Jane, shut behind a red moreen curtain, watches "ceaseless rain sweeping away wildly before a long and lamentable blast." But sensation and even horror underlie this peaceful scene. Jane's choice of reading matter is that irreproachable Victorian text, Bewick's *History of British Birds*, but the impressions she draws from it are far from pastoral: "Death-white realms," a "fiend pinning down the thief's pack," and a "black, horned thing . . . surveying a distant crowd surrounding a gallows." And what is more, while engrossed in these sensational "innermost little thoughts," Jane is in fact interrupted by someone appearing and pitching her onto the floor, if not out the window: John Reed, who (like a comic-book villain) embodies the violence of the gender and class inequalities controlling Jane. And then comes the scene in the Red Room.

Night terrors, isolation, persecution by bullies who terrifyingly mimic adult prejudice and power are important issues for any child, in any era. From the example quoted above as well as from the tone of the rest of his book, it is clear that Wertham, like so many well-intentioned knights crusading against new forms of mass culture (including the serialized novel, film, jazz, and TV, as they appeared in successive ages), seeks a return to a quieter, gentler age and has consciously or unconsciously distorted the truth and invented an "enemy" to accomplish this goal. On the other hand, it is important to acknowledge Wertham's very sound reasons for undertaking his campaign. Not simply a watchdog of "high culture," he was hostile to the politically conservative agenda of many of his admirers. For example, he turned down Lyle Stuart's offer in 1954 of the position of commissioner of the new Comic Book Code Authority and Advisory board appointed by comics publishers as a public-relations measure (Gilbert, 107). And some of his objections to comics are both unarguable and backed by personal experience. His comments on the "race hatred" inculcated by comics reflect a real, ongoing concern with America's systematic oppression of minorities as well as considerable firsthand knowledge of the consequences. In 1944 Wertham, Richard Wright, Ralph Ellison, and others opened the LaFargue Clinic, a low-cost psychiatric clinic in Harlem. Wertham had developed a psychophilosophy which resembles that of Frantz Fanon (though Wertham's is not explicated with the theoretical sophistication and empirical evidence of Fanon's) and was convinced of the emotional and psychological ravages of segregation, cultural deprivation, and racism on *both* oppressor and oppressed. He therefore intended the clinic to work toward eradicating the psychoses of institutional racism.

However, Wertham's positive motivation for attacking racism had a terribly negative effect: it intimidated cartoonists, of strips as well as of books, into avoiding ethnic images altogether. The Comic Book Code Authority (first appointed in 1949) as well as the subsequent 1950s crackdown produced a dramatic decrease in ethnic characters of any sort. Although comic fans of the 1930s saw a wide range of ethnicities in the action-adventure strips set in Africa and the East, in the post-World War II years these often derogatory images ceased. Wertham's attack coincided with other events such as the United Nations delegation from Africa criticizing "Tarzan's" depiction of the African jungle in particular and the NAACP's lobbying against racist images in comics in general (Hardy and Stern, 8). Syndicates, papers, publishers, and artists responded by evading the issue altogether. There was no development, no dismantling of stereotypes. African Americans, Asians, Indians, and other previously exploited Others simply ceased to exist. Caniff followed the general trend in his treatment of Connie. Although this character had slowly been humanized over the years, suddenly in the 1940s he vanishes, his role being filled by the all-American-appearing Charles Charles of Boston. And this is just one example of the mass retreat: a 1962 study sampling comic strips between 1943 and 1958 found one African American and no Jewish characters. Of a total of 532 characters counted in the study, 80 percent were found to be "'100% Americans,'" and 93 percent were of Anglo-Saxon or Nordic ethnicity (Hardy and Stern, 9).

Wertham's well-meant war on comics was, of course, just a small part of the epidemic of attacks in the 1950s on all forms of mass culture. For example, there was the infamous Dr. Louis Berg, who in 1942 determined that radio soap operas produce symptoms ranging from hysteria to psychosis in their audiences, including "acute anxiety state, tachycardia, arrhythmias, increase in blood pressure, profuse perspiration, tremors, vasomotor instability, nocturnal frights, vertigo, and gastro-intestinal disturbances" (Allen 1985, 21). After launching a crusade to banish soaps from the airwaves, Berg was discovered to have derived his "evidence" by the very scientific method of hooking *himself* to monitors while listening to soap episodes (Allen 1985, 22). Like the sermon of Thomas Arnold cited in the introduction, Berg's list of symptoms invokes the discourse of addiction and withdrawal and reinforces D.A. Miller's view that it is the ability of sensation fiction to provoke physical effects that produces fear among critics.

In the narrative of serial development I have traced so far, Dickens's part-published novels were feared for their addictive power and extended duration, both seen as increasing their pernicious influence on readers. It should therefore come as no surprise that comic strips have been condemned for both of these factors, as well as for the efficiency of consumption that implies, for many critics, superficiality. And while cultural critics of other media are beginning to move away from a single-minded focus on purely formal factors as we realize the importance of audience activity in determining the use and value of a text, comic-strip critics have so far steered clear of such studies, no doubt partly because of the difficulties of investigating the vast and amorphous newspaper audience.

In fact, apologists of comic art still occasionally seek to justify the inclusion of their particular brand of mass culture by mobilizing the high-culture strategy of denigrating other, "lesser" mass texts. For example, catherine yronwode (1987) introduces a collection of Caniff's work by explaining: "To those unfamiliar with Caniff's work, it may seem folly to invoke a word like 'literature' in reference to newspaper comic strips. Suffice it to say that one of the things that distinguishes high literature from low soap opera is a concern with the larger issues in society and in life, and Caniff delivers these in spades" (4). As Jane Austen so succinctly put it in reference to another genre's struggle for validation as "high culture": "Alas! If the heroine of one novel be not patronised by the heroine of another, from whom can she expect protection and regard?" I turn, in conclusion, to low soap opera and its concern with the larger issues in society and in life.

3

The Future of the Serial Form

—Today's the big day, huh?
—Oh, every day is a big day here in Pine Valley.[1]
—Skye, All My Children

PUSHING THE DICKENSIAN serial narrative to its logical conclusion, both comic strips and soap operas were created to *vanish*. Each episode gives way to the next, repeatedly renewing an experience that eternally changes and eternally remains the same. But serial fictions are neither consumed nor interpreted in a vacuum. An individual, or group of individuals, filters the familiar tropes of soap opera through a specific set of cultural references or habitus. And the meanings audiences produce as well as the ways they use their texts in turn influence the circumference of the familiar.

The serial languages discussed in this study—Dickens's narrative techniques, comic-strip conventions, televisual tropes—have been shaped and reshaped in response to mass audiences' desires as expressed by sales figures, fan mail, reviews, and other forms of input. Serials receive more direct feedback over a longer time period than any other form of mass-fiction narrative, so their long-term structure encodes the shifting context of their consumption. Thus the daily episodes of comics and of soaps in particular create a new relation to time and text. The sheer volume of textual production virtually negates the possibility of reexperiencing earlier installments. Unless we save each day's strip or videotape or buy one of the histories created and marketed as a solution to exactly this problem of serial ephemerality, there is no way to perform the kind of reality check we often run on novels, glancing back through the text to see what we have missed or forgotten. There is also no way to read early cues differently in light of later developments.[2] Thus readers become reliant on other fans, who may be able to confirm or correct fading memories of past storylines. The occasional rewriting of soap history by writing teams reveals the contradiction within today's serials between contemporaneity (current social issues, fresh writing talent to boost ratings) and longevity (timeless plots, thirty-year show histories and fans who know the show better than writers).

Serials are paradoxically perhaps the most present of any narrative form in that characters are always frozen in the *now*; it is audiences who must think of the future and recall the past in order to interpret the present. A text so ephemeral, and yet so absolutely reliable, creates an unprecedented kind of narrative experience. Each day's reading or viewing becomes the *same* experience: slotted into the same space in the day's schedule, taking place in the same surroundings, involving the same characters. Between one episode and the next, serials imply, the world slips away. Critical castigation of the "eternal same" of serial fiction is thus not difficult to understand, given the fact that few critics are fans. Only a cumulative process of serial involvement enables understanding of the complexities of the text over time and of the concomitant delights of repetition-with-a-difference. Glancing at a single installment of *Terry and the Pirates* or *All My Children*, or even reading a single part of *Our Mutual Friend*, the serial slummer gains almost nothing. The text will appear to contain only a series of unconnected, irrelevant, and melodramatic exchanges between interchangeable characters against meaningless backdrops: narrative in a vacuum. Each serial episode means little in isolation from its long history and contextualizing narrative flow; each modifies the previous installment while simultaneously tilting forward to the next, reaching out of the last frame to grab a hint of the one to come. For this reason, the neophyte TV series fans that Henry Jenkins discusses in *Textual Poachers: Television Fans and Participatory Culture* make a practice of watching old episodes with long-term viewers in order to be introduced to the culture of fandom while simultaneously learning the show's past history and the complex interrelations of characters and storylines. Similarly, most soap fans are initiated by another viewer or group of viewers.

Paradoxically, though, with the short-term impermanence of the serial comes a long-term stability. These stories that appear so briefly every day and are not saved or stacked on shelves (and even Dickens's novels had to appear in volume form before this could happen) nevertheless serve a parallel function to the one I argued as crucial to the sudden rise of nineteenth-century serial fiction and the popularity of newspaper continuity strips: all provide steady, reliable, unchanging communities of both characters and viewers. As French comic theorist Pierre Couperie explains, "the American spends his [or her] entire life in the company of the same heroes, and can establish his own landmarks in relation to theirs. They are connected with his earliest memories; they are his oldest friends; often, through wars, crises, changes of residence and changes of job, and divorces, they are the most stable elements of his existence, to the point, according to Bogart, that adults experience a hostile reaction to new strips, which introduce a change in the immutable circle of familiar faces" (151). This statement implies a psychotic nation, clinging to a network of false faces. Although there is a grain of truth to Couperie's assessment, attentiveness to fans' own accounts of their activity reveals that this reliance on serials has more to do with the *ritual* of (often collaborative) reading or viewing than with a psychotic substitution of comic or soap characters for actual friends. In addition to enjoying the reassurance of the familiar, readers take pleasure in the rhythms of seriality. This process works on several levels. First, there is the daily experience of reading or watching, which usually takes place at the same time and in the same location and can serve, for example, as punctuation or accompaniment to the rhythms of housework or as a transition between home and work or school. Second, discussion of soaps can form an integral part of a daily routine and work to bond discussants who do not know each other (new office mates, sports team members, or college students, for example: thus Allen cites Dorothy Hobson's finding that office workers actually began watching a particular soap so they could discuss it with colleague [Allen 1992, 110]). Third, reliability of character types, plots, and generic themes satisfies by means of the very predictability often cited as proving serial worthlessness.

Of course, since the genre began, the social and economic functions of serials have been transformed in response to shifts in the material context of serial production. To briefly recapitulate that narrative as developed here, nineteenth-century advances in printing and mass production technologies combined with increased literacy rates to change the printed text from luxury to commodity while shifting its audience from elite patron to mass consumer. With the *Pickwick Papers'* unprecedented success in 1836, publishers and writers realized the key to cashing in on the new market for entertainment: simultaneously lowering the cost per unit to permit mass consumption and stimulating an endlessly deferred desire for textual gratification. After completing their run as continuing narratives, Charles Dickens's works were repackaged and marketed as traditional three-volume novels. Transformed both materially and hermeneutically, slender, green-backed, paper parts metamorphosed into sturdy leather-bound books, while open-ended, gradually unfolding tales became finite novels with the conclusion literally in the palm of the reader's hand. Knowing that this transformation would take place, the consumer of a Dickens serial expected eventually to own narrative resolution.

Comic strips served a very different function. The rationale behind issuing novels in successive parts was essentially to create a sort of payment plan for buying a novel, with financial investment both diminished and extended over a longer time period. With Dickens's novels, as with *The Perils of Pauline* and other movie serials, readers expected ultimately to have bought a completed text. This expectation does not apply in the case of comic strips, which, like soap operas, are often produced with no end in sight. For comics readers, the cost of their habit is justified not by eventual text ownership but by the pleasures of comic reading and the need to buy a daily paper. Thus strips are not a commodity in themselves but are used to increase sales of the real commodity, newspapers. The act of buying and reading a paper may be performed out of a sense of civic obligation, guilt, interest, or pleasure, but the choice of which paper to buy is often made by a family rather than an individual and depends not on the quality or slant of its news coverage but on "extra" features: sports, entertainment, comic strips.

Soap operas create a new relationship between audience and text. Their medium, the airwaves, is inherently even more ephemeral than that of comic strips. Although newspapers are throwaway items, newsprint can still be touched, smelled, crackled, even saved in scrapbooks. Until the invention and popular appropriation of the video recorder, soap audiences could not capture their text and were forced to return day after day to renew its pleasure. The narrative was not meant to be owned; each moment, even each character, was brief, passing, and prone to alteration by memory—or new scriptwriters.

Since each day's episode survived only in memory, the first soap operas moved slowly: the weight of tradition, fifteen-minute segments, and sporadic listeners prevented quick-moving plots. Even when soaps moved to television and to half-hour and then hour-long segments, key scenes carried over from day to day, and significant bits of information were repeated several times to ensure that viewers who missed episodes would not fall too far behind and therefore abandon the show. Soap-history revisions such as characters returned from the dead, long-lost sons and daughters, and dramatic changes in character all rely heavily for their existence on the absence of material evidence of past storylines. Although credibility is not the point of these plot moves, the instability of memory and history that *is* the point is enabled, even reinforced, by the impermanence of the text. And as we will see, this shift in the materiality of serial fiction parallels an equally radical shift in its production context.

In the first decade of the twentieth century, music halls gave way to silent films. Producers capitalized on the proven power of continued narratives: the 119 episodes of *Hazards of Helen* left Helen tied to railway tracks week after week, and her devoted fans returned to the theater every Saturday to watch her escape last week's hazard only to land in a new one. "Chapter plays," as these short segments were called (other favorites included *What Happened to Mary, The Active Life of Dolly of the Dailies*, and *The Perils of Pauline*) were the most popular form of early movies.[3]

In 1922, radio producers convinced manufacturers that radio was an ideal advertising medium, which impelled demand for narrative vehicles to "carry" the advertisements. Through the 1920s, radio began developing serials. Daytime listeners were initially considered an "undesirable market," but soap and food manufacturers such as General Foods, A&P, Kellogg, and Procter and Gamble eventually realized that their products, though consumed by a diverse population, were primarily purchased by a particular subsegment—mothers of families, or housewives. Both advertisers and networks perceived their target audience as afflicted with a short attention span and low intelligence and therefore sought daytime programming guaranteed to catch, and hold, the attention of even the most distracted listeners.

The first soap opera (defined in that era as a serial aimed at a female audience and marked by a domestic setting, emphasis on emotional and interpersonal concerns, and continuing narrative) is credited as Irna Phillips's *Painted Dreams* (1931), which followed the activities of a strong, courageous woman, Mrs. Moynihan, and her daughters. Immensely successful, the show inspired a plethora of continued radio dramas, which quickly proved themselves the most powerful advertising vehicles yet developed. Broadcasting regulations did not yet forbid the plugging of particular name brands, and in fact shows were usually sponsored by a single manufacturer. Audiences demonstrating an astonishing loyalty to "their" shows—as soap audiences overwhelmingly did—could be encouraged to transfer that loyalty to a sponsoring product. For example, in 1931 a manufacturer checked the effectiveness of a comedy program, *The Oxol Feature*, by offering a free rag doll in exchange for an Oxol label; the show received seventy thousand responses. By contrast, just three years later Procter and Gamble checked their soap opera "Oxydol's Own Ma Perkins" by offering flower seeds to be sent in return for ten cents and a box top. Not such a great deal, by comparison, but still more than a million listeners responded—perhaps because Ma herself was planting begonias on the show that day (Allen 1984, 106 and 116).

In 1951, *Search for Tomorrow* made the transition to television, and other serials followed its example. In 1960 all remaining radio soaps ended abruptly in mid-narrative (in America, that is; the British pattern of development was very different, and in fact *The Archers* still airs on the radio and has a devoted following). Television's added visual dimension introduced complications, among them the need for a greatly expanded cast since viewers could now identify characters by appearance as well as voice. Larger casts required more involved plots, which in turn demanded lengthened segments, and this development eventually worked to encourage multiple subplots and to complicate plots even further. The initial fifteen-minute episodes were extended to a half hour in 1956 and to a full hour for most soaps by the late seventies.

Then came the VCR. On January 9, 1990, the editor of *Soap Opera Digest* opened the new year with these remarks: "To my mind, the most significant change of the 1980s was the advent of the VCR. This little machine, which is now in half of all American households, changed viewing habits forever. . . . The videocassette recorder forced soaps to be faster-paced and to appeal to a broader audience." Time, shifting. No longer are soap audiences at the mercy of the networks' scheduling decisions. The *TV Guide* becomes a timetable for the week's recording, rather than a dictate for scheduling leisure.[4] Like the remote control, VCRs increase audiences' power over the televisual text. Viewers have the technology to "channel-surf"—catching the wave of one show, skipping to another, jumping over the trough of advertisements—and watch one show while taping another to be viewed later as they skim efficiently through commercial breaks. Advertisers are understandably unhappy about these new technologies, and the shifts in viewing habits they have produced have already effected changes in soap narrative construction and production values. For example, VCR technology has changed demographics since working viewers can catch up on shows in the evening, and the fact that viewers can now record shows means increased pressure to compete for overall viewer hours against prime-time shows and cable as well as other soaps. Therefore soaps try to keep ratings up by incorporating MTV and prime-time conventions into the shows, with apparent success: according to the network, *All My Children* is the most taped show on television. Also, since dedicated viewers can now watch every episode, sharply decrease viewing time by fast-forwarding through commercials and less interesting subplots, and save and rewatch favorite episodes, soaps have had to quicken their pace. They now include faster moving storylines, less repeated dialogue and scenes, high-action mystery and adventure subplots, and location shoots.[5] Really crucial scenes in Friday's cliff-hanger may still be "rewound" or repeated on Monday, and the day's teaser (the first segment of the show) may still repeat a locating phrase from the previous day (or reair especially expensive special effects—producers like to get the most for their money), but overall there is much less explicit repetition in present-day soaps.

In addition to transforming narrative aspects of serial fiction, the translation to a new medium produced essential changes in the economic exigencies of serial production. Unlike both serial novels and comic strips, radio and television segments are free. Once the initial investment in a set has been made, there is no direct cost per episode; profits depend upon advertising revenues. Of course, part-issue novels and periodicals also relied on paid advertising, but in both cases a per-unit cost reinforced the link between the consumer exercising "free choice" and the commodity he or she chose to consume. The airwaves elide this direct economic relationship. The text is no longer the commodity: it is the reader of that text who generates profit when packaged in units of a thousand and sold, or "delivered," to advertisers. Networks, the middlemen in this transaction, seek to acquire as many units of the listener/viewer commodity as possible. A complex network of ratings systems attempts to convince both current and potential advertisers of the effectiveness of their investment in terms of viewers reached and influence obtained. Obviously, networks have an enormous stake in maintaining high ratings day after day, week after week. This compulsion directly inflected soap structure in its extension of the long-standing serial tendency of deferred and problematized closure into a *refusal* of closure. In other words, the narrative structure so often seen as determined by a female audience actually has more to do with the material conditions of the genre's development. Tune in tomorrow, same time, same place—the soap slogan makes visible its economic imperative.

Critics such as Tania Modleski and Robert C. Allen have seen soaps' decentered narratives and refusal of closure as reflecting essential differences between male and female ways of knowing and experience of temporality. For example, Modleski characterizes the generic "placing of ever more complex obstacles between desire and fulfillment, which makes anticipation of an end an end in itself," as related to patterns of female sexuality as well as to female work patterns; and as just discussed, in some ways the early history of soap opera confirms these views. On the other hand, the narrative of serial development in this study shows that in fact the trope of refusal of closure reflects the material conditions of generic development. It was not developed in response to the desires of a particular gendered audience but is an essential quality of the serial form itself, one whose incipient formulation can be seen in nineteenth-century novels like *Our Mutual Friend*. As a partial consequence of the lack of attention to the historical development of the serial genre, its intimate focus, emphasis on interpersonal relations, melodramatic tropes, and deferred closure—among other qualities—have been erroneously labeled "essentially female" by association with the serial's most visible contemporary incarnation, soap opera. Although it is important to explicate the privileging of such elements as teleology, dominant narrative voice, and a single (often male-dominated) literary tradition in literary criticism and history so as to enable more accurate and flexible perceptions of the uses of narrative, it is equally crucial to avoid easy and essentializing relations between gender and narrative form. As Lynn Spigel points out in her review of Modleski's *Loving with a Vengeance* (1985), "Modleski's subject appears to be a historically unchanging and universal category. . . . [which] elides the possibility that female desire undergoes historical variation" (226).

This elision is produced primarily by a gap in Modleski's study, a failure to address the material context of cultural production. As Spigel affirms, this failure undermines Modleski's claims for a relationship between sexual identity and mass-cultural forms. Spigel herself urges the need to repose the questions asked by feminist critics: "I would suggest that we ask how mass culture reacts to (as well as contributes to) the social and historical construction of femininity" (228). Her call is particularly relevant to the history of serial fiction, which has certainly been pushed in new directions by the female creators of soap opera but is by no means an "essentially" female narrative form. Although the demonstrable links between early soap opera and women's rhythms of work, for example, are certainly worthy of notice, it is actually the content and themes of this particular incarnation of serial fiction, rather than its narrative structure, that mark it as a form developed by and for women.

Martha Nochimson has pointed out that radio soap narratives were carefully contained by a male announcer who "intoned a ritual prologue at the beginning of each show, set the scene, and provided omniscient commentary on the events of the story" (53). In a sense, this narrator effectively circumscribed the soap heroine by acting as master of ceremonies to the narrative itself. On the other hand, like the Dickensian narrator, the announcer's apparent authority was subverted by the eruption of the heroine's own voice, as her narrative "persistently undermined the belief that this is a man's world by presenting us with heroes who were neither as effective nor as aware as the heroines" (47). Radio soaps often worked to redefine, in fantasy, (male) value systems based on class, money, and power by decentering these values in favor of empathy, reciprocal relationships, intimacy, and community. This subversion was enabled, in part, by the proliferation on these early shows of men who are, or become, ineffectual for one reason or another. Discussing *Painted Dreams* and other early soaps, James Thurber coined the term "wheelchair syndrome" to denote the alarming predilection of soap men to become crippled, paralyzed, blinded—all symbolic castrations intended to excuse the threatening strength and centrality of soap women. This centrality is not so surprising when we realize that radio soaps were one of the few forms that could truly claim to be women's shows, not just consumed but also created and produced primarily by women.

In the early days of television, women seeking to break into the business could often find jobs only on the soaps, while men were reluctant to work on a form seen even at its inception as trash. The shows therefore quickly became female-dominated by default, reinforcing their reputation as women's shows, satisfying either essential or socially constructed desires of women. James Thurber's term "wheelchair syndrome" speaks not only to the construction of men within early soaps but also to male attitudes toward the shows themselves: they were simultaneously denigrated and feared by critics, seen as actively working to cripple the men who ought to be in control.

Now, forty years later, the women who produced soaps when men would not are in control of an enormously valuable commodity, and one no longer associated with an exclusively female audience. Although the portrayal of soap opera men has become much more complex in the last twenty years as women acquire more real power in the external world, and the form now claims many male fans (30 percent of the audience, according to some Nielsen statistics), soaps remain unique both in positively portraying strong women and in being a form still produced primarily *by* women. Female soap producers have begun to redress gender imbalances by tending to hire and train other women, who then move up through the network and continue the legacy. Agnes Nixon, who created many of the most popular soaps (including *All My Children* and *One Life to Live*), is often dubbed "the mother of Daytime." Despite the condescension implicit in this title, she is an enormously powerful woman who steps in when she sees her shows going off track and generally manages to save them.[6] And women play an active part in soap production all the way down the line. In 1992, for example, the creator, producer, associate producer, head writer, and all but one of the "stable" of outliners and dialoguers who write the actual scripts of *All My Children* were women. One of the show's production assistants described an apparently unique television production experience: being in the editing room when putting an episode together and realizing that all the people involved, from head writer to technical crew, were female.

Given this history, it is not surprising that soap opera is strongly marked by contradiction. As mass entertainment, it is generated by the imperatives of a patriarchal and capitalist entertainment industry; as "women's fiction," it is primarily generated not only for but *by* women, a still marginalized subgroup within that industry. In the last decade, though, daytime drama has become slightly more prestigious and infinitely more profitable. As a consequence, men are increasingly involved in soap production. In contrast to the primarily female production team of ABC's *All My Children*, in 1994 the same network's *One Life to Live* had two male head writers and a stable of six male and three female scriptwriters.[7] This shift toward male representation in both production and consumption raises an important question: is soap opera also shifting in response to the increasing percentages of male viewers, producers, creators, and writers? At the end of this chapter I will discuss the handling of an ongoing rape storyline on *One Life to Live*, asking whether the departure from earlier rape plots indicates the perspective of a male writing team, the producers' acknowledgment of an increasingly male audience, a shifting cultural climate, or simply the normal variations in recycled storylines as writers seek to tell the same story differently.

Audiences and Soap Opera Production

> As twisted and sick as it is, he's going to have to be told the whole story.
>
> —All My Children

In discussing the potential of mass-cultural forms of production, Walter Benjamin emphasizes the need for development of texts responsive to their audience, texts that can work to turn consumers into producers, "that is, readers or spectators into collaborators" (1986, 233). Although he would almost certainly have disagreed, soap opera partially concretizes Benjamin's abstract imperative. In an admittedly negotiated way, his utopian ideal has become virtual reality (to use a loaded but appropriate term). Thoroughly enmeshed in the social and economic network, soaps provide ways of visualizing and acting out social issues in a space apparently free from consequences.[8] They are collaboratively produced and consumed, respond to the desires of audiences, and, finally but not least importantly, allow audiences to play an active role in determining the uses and meanings of their texts.

Television offers unique benefits in its appropriation of the serial genre. Parts are issued regularly: every day for American daytime soaps, twice a day for the Australian show *Neighbours* as it airs in Britain, once a week for nighttime soaps like *Dallas* or *Melrose Place*. Audiences are vast and diverse, and because of their longevity, quotidian recurrence and themes, and—not least—audience familiarity with actors as well as characters as a result of media's obsession with itself, soaps intensify the intermingling of fictional characters with audience lives that is so characteristic of the serial form. As we saw with regard to Dickens, this intermingling has long been a subject of debate by mass-culture critics, many claiming serial audiences as entangled in or duped by the products they consume. Despite the arguments for ethnographies of audiences discussed in the introduction to this study, much American soap scholarship still focuses on an attempt to "discover" that soaps have produced a distorted view of reality in viewers. For example, like many other studies, Rodney Andrew Carveth's "Exploring the Effects of 'Love in the Afternoon': Does Soap Opera Viewing Create Perceptions of a Promiscuous World?" uses a methodology based on Gerbner's "cultivation effect" to determine the extent to which television "functions as social reality for its viewers"; practitioners of cultivation analysis often end by arguing that heavy TV viewing produces distorted worldviews (4). Based on the responses of viewers, however, Carveth himself is forced to conclude that the effects of soap viewing on his college-student subjects' attitudes toward sex and promiscuity are weak or negligible. He further urges the impossibility of simply counting promiscuous incidents on television and then adducing their effects, as many researchers have done, since "there are multiple and conflicting messages about sex in soap operas. . . . [which] supports Butler's (1990) notion of soap opera's *structured polysemy*—that is, there is not one meaning, but multiple meanings available to the soap opera viewer by which they negotiate an understanding of the genre" (15). This acknowledgment effectively returns agency to the viewers themselves, a much needed corrective to traditional cultivation effect studies.

On the other hand, another recent study, "Everyday Sex in Everyday Drama" by Suzanne Frentz and Bonnie Ketter, comes to exactly the opposite conclusion. The authors argue that "the frequent sexual themes on television, and on soap operas in particular, affect viewers in their perceptions of sex. They cause viewers to see sex in an unrealistic light" (45). Unlike Carveth, Frentz and Ketter did not survey audience responses. Instead they provide a variety of "evidence" in support of their conclusion, including the statement that "soaps' constant exploration of sexual themes is of particular concern because of the tendency of their fans to see them as real. Some soap opera fans confuse soap characters with real people, and most soap stars have at least one story of receiving birthday cards for their character, or warnings on his/her behalf" (35). As far as can be told from the essay, the authors have never asked fans whether they truly believe that soap characters are real people, nor do they take into account the research attesting to the double-edged pleasure for fans of seeing popular texts as both real and constructed.[9] Again, and even less responsibly, the authors insist that "if sexual messages are having an effect, and it is hard to argue that they are not, then sexually responsible programming should have some, if not an equal, effect" (33). The sole documentation these authors provide is a counting and coding of twenty episodes of ABC soaps, a method that ignores the cautions provided by Butler and Carveth, among others.

It is depressing that even recent criticism still invokes the same outworn and unsupported assumptions. Carol T. Williams traces "calls for action" attesting to the need for soap audience studies as far back as Horace Newcomb (1974) and Robert C. Allen (1984), and Allen has repeatedly worked to bring exemplary audience studies to our attention (1987, 1989, 1992). The surge of recent ethnographic accounts of fandoms of other popular texts may inspire soap studies along the lines of Seiter, Borchers, Kreutzner, and Warth's "'Don't treat us like we're so stupid and naïve': Towards an ethnography of soap opera viewers," a 1989 study using viewers' accounts of their own interpretative practices to dismantle theories like Modleski's that seem to posit a single spectator position into which the viewer is ineluctably coerced by the text. Seiter et al. find that their viewers "consciously resisted and vehemently rejected" the position of "ideal mother" (237). To explain these resistant readings, the researchers cite their consistent finding that "soap opera texts are the products not of individual and isolated readings but of collective constructions—collaborative readings, as it were, of small social groups such as families, friends, and neighbors, or people sharing an apartment" (233). Similarly, Mary Ellen Brown's *Soap Opera and Women's Talk: The Pleasure of Resistance* studies the discursive practices of actual soap viewing groups. Brown quotes extensively from these groups' discussions to emphasize elements that distinguish soap viewing practices from dominant TV viewing practices. For example, the conventional "suspension of disbelief" that audiences supposedly bring to televisual texts is continually challenged by soap viewers as they factor producers', writers', and actors' decisions and motivations into their understanding of the fictional text (119). In fact, even some researchers in search of data to support the cultivation hypothesis end by being forced to acknowledge the social function of serials. For example, one critic discovered in the course of a survey of young soap viewers that "*the most surprising finding* from these surveys was the large number . . . who indicated watching soaps with friends as reasons for watching soaps" (see figs. 3.1 and 3.2).[10]

Unlike many critics, all networks are forced to acknowledge, at least to some extent, the actual viewing practices of soap audiences as well as their active involvement in the interpretation, uses, and even creation of the shows they watch. In the soap world, all aspects (creation, production, advertising, consumption) interact. To produce a profitable show, networks must increase advertising revenues; increasing revenues requires keeping ratings up; high ratings imply satisfied viewers; and viewer satisfaction demands a compelling show, which means networks must keep close tabs on what viewers consider compelling. And audiences are more than willing to inform networks of their desires. Phenomenal in emotional investment as well as in sheer numbers, soap fans cluster outside the studios from early morning till evening, waiting for the actors to emerge; write letters praising particular performers and storylines, condemning others, and suggesting possible developments or romantic pairings for the future; and threaten to stop watching if their suggestions are ignored. They play an active role in interpreting the narrative and televisual codes that soap producers have developed, and soaps, thoroughly enmeshed in the social and economic network, respond—in some of their manifestations and in limited ways—to the desires of audiences.

Figs. 3.1 & 3.2: College student fans watching *Days of Our Lives*. Matt Dilyard, College of Wooster photo.

The soap genre has recognizable themes and codes, most of which can be traced to the Dickensian techniques outlined earlier. These themes have been inflected, however, by the originally female creators and viewers, so that soap sensibility is qualitatively different from Dickens's or Caniff's. According to Robert Allen, the standard soap themes are family interrelations, romantic triangles, money and its relationship to power, and social issues; I would add a recent focus, in some shows, on adventure or mystery and on self-reflexivity. The narrative codes by which these themes are realized are resistance to closure, producing attenuation of events instead of the temporal compression of most other narrative forms;[11] an episodic structure of six distinct "acts," each separated by commercial breaks and ending on a note of indeterminacy; cutting, within each act, from one to another of three or four scenes involving distinct characters and storylines; and construction of an interior world and of a complex network of character interrelations.

Soaps keep their viewers coming back by skilled appropriation of serial techniques that have existed for centuries. For example, like Dickens they draw heavily on theatrical plotting and in particular on the nineteenth-century "well-made play." However, soaps adopt this structure only insofar as it is useful, given entirely different production and consumption strategies. The Scribean model dictates a fairly rigid five-act progression, from exposition through conclusion: "Each scene has its initial situation, its progression, complication, climax, peripeteia, and conclusion, so that it formed an autonomous whole within the total arrangement. It was, consequently, quite possible to come to the theatre in time for the performance of a favorite scene, and to leave immediately after, having enjoyed a complete, and often sufficient, dramatic experience."[12] Obviously this instant spectator satisfaction would be less than gratifying to soap producers. Theatergoers pay the same admission price whether they stay for the whole play or leave after one scene, but a television viewer who wanders away, sated, from a single scene or episode will not help in the long-term ratings game. Therefore, in soaps no single scene gratifies in and of itself, and the fifth (concluding) act is scrapped in favor of interweaving the first four to maximize narrative draw. Moreover, soaps shift the emphasis from one central plot to a succession of subplots. On the largest temporal and structural level, each show runs three or four storylines simultaneously, making sure each transpires at a different rate. As a general rule, only one storyline will climax in any given week; the rest serve as ancillaries to this temporarily central issue. In October 1991, for example, the climactic story (developed over six months) of *All My Children* involved Natalie Chandler's psychotic twin sister Janet, who—after flinging Natalie into a well months before, impersonating her, and marrying Natalie's fiancé Trevor Dillon—has finally been discovered as an impostor, and therefore takes Trevor's niece Hayley hostage. Almost every episode ends with the psychotic Janet waving a gun in the terrified Hayley's face, threatening her with instant oblivion. Viewers who care about Hayley (or who want to check out the special effects of a shooting, which is a more likely attraction since Hayley was voted "Most Annoying New Character" by viewers) will return the next day to watch, yet again, resolution deferred.

The ancillary storylines include both exposition (Natalie, too terrified of Janet to make her existence known to friends or family, bonding with her rescuer Dimitri Merrick) and complication (Natalie and Dimitri planning to leave for Europe permanently, not knowing that Janet's "passing" has finally been discovered and that she is now waving a gun at Natalie's adored Hayley). Another thread, combining complication with a possible peripeteia, is Erica Kane's sympathy toward Adam (Hayley is his daughter) since her help in attempting to free Hayley implies a possible resolution of their ongoing conflict (Adam forced Erica to marry him—it's a long story). And for those who find the hostage crisis a bit overwrought, there are more upbeat plots such as a new love affair (between Dixie and Craig) and a return to an old and popular passion (between Erica and Jack; as Opal Cortlandt so self-reflexively puts it, this recycled romance is "Jackson/Erica: THE SEQUEL").

All these subplots develop over months, even years, and are carefully juxtaposed and paced to ensure viewers' return. As can be seen from the examples above, soap operas follow the well-made play model on two levels: by continuing a balance of ongoing well-made storylines from episode to episode and by encapsulating, within each episode, an all but complete dramatic experience including exposition, complication, and crisis. The necessity of *crisis* can become forced, of course. After writers ended each episode for over a week with Janet waving her gun more wildly than ever, about to shoot—*really* this time, folks!—Hayley, viewers became restless and complained loudly on computer networks and in letters to producers. Each "act" also works as a drama-in-miniature, intertwining and developing the day's three or four subplots. And finally, individual scenes reinforce structural unity by reiterating the trajectory of the whole: each establishes a situation, provides progression, and ends with an unanswered question, unexpected arrival, sudden ring of the telephone, or some other bit of unfinished business.

Although appropriating aspects of the well-made play, soaps depart from that model in crucial ways. First, they provide not just one but several ongoing storylines, carefully balanced to satisfy very different levels of interest—romance, humor, intrigue, suspense—and to unfold at different rates so that the crisis of one subplot is juxtaposed with the exposition or complication of another. Second, while each storyline and episode contains exposition (a quick recap of the previous episode, for occasional viewers), complication, and crisis, shows almost invariably end just before, or during, the climatic moment, leaving resolution forever postponed.[13] Each "solution," then, impels increased difficulties. Although there *are* small, temporary conclusions in soap opera (Janet seemingly safely locked behind bars, a long separated couple blissfully reunited, a racist thug successfully prosecuted), viewers know above all that consummation of an affair, a marriage, or a plotline will always be disrupted: diegetically by old lovers, new passion, fatal disease, new outbreaks of intolerance; structurally by the successive levels of subplot, commercial, interepisodic, and weekend interruptions.

This formulaic narrative disruption signals an insistence upon the inevitable interposition of obstacles between Self (character/viewer) and Other (love object/text). Significantly, fissures are usually predicated upon language: false information or inaccurate interpretation. Characters who fail at interpretation (by trusting someone who betrays them, for example, or by believing a false witness and therefore failing to trust someone who is loyal) usually experience, and articulate, a temporary paralysis. To reinvoke Natalie Chandler's dismal scenario—flung into a well by her psychotic twin Janet months ago and only rescued at the end of the summer ratings sweep by the mysterious Dimitri—poor Natalie desperately attempts to interpret (false) "evidence" that her true love Trevor has embraced Janet-as-Natalie without noticing the essential difference beneath superficial appearance. Dimitri, eyes fixed on Natalie's while telling her how hurt she must be by Trevor's apparent betrayal, does not help the process of conducting an "objective" reading of events. His words invade her perception of reality until she finally succumbs to the paralysis caused by "discovering" that what she had considered the center of her life was never there at all. "Nothing matters anymore, anyway," she repeats, abandoning her life to Dimitri's control with a passivity unworthy of a true Gothic heroine.

And we the viewers—having been dragged through Trevor's summer-long anguish as well as Natalie's and seeing all sides of the story, an objectivity reinforced by soap televisual techniques, as discussed in the next section—experience firsthand the radical disjunction between appearance and reality, word and world. We had been promised the wedding of the year and the Nick-and-Nora repartee of Natalie and Trevor; now we have relentlessly sincere Dimitri to contend with instead, not to mention a Natalie who has not only become annoyingly passive but whose acting style appears to have been strongly influenced (and not for the better) by the tricks she has acquired to play a psychotic twin as well as her original character.

Soap narrative structure as well as soap character relations, then, vividly embody that vexed relation to the Other which produces the "radical oscillation between contrary emotions" (certainty/doubt, excess/lack, triumph/ despair, love/hate) and positions (subject/object, victim/victimizer, exhibitionist/voyeur) and which characterizes both subjects trapped within Lacan's imaginary order[14] and actors trapped within a melodramatic script. And radical oscillation describes not only the relations of subplots and characters to each other but also those of viewers to their text.

Knowledge and Power: Soap Narrative Strategies

> *Love is glorious, but it's fleeting. Whereas money is forever. Money is power.*
>
> —All My Children

Although romance and sex have generally been perceived as the primary themes of soap opera as well as the motivating factor in audience addiction, the dynamics are actually much more complex. Viewers certainly enjoy attractive actors and steamy scenes, but romance occupies only a third—if that much—of soap narrative, with family, social issues, business, suspense, and crime equally central. But all these threads have a common factor: they remain open-ended. Obvious examples are the Janet crisis discussed above or the long-running rape storyline (begun in the spring of 1993 and ending with the rapist's "death" in 1996) on *One Life To Live*, during the height of which most episodes ended with the rapist/stalker Todd menacing yet another victim. Sometimes the narrative hook is not fear or suspense but desire. A moment beautifully dramatizing "the desire to desire" (to borrow Mary Anne Doane's useful construction in its pure sense) came when the *All My Children* character Nico said to his legal but not actual wife Cecily (the subtext being that sexual tension between the two had been building for months, but though both were attracted, neither would admit it): "If you don't let me go now, I'm going to kiss you. And once I start, I'm never going to stop." Cut to commercial.

But we never get to the point of not stopping, of desire's saturation. In Cecily and Nico's case, the kiss was deferred long after this scene; as a general rule, moments of near consummation cut to months of frustration. The informal contract between producers and consumers of texts—narrative responsibility on the one hand, trust on the other—is an unstable one here, since generic codes actually inscribe radical indeterminacy of interpretation and even of event.[15] It is crucial, however, to stress that soap viewers, far from being "tricked" into expecting a climax that never arrives, profoundly enjoy the extended suspense, which has been refined to an art over two centuries of serialization. As cult filmmaker David Lynch remarked about

Twin Peaks, a show that at least temporarily attested to the power of the serial genre to produce an international media experience, "It's human nature . . . to have a tremendous letdown once you receive the answer to a question, especially one that you've been searching for and waiting for. It's a momentary thrill, but it's followed by a kind of depression. And so I don't know what will happen. But the murder of Laura Palmer is. . . . It's a complicated story."[16] Making explicit the pragmatics behind the disappointing narrative strategy of *Twin Peaks*, Lynch provides a solution to the show's eventual failure. In addition to the soap opera, the show's other strong generic influence was the murder mystery, and "Who killed Laura Palmer?" became the question obsessing not just viewers but virtually all *characters* within the show. Because the focus remained so fixed for the first eight or ten episodes, by the time Lynch and Frost began attempting to diversify their portfolio, the new plotlines seemed gratuitous. Even the soap-within-a-soap, which paralleled the show's master narrative in amusing ways, could not save it. The "complicated story" was not complicated enough; depression could not be dispelled by alternating subplots.

True soap operas, on the other hand, fully aware of the depression following narrative conclusion, diffuse and defuse that disappointment by interweaving multiple *and equally weighted* plot strands right from the beginning. Disjunctive romances like the Natalie/Trevor fiasco or the Janet/Hayley cliff-hanger are balanced, denied, even partially recuperated by simultaneous subplots featuring humor, peace, or reconciliation (Erica and Adam approaching a barb-tongued but compassionate friendship, for example) or by characters whose romantic/infantile merging of Self and Other seems (for a time at least) blissfully undifferentiated (the Dixie/Craig and Erica/Jackson romances).

Soap operas satisfy, then, by essentially disseminating the disappointment—or the death, as Benjamin might argue—structurally inscribed within traditional narrative, which marks its crucial difference from, for example, the nineteenth-century serialized novel. Although all serials work by producing desire for *more* about characters and plots, soaps paradoxically arouse desire that audiences know will never be satisfied, disrupting the parameters of knowledge by making knowledge itself—its possibility or impossibility— a subject of narrative. The ubiquitous "cliff-hanger" endings and secrets combine with the plot devices of amnesia, long-lost relatives, mistaken identity, and so on to expose the shifting and subjective nature of "fact." All attest to the ways in which soap plots are impelled by exploration of the difficulty or impossibility of *knowing*, of keeping "facts" straight despite the shimmering distortions of memory and subjective desire.

Fans have found ways to participate in this generic theorization of knowledge. The proliferation of a kind of parasite industry—soap magazines, radio spots, cable shows, 900 numbers, web sites—has inflected the game of fandom. Fan discourse has in turn produced an increased intertextuality in soaps, especially regarding the economics of actor contracts. Regular viewers realize the direct connection between the plots of their shows and the hiring and firing of actors, and therefore tend to follow fan magazines and other media sources to gather facts about contract disputes and ratings, using this knowledge to inform their reading of the show itself. Producers actively encourage fans in their desire for extratextual knowledge. In fact, for a time ABC produced its own magazine, *Episodes*, devoted exclusively to the network's shows. Thus viewers knew that Todd, the demonized rapist on *One Life to Live,* would be "redeemed" even before narrative cues began to indicate this development: not only did actor Roger Howarth win an Emmy Award for best younger actor in 1994 but soap magazines cited the incredible volume of fanmail he received as well as the even more telling fact that he had just signed a new two-year contract with the show. And intertextuality cuts both ways; even if soap magazines contain no warning, certain plot moves can be read as clear danger signals for the longevity of the actor concerned. For example, *All My Children* ended an (unpopular) engagement between a white man and a black woman, Cliff and Angie, by having Cliff's former wife, Nina, return to Pine Valley after an absence of several years. Viewers who knew from fan magazines or trade gossip that Taylor Miller (the actress playing Nina) only had a one-month contract could infer that Cliff's revived love for her implied a fast exit for Cliff as well as Nina when that month expired. On the other hand, even viewers unaware of Miller's contracted departure were alerted by her sudden return, which clearly signaled doom for Cliff's romance with Angie. Since the Cliff/Nina storyline had been dormant for so long and had always been coded as destined and eternal, its revival signaled something unusual behind the scenes, so fans guessed (though a writer I interviewed denied it) that the *All My Children* team was desperately searching for a quick end to a too controversial interracial romance, hoping that neither Cliff nor the producers would be blamed when he jilted Angie the Other woman for Nina his "long-lost love." Mary Ellen Brown follows Fiske in dubbing this game of informed prediction "vertical intertextuality" (121).

Although viewers do engage with the soap text by means of an economy of information and interpretation—the more we know, the bigger the pleasure payoff—soap structure encourages accumulating knowledge of character relationships, subplot complications, and industry maneuverings not as a set of "keys" that will eventually buy narrative resolution, but as part of an intricate game with no teleological purpose, a game whose interest lies in the accumulation of (unmarketable) information. In view of recent debates as to whether developing information technologies are as democratizing as has been claimed, it is interesting to note that while access to marketable information has remained radically unequal, relying as it does on possession of both economic and cultural capital (to buy a modem, to know how to use it), the mass media encourage obsession with scraps of knowledge about the lifestyles of the rich and famous. Although information technologies are highly profitable, the average American's (often considerable) knowledge of, say, early episodes of *The Addams Family* or the intricate four-generation history of the Martin family of *All My Children* is unlikely to benefit him or her in any material sense—unless he or she happens to get lucky on *Jeopardy*.

On the other hand, soap viewers have appropriated the game of information trading in ways that enhance their own pleasure. For example, exigencies of production may lead to viewers feeling betrayed by sudden shifts in clearly established storylines that effectively deny what the viewer experienced as narrative *fact* in previous episodes. In response, members of an online discussion group, rec.arts.tv.soaps.abc, mock soap writers by collaboratively scripting a lengthy set of "soap rules." Rule S1.023, for example, references the recurrent "evil twin" plot, used to capitalize on a talented actor or to extract the show from the dilemma of having placed a terrific actor in an unredeemable role. In keeping with this rule, many fans of *One Life to Live* are still convinced that Todd the rapist will eventually return to the show as his own "good" twin. The rule reads as follows: "All residents [of soap communities] are required to have one of the following: a) identical sibling, b) identical sibling capable of taking over their lives, or c) person who looks identical to them, although they are not related." Rule S1.025 deals with the opposite syndrome: the recasting of characters, generally unaccompanied by any acknowledgment within the world of the show (though there is always a voice-over announcing, "The role of Joe Blow will now be played by New Guy"). Because fans take a long time to adjust to a new actor playing a character they have become familiar with, any intradiegetic acknowledgment of the change is deeply appreciated but all too rare; even hairstyles are generally ignored. Hence this rule: "Residents are prohibited from mentioning other residents' sudden and unexplained changes in physical characteristics, including, but not limited to, height, weight, eye color, hair color and foot size."[17]

In these rules, and there are hundreds altogether, we see viewers' response to the fact that the informal contract of narrative responsibility on the one hand and trust on the other which exists between producers and consumers of texts is an unstable one in the case of soap operas. Producers' frequent rewriting of soap history and ignoring of soap chronology or real world temporality are necessary consequences of soap creation. In narrative terms, interminable serial reproduction requires that each small, temporary "conclusion" shift, give way to a new instability. In production terms, the sheer volume and longevity of each show, coupled with the imperative of maintaining at least the illusion of newness while preserving favorite characters, introduce an instability of memory, personality, and history which far exceeds that of the multiple sets of doubles and radical character transformations of *Our Mutual Friend*. Experienced viewers understand that the revival of killed-off characters, invention of long-lost parents or children, radical personality changes, and so on all mesh with soap opera imperatives. Uncertainty forms the structural essence of any serial, and in this way soap audience positioning parallels, to some extent, the relation of Caniff's fans to the constant predicaments of Terry and his friends or that of Dickens's readers to his alternating plot strands and interrogation of identity.

Still, the differences are crucial. Most important is the peculiar viewer relation created by televisual narrative. The issue of televisual spectator positioning has recently received some much needed critical attention. E. Ann Kaplan (1987), for example, says of MTV that "the spectator has the illusion of being in control of the 'windows' of television whereas in fact the desire for plenitude that keeps him/her watching is, in this case, forever deferred. The TV is seductive precisely because it speaks to a desire that is insatiable—it promises complete knowledge in some far distant and never-to-be-experienced future. TV's strategy is to keep us endlessly consuming in the hopes of fulfilling our desire" (4). Of all TV narrative forms, soaps are arguably the most skilled at deploying this strategy of seduction. Viewers use the discourse of addiction: they are hooked, have to get a fix, go through withdrawal, are in *All My Children* ecstasy. Clearly soaps work, as Kaplan says MTV does, to arouse some need that can only be satisfied by—more soap. But what exactly is the mechanism by which this desire is aroused, and is it as controlling of the viewer as Kaplan implies?

To complement their narrative strategies, soaps work visually through a distillation of Hollywood conventions pushed to their hermeneutic limit. Like all serials, the development of soap opera is inextricably intertwined with the actual workings of the economy in which it is produced: its setting, characters, format, even subject matter are determined by economic imperatives. For example, soap scenes usually center on a dyad or triad because intimate conversation is infinitely cheaper to tape than group or action scenes and can be set in any one of a number of small, reusable sets that fit easily into the studio. Although clearly economically determined, this interiority enhances daytime's "women-centered" atmosphere since its dyadic structure and familiar setting necessitate a primarily emotional and interactive, rather than action-oriented, narrative. Paralleling women's entry into the work force and their consequent escape from the confines of the home, increasing soap profits led to larger production budgets, which in turn enabled soaps' escape from the ubiquitous kitchen, living room, and hospital waiting room sets to explore the narrative possibilities of restaurants, hotels, health clubs, nightclubs, and outdoor sets. Still, the sets are not hermeneutically crucial in themselves, as they are in cinema. Soaps focus on what characters say to one another, not where they say it.

Since they are taped in cramped studios with limited budgets and extremely limited production time, soaps must *mean* as economically as possible, restricting visuals to one or two camera positions and one small set per scene. Camerawork is highly coded, delivering well-established cues to viewers trained to read them. As Bernard Timberg argues in "The Rhetoric of the Camera in Television Soap Opera," "Like the visibility of the purloined letter in Poe's short story, the very obviousness of the cinematic codes of soap opera keeps people from thinking about them and thus makes them more effective in doing their job: to shape and direct the audience's point of view" (166). Soaps rely almost exclusively on a long shot to set the scene, tracking in to alternate between the standard two-shot and a modified shot-reverse shot and ending each scene with a close-up to catch every nuance of character reaction to the usual cliff-hanger. An intensification of classic cinema's reaction shot, this close-up becomes temporally extended to a sometimes disconcerting extent at the end of each "act," or group of three or four scenes between commercial breaks. This much mocked soap "freeze" is actually highly functional in creating soap meaning. Like the cinematic close-up, it invites viewers to attend to an actor's reaction, to imagine his or her thoughts. As Timberg expresses it, the camera's slow truck-ins and "elegiac movement" toward a character's face have "the effect of bringing the viewer closer and closer to the hidden emotional secrets soap opera explores: stylized expressions of pity, jealousy, rage, self-doubt" (166). We are so close, this shot tells us, that we *must* be almost inside the character's mind and therefore must know what is happening there.

However, while actors do occasionally manifest the emotions Timberg describes (as in fig. 3.3, a closeup ending a highly charged scene between rapist Todd and rape survivor Marty), in most cases they are actually trained to keep the expression intense but neutral: projecting strong, concentrated, *impenetrable* emotion (see fig. 3.6).[18] What fascinates about the soap version of reaction shots is their strategic purpose. Since it is so difficult to read—and thus impossible to predict—exactly what a character will do or say next, the freeze's intense neutrality fosters doubt and suspense, which in turn ensures that viewers stay tuned through the commercial break. So the shot has

Fig. 3.3: The closeup: Todd (Roger Howarth), with Marty (Susan Haskell) in the background. © 1996 Ann Limongello/ABC, Inc.

a dual and seemingly contradictory purpose, functioning both to pull us into empathy by zooming, as Timberg elegantly describes it, almost into the actor's thoughts and to push us into objectivity by making strange the contours of a face so minutely scanned, forcing the realization that in fact we cannot possibly enter this Other's thoughts.

This paradoxical function signals a larger ambivalence reverberating across soap televisuals and echoing within soap narrative, as we will see shortly. On one level, soap techniques work to create intimacy with the characters. The camera literally pulls us into each scene, positions us at eye level with the actors, situates us inside living rooms, kitchens, and bedrooms, enables us to share with certain characters knowledge unavailable to others. We hear the most intimate details of characters' lives, individuals who have become familiar over years or even decades, to the extent that viewer letters claim to have known them longer than many friends or even family members.

On another level, this familiarity is paired with estrangement. Though pulling us into the action, soap televisual techniques have the peculiar effect not of establishing viewer identification with one character (as cinematic point-of-view shots do) or of effectively inserting the viewer into the scene as *voyeur*, but of maintaining a certain distance between viewer and text. We remain a little outside every scene, quite literally: the shot/countershot or glance/object editing that works in Hollywood cinema to suture viewers into one point of view is practically unavailable to the soap director, since it requires too many camera positions and too many takes. Most soaps are shot from the fourth wall of a long row of three-sided sets packed into an urban studio. Like a theater audience, then, we remain cut off from the action and cannot be sutured into it by the ability to see exactly what any one character would see. Glance/object editing is rare because it is technically difficult and expensive. Even the standard shot/reverse shots used to establish conversation between two people have to be carefully angled, their width kept well under the cinematic 180 percent. This method leaves a large gap of absent space in which we as viewers are positioned, but crucially we are rarely assigned a specific, voyeuristic perspective.

And soap narrative follows the restrictions imposed by production exigencies; thus we see all sides of every story. In the summer of 1993, for example, the ratings-sweep storyline of *One Life to Live* was the gang rape trial of three fraternity brothers: Todd Manning, Zachary Rosen, and Powell Lord III. All characters involved in the trial know part of the story: Marty Saybrooke knows she was raped and by whom, the perpetrators know they are guilty as well as where they hid the evidence, the Llanview community knows these are "fine boys" from good families whereas Marty is a notorious liar and "bad girl." However, we—represented by the camera—see all these sides and more. For example, we watch the increasingly guilt-ridden Powell try to convince his "brothers" to admit what they have done, and later see him telephone his attorney Nora Gannon to confess and then hang up the phone; we cut to Nora, puzzled, staring at the silent receiver. So far, so *The Accused*; but the difference is that many of these are characters we ourselves have "known" for years. We are familiar with the histories and interrelations of all participants in the rape and in the trial, and the multiple points of view thus encourage us to weigh motivations and personal agendas as well as facts, arriving at a more complex interpretation of the case than would be possible without this sense of history and perspective. While each character involved understands only a small part of the total whirlpool of events, "we," represented by the camera, see all—and what is more, we *know* that we alone are privileged. Like the freeze that ends most "acts," these technically dictated techniques create an interesting interpretive confusion. We are privileged to see and hear the most private moments, a voyeurism even more intimate because more familial/familiar than that of cinema. At the same time, we see more than any character and are thus distanced from them. Soap camera work parallels the form's multiple and intertwined narratives in that both enable the viewer alone to understand all sides of the story. Thus while Marty was seeking evidence to support her claim of rape, many episodes ended with a tight shot of the sweatband used to gag her and now hidden in the woods behind the frat house; this clue was "seen" and fetishized by the camera but remained unseen by any of the characters.

Soap directors occasionally depart from these conventions, and when they do it is worthy of notice. For example, while most of the rape storyline is shot using traditional soap camera work, scenes of the rape itself depart in significant ways from the conventional. First, our spectator positioning changes. As we have seen, soap point of view virtually never positions us with any one character; instead, we see all action from the fourth wall of a three-sided set. During the rape, however, the director made the highly unusual decision to position us with Marty. We saw, through a hand-held camera's jumpy eye, the rapists approaching, weaving in and out of focus, and pinning us/her down. Next we saw each rapist's face distorted through a fishbowl lens, looking down into the camera and victimizing us, the hapless spectators, just as each victimized Marty (see figs. 3.4 and 3.5). Clearly, and for obvious reasons, these visuals refuse the distance that generally works to encourage empathy with all points of view. After the rape, however, the camera's view of Marty reverted back to the objective in order to carry out one of soaps' most valuable functions: forcing public attention to and debate about difficult but important social issues while educating viewers about these issues. Marty's post-rape visit to the hospital was carefully chronicled, using traditional camerawork so as not to distract from the information presented. Her choices were clearly explained and each stage of the physical examination, collection of evidence, and police report was carefully followed.

In this context, it is important to emphasize the very different feel of televisual, as opposed to cinematic, spectatorship. First, the camera positioning, production values, scene construction, even acting style are much "smaller" and more intimate in television. Second, the viewing context is very different. Dominated by the vast screen above, surrounded by darkness and strange bodies, the cinemagoer's viewing experience is both spectacular and specular. Glancing at a small screen, surrounded by familiar objects and people, the television watcher's viewing experience is both intimate and distracted. She or he virtually exchanges glances with the smaller than life-sized actors, placed at eye level, watching them within the private space of the home rather than in a public theater. If others are present, they may or may not be watching (but in either case will probably be talking over, wandering in front of, and otherwise distracting attention from) the television, a small, familiar piece of household furniture. Perhaps most important, the viewer has power over the images. As Ann Kaplan pointed out in the passage quoted above (155), this feeling of control over the "windows" of television is to

Figs. 3.4 & 3.5: Distorted camerawork: a rape scene. © 1996 Ann Limongello/ABC, Inc.

some degree illusory. Nevertheless, viewers can certainly choose, at any time, to "channel-surf," mute, or turn off the set.

John Ellis, in his *Visible Fictions*, discusses the distinction between cinema and television. Citing differences in both visual qualities and viewing contexts, Ellis points out that television "engages the look and the glance rather than the gaze, and thus has a different relation to voyeurism from the cinema's" (128). In the close-up, for example, cinema iconicizes vast, god-like actors; by contrast, television close-ups explore a face scaled to approximately normal size and located close to the viewers' own eye level, producing equality—even intimacy—as opposed to the "distance and unattainability" imposed by the size and positioning of the cinema screen (130–31). The cost of this intimacy is that "the voyeuristic mode cannot operate as intensely as in cinema," the advantage that the physical presence of the television set pushes us into awareness of the activity of watching, thus defusing the rapt voyeurism that films can produce (137–38). TV watching is a conscious activity, a fact enforced by commercial breaks as well as by the freedom most viewers feel to talk during or comment on shows, a practice that is firmly hushed in movie theaters. Modleski has related the subject position of the television viewer to that of the "(ideal) mother" (1982, 101 and passim), but a closer analogy might be Jane Feuer's "fully socialized family member."[19] Thus soap opera is well-suited to storylines encouraging cooperation, understanding, empathy, forgiveness. These are all qualities necessary for the interrelationships typically thought of as constituting the family. They are also qualities that could, if coupled with real social, economic, and legal change, work toward overcoming the gaps in understanding which help to produce racism, homophobia, and other forms of discrimination.

In July 1992, ABC's *One Life to Live* tackled an exploration of homosexuality and AIDS. Having spent weeks building the teen storyline most soaps develop over school holidays to attract students, the show plunged viewers into the problems faced by one of the most popular characters, sixteen-year-old Billy, as he "comes out" to his closest friends, to a local minister, Andrew Carpenter, and indirectly to us. As usual, we have been prepared for increased objectivity by following all sides of the story as they develop: Billy's vexed relation to his snobbish and dictatorial parents; their terror of homosexuality and well-meant though misguided overprotection of their only child; Billy's friends' reactions, both positive and negative, public and private. We simultaneously track troublemaker Marty, following her to various covert vantage points as she spies on Andrew and plots against him; the camera then pulls back to allow us to catch *her* reaction. And finally, we watch Andrew as he prepares and delivers a funeral service for a parishioner who died of AIDS. He urges the importance of AIDS education in schools, lashes into the upper classes who ignore the epidemic because of class- and race-based imaginary immunity, announces the fact that his own brother died of complications resulting from the disease, and publicly pins the red badge of HIV awareness onto his surplice. These independent subplots begin to converge when Billy's parents, already falsely "warned" that Andrew is gay by jealous Marty, spot the minister (who has been counseling Billy) holding the boy's shoulders and looking into his eyes and—

At this point in the narrative, a witch-hunt seemed imminent, but all was ultimately resolved when the NAMES project memorial quilt came to Llanview, its names intoned in a reconciliatory ritual that united previously antagonistic characters. Although using the quilt, sacred to so many people, to resolve a soap storyline might seem cynical, it also gave millions of viewers the chance to experience, albeit vicariously, the power of the quilt as a symbol and source of communal mourning. When Andrew and others added a square they had made for Andrew's brother William, their act drove home the fact that each square is a narrative in itself, an iconic representation of an individual life.

Citing the dynamics of television watching—its familial give-and-take, the distraction inherent in the activity, and the "flow" of televisual life—Ellis and Feuer underline the crucial role viewers play in creating the meaning of a television text. As with the rape storyline discussed earlier, in following the Billy Douglas saga viewers can choose to respond on any one of a number of levels, including fury at the violence of homophobia (which positions us with Billy himself as well as with Andrew Carpenter, Viki Buchanan, and a number of other characters who are both open-minded and safely "straight"), disgust at the idea of homosexuality (which positions us with Andrew's father, Sloan Carpenter, Billy's father, and Viki's husband, Clint Buchanan), or simply desire to find out *what happens next*. Perhaps most important, most viewers discuss their reactions to this controversial plot with others, thus allowing a more open exchange of ideas than might be possible if discussing actual people rather than television characters. Like Andrew's and Billy's fathers, we may learn to overcome prejudice through emotional involvement with characters we have grown to "know" and respect. In response to this storyline, the Usenet group r.a.t.s., which is devoted to discussion of television soap operas, became very active. Participants heatedly debated homosexuality, AIDS, and related topics and exchanged their own narratives of "coming out" or of involvement with HIV or the NAMES project quilt.

As a women's narrative form, soap opera initially restructured gender relations by focusing on women's emotions and relationships and figuring men as peripheral in many ways to the bonds between women. In its present incarnation on television, some of the most interesting soap storylines remain female-centered in a stereotypical but perhaps still useful sense in that they seek to produce empathy and even identification with characters. The real force of storylines like that of Billy fighting for acceptance, Marty surviving the aftereffects of rape, or the black *All My Children* character Terrence struggling to understand racism after his house is bombed by a white supremacist group comes as we experience such characters' anguished lack of control, rejection of even long-standing (straight, male, or white) friends who prove unable to understand that anguish, and (of course) the community's eventual ability to at least partially heal itself through increased tolerance and understanding. Despite the often facile resolutions of these stories, their sheer duration, our long-standing history with the characters involved, and above all the collaborative viewing practices favored by soap fans mean that these stories can have enormous impact in impelling open debate about underlying issues. And this impact is heightened by televisual dynamics. Because the physical qualities of the TV set itself unplug us from voyeurism, soaps' value as catalysts for discussion is increased. It is not surprising, therefore, that audiences find their greatest pleasure in the collaborative viewing practices they engage in and the degree of power they are increasingly able to wield over "their stories."

Audiences and Power

> *I want to thank, most of all, the fans—because without you none of this would be happening. And we all know that.*
> —*actor David Canary, accepting* Soap Digest's
> Outstanding Lead Actor award.[20]

In this section, I draw on two bodies of evidence—letters from soap fans to the ABC network and the vast resources of a Usenet computer network discussion group, r.a.t.s. (rec.arts.tv.soaps, now known as rec.arts.tv.soaps.abc since the traffic became so overwhelming that the group voted to split the discussion by network)—to undermine some of the most common misperceptions of the soap watching experience. Fans have long been considered passive victims, entangled in an ideologically sticky web of narrative and televisual brainwashing. It is certainly possible to interpret the bags of fan mail and the birthday and wedding presents that all soaps receive as evidence that the narrative cycle of desire and loss discussed above is not restricted to the diegetic world of the soap characters but moves outward to entangle the audience—that fans are, in other words, trapped in a plot structure they had no voice in determining. But while it is easy to understand how outside observers, stunned by the pleasure and passion involved in fan activity, could misinterpret it, analysis of the contents of the bags of letters sent in to every soap and conversations with soap fans suggest a very different reading. As Mary Ellen Brown puts it in her ethnography of soap audiences, "It is clear with these groups of fans that talking about soaps [*sic*] characters as if they were real is actually a manner of speculation about soaps and is also a kind of shorthand sparing one the trouble of mentioning actor as well as character" (121).

Oprah Winfrey, in a show devoted to untangling soaps' mystique (May 1991), uncharacteristically echoed the popular misconception that soap viewers become unable to distinguish between soap excess and real life when she solemnly informed her panel of "soap addicts" and her audience that "It's all really kind of acting. Don't—everybody realizes that, right—that it's all really acting? But that's still okay?" One of her "addict" panelists, a woman named Vicky, responded, "That's wonderful. That's what makes it so much fun." Oprah replied, "Uh-huh. That it's—that—'Cause you know it's—Do you find yourself worrying about their problems sometimes, Vicky?" And Vicky patiently answered, "Beyond our conversations with the days' soap opera, my daughters and I—we're trying to figure out things, but I don't worry about them, no." This exchange underlines one of the most important and least understood aspects of soap pleasure: texts become an ongoing narrative game in which viewers puzzle out clues and meanings. Pretending to take soap events as real is part of "what makes it so much fun."

Vicky's comments also imply a crucial function of serials. Like serialized novels and comic strips, soaps provide communities both extradiegetically in bonds formed with other viewers and diegetically in extended familiarity with characters. Almost every long-term viewer I have spoken with stresses one or both of these aspects as an integral part of soap pleasure. The historical timing of soaps' incredible popularity, which exploded in the postwar years as America became increasingly mobile and extended families increasingly fragmented, confirms the importance of the stable "family" provided by soap communities. Soaps function to open lines of communication between viewers. For example, daily discussions about the soap community clearly strengthen Vicky's relationship with her daughters; how much more crucial, then, for workmates or neighbors who may have no other common interests. Early soaps provided a shared community and a neutral field of discussion for women isolated in their respective homes and nuclear families. Contemporary shows serve a similar function for homeowners as well as college students, office workers, and NBA and NFL teams. Given soaps' explicit commitment to "socially relevant" storylines—AIDS and HIV, racism, homelessness, addiction, rape survival, gang membership, the importance of voting, and instructions for registration have all been covered in recent ABC soaps—a daily show discussed by so many disparate people can have a powerful impact on society. Soaps act out conflict in a space apparently free from consequences, thereby offering low-threat opportunities for debating politically charged issues.

Although much work remains to be done, recent ethnographic exploration suggests that what might be called a vulgar Frankfurt vision of mass audiences as cultural dupes (a vision that Winfrey, for example, echoes in fearing that soap audiences are unable to separate reality and fiction) is much too simple: fan engagement with texts suggests a much more active engagement with the processes of fiction making. Networks acknowledge audience involvement in the interpretation, uses, and even creation of "their" shows, and facilitate this by holding "forums" in which they invite panels of fans to view an upcoming episode and discuss their reactions to characters and storylines while producers and writers note responses, which are then brought into weekly planning sessions. Each show also has a fan mail department where letters are analyzed quantitatively and qualitatively. Producers and writers study a monthly report detailing the number of letters each actor received, the number of letters the show received, an abstract of particular suggestions regarding each storyline and couple, and a synopsis of attitudes toward the show. If strong reaction occurs in favor of or in opposition to a storyline, couple, or character, writers may alter planned scripts accordingly. For example, viewers expressed their anger that Powell Lord was essentially excused for his part in the rape because he had "simply" succumbed to peer pressure. Their responses may well have led to revised treatment of the character and ultimately to his departure from the show. Similarly, when actor Billy Husfey left *One Life to Live* because of contract disputes, ABC received forty-five thousand letters requesting his return and quickly rehired him, an affirmation of viewer power soon splashed across soap magazine headlines.

The following paraphrases of *All My Children* fan letters attest to the confidence of these viewers that their voices will be heard.[21] Letters discuss characters as distinct from actors, revealing their considerable knowledge of offscreen relations between actors and how these may affect onscreen chemistry. Not incidentally, such letters also prove that fans do not in fact confuse character and actor. Letters harangue the show's producers, suggesting that they get the wheels rolling and give devoted and very disappointed fans what they want. In reference to the recently split soap couple Travis and Erica, for example, a writer asks producers how, after watching these two on the monitors (this fan is clearly aware of the monitor installed in executive offices, allowing Big Brother to spy on rehearsals) and observing their "chemistry," they can persist in splitting the couple.

Fans also complain about the predictability of certain characters, as in a two-page letter concerning Palmer Cortlandt (who has a fascinating predilection for keeping young female relatives all to himself) pointing out that soap writers first gave him Nina to torment, then Julie, now Melanie, and viewers are getting bored. This letter writer goes on to imagine the plotting possibilities of Palmer's death and to reassure producers that if they want the actor to stay on the show, they can always (since they do not seem to mind being predictable) bring him back to life or give him a twin. These suggestions show strong awareness of the menu of narrative tropes soap writers have at their disposal and also imply that viewers take pleasure in their knowledge of these patterns of repetition.

Another letter asks *All My Children* writers to please ax the couple Melanie and David, who, the writer says, give the word "boring" a meaning all its own. This writer adds that the Jeremy-Marissa storyline is an equally weak link, asserts that this fact is not surprising since Jeremy's storylines always are, and asks in closing that Jeremy's story receive less airtime since fans are already suffering enough with Melanie and David. (This wish eventually came true; Jeremy was moved to another soap, *Loving.* For the first few months of the transition, writers on both soaps collaborated so that he traveled back and forth between Pine Valley and neighboring Corinth, site of *Loving,* in the vain hope that the intertextuality would attract *All My Children* viewers to its dying fellow soap.)

There is also, of course, praise for the show from fans who want to let producers know what they particularly enjoy. Interestingly, most of these letter writers see themselves as spokespeople for a viewing community, and phrases like "my friends and I," "the majority of viewers I know," "I and all my friends who watch" are common. For example, one letter praises the Cliff/Angie interracial storyline, which exposes the problems interracial couples face as well as the racism of the 1990s. She cites the approbation of other black viewers in Atlanta, saying that they have discussed the storyline and feel it to be realistic.

Almost all those viewers who bother writing to the show (admittedly a small percentage of the total audience, though the minimum number of letters received, twelve hundred per month, is not inconsiderable) are both articulate and sophisticated, demonstrating awareness of the role of production factors in determining storylines. They have a strong stake in articulating opinions about "their" show; many apparently expect to have a voice in its creation. The only correspondence that did not demonstrate some degree of awareness of the production process and the economic factors underlying soap fictions was brief notes requesting autographed pictures.[22] Letters often close with thanks for the interest they feel the show takes in their opinions, an expression of confidence that soap fans' voices are heard and heeded.

A more collaborative forum for soap discussion is the Internet. The Usenet discussion group r.a.t.s., for example, is a powerful testimonial to the alternative uses to which mass culture can be put. A loosely linked collection of "net friends" and "lurkers" who collaborate to increase their enjoyment of soap watching, group members volunteer to write daily updates of the show's events so that others who missed the show can find out what happened. These updates go far beyond a simple blow-by-blow recounting of the episode to include clear awareness of the narrative structure of soap opera, as well as ironic commentary on the text, past history to clarify plot twists, and other insider knowledge. Group members also organize themselves into subgroups devoted to discussing particularly ludicrous storylines. For example, reproduced below is a post from an *All My Children* viewer and member of 'SPERM,' a "Society for the Prevention of Enmity toward Repentant Mothers." Members of this listserv subgroup take note of soap writers' tendency to punish mothers by killing off their children, or, conversely, to overuse the plotline (in use since the nineteenth-century serial novel, and perhaps most closely associated with the 1950s maternal melodrama) of the "bad" mother who refuses to sacrifice herself for her children.

A brief recap of the story giving rise to this post will be useful. Dr. Maria Santos Gray, long infertile, has finally conceived, much to her joy and that of her husband, Edmund Gray. Unfortunately, in a moment of desperation produced by events much too complicated to go into here, Maria spent one night with her husband's half-brother, Dimitri Merrick, so she cannot be sure the baby is Edmund's. To make matters worse, Dimitri suddenly learns (though this has never been part of the show's history) that he is a carrier of the rare blood disorder thalassemia, that an infant sister died of the disease, and that any fetus that might be his needs to be tested to ensure its safety. For reasons that viewers cannot fathom, *All My Children* writers decided to throw yet another kink into the works by having Erica Kane, Dimitri's wife, announce that she too is pregnant. One post on this storyline reads:

Subject: AMC: The SPERM Count: A Tale of Too Twitties
Date: Tue, 14 Jan 1997 09:21:19 -0600
Well, Tante's in Texas, running a background check on a certain frequent applicant for SPERM protection, so here I sit with the extremely unpleasant task of examining recent instances of mothering in Pine Valley.
Yes, it's "no room at the womb" season on the Main Line, and everyone who's anyone is gearing up for a blessed event. But blessed for who? Little

Hectoria, who by now has picked up more bad amniotic vibes than most fully formed humans could stand? Poor wee Mona Marrick, who will probably never even hear mention of his half-sister Kendall (with any luck, though, Mona will be spared undue exposure to his father's halting speech patterns)?

"Blessed," it seems, is an extremely relative term. From where I'm sitting, neither of these tots-in-progress stands much of a chance, and we can trace it all back to the mama of all Big Mamas, Francesca James.

Yes, easy as it would be to blame Maria, Dimitri, Skye, Binky, Alf, Hugo, Flora, or any number of other usual suspects, I fear the sorry state of these sad fetuses must be pinned on the harebrained EP who green-lighted this little round of "Rare blood disorder! Rare blood disorder! Who's got the rare blood disorder!" (The answer to that question, BTW, all laws of genetics aside, would seem to be "No one.")

So, basically, just for *fun*, we get to watch two women spend an inordinate amount of time gnashing their teeth needlessly over the well-being of their little ones. More than likely, we'll also get to watch them go through the whole experience without the support or comfort of their much-beloved significant others, just to give the whole scenario a little tweak. I never thought I'd live to see the day where anyone would actually *root* for a miscarriage, but I apparently underestimated Ms. James and her crack team of lunatics.

I have visions of the story meetings that served as the primal ooze from which this tale sprang.

Writer #1: "I just don't think Maria thinking she's pregnant by Dimitri is depressing or improbable enough, do you?"

Writer #2: "Definitely not. Plus, we've got this 'bad sperm' thing going with Dimitri and it's not even *his sperm*. What sense does that make?"

Writer #3: "We really should use the bad sperm, I mean, if we have it."

Writer #2: "That's all I'm saying."

Writer #1: "Well, Dimitri could get someone else pregnant . . . but who?"

Writer #3: "What about Erica?"

Writer #4: "Didn't she have some bad baby thing? Toxi-whatdo-youcallit?"

Writer #2: "Please, that was years ago. Nobody will remember that. They'll be too worried about the sperm."

Writer #4: "I don't know."

Writer #1: "Besides, we're not worried about *old* viewers. We want *new* viewers."

Writer #2: "Yeah, and I think bad sperm is *just* the way to get them hooked, I mean just the *sound* of it! 'Bad sperrrrrrm!'"

Writer #3: "Ooooh, I've got chills!"

Writer #4: "Should we run this past Francesca?"

Writer #1: "No, she's really busy interviewing models for the role of 'Tank.'"

Writer #2: "Y'know, I haven't seen any story on him, but I just *know* he's going to be a great character. Have you *seen* the guys casting sent over? Yowza!"

End of Scenario.

But I fear I've abused the power and privilege of SPERM Counting just a bit too much for the moment. I'm going to go huddle in a corner under my new "A Match/Not A Match" quilt and wait for this horror to come to an end.

Courage, one and all . . .[23]

This post is worth examining in some detail, since it responds to this storyline by engaging in a number of activities typical of soap viewers. For example, like many viewers, this one uses humor as a way of preserving viewer pleasure in unrealistic, degrading, or just plain uninteresting storylines. His closing comment, that he will "go huddle in a corner under my new 'A Match/Not A Match' quilt," refers to one of this storyline's most ludicrous moments, when the paternity test results appeared on a computer terminal as nothing more than a flashing "Not A Match" and were quickly and easily changed by a jealous troublemaker to read "A Match." Despite the bizarre phrasing of this, the anxious expectant parents accepted the printout without a second thought—although one would imagine that Maria, as a doctor, might question the printout's laconic wording.

This viewer creates a mock-dialogue between the soap writers which not only echoes David Mamet in its ability to capture the rhythms and repetitions of conversation, but also exposes a number of complaints made by list members in the months before this post. First, many viewers feel that writers reveal their disdain for viewers and for their craft by completely ignoring medical fact, as in this storyline on thalassemia (the "bad sperm"). The facts of the disorder's transmission were initially glossed over by the show's writers, but eventually they did present the facts more accurately, perhaps in response to protests by numerous astute viewers. Second, viewers complain that writers have far less knowledge than viewers of the long-term history of the show and don't seem to care enough to research that history ("Didn't she have some bad baby thing? Toxi-whatdoyoucallit?" "Please, that was years ago. Nobody will remember that."). Third, toward the end of 1996 viewers began to protest the casting of a number of male models with little discernible acting ability. The "Francesca" who is too busy interviewing models to approve or revise the "bad sperm" storyline in this viewer's post is Francesca James, executive producer of *All My Children;* note that she makes three appearances in this post, a clear signal that viewers know who is ultimately responsible for their disappointment in the quality of their show.

Other types of net activity include "spoilers" from those who have read a soap magazine and picked up rumors about future storylines or about contract disputes that may affect storylines; in-depth discussions of particular characters, storylines, or social issues; jubilant enumeration of writers' lapses in continuity, plausibility, or awareness of show history; and "TANs," or tangents leading out from discussion of the show itself. In the past few months these TANs have included exchanges about viewers' weddings, births, relationships, upcoming operations, and other personal issues as well as debates on issues raised by the show (including racism, homosexuality, the reaction of rape victims to the rape storyline on *One Life to Live,* and the pros and cons of chest hair on men). Debates on controversial storylines often spill over into exchanges of personal opinion and information from which group members say they learn a good deal.

The existence of this group clearly supports the argument that serial fictions encourage collaborative readings of texts. In addition, the net enforces my contention that serial fictions, unlike many mass texts, actually do respond more or less directly to audience feedback. Soap producers publicly insist with increasing vehemence that they respond to audiences, but soap writers and others behind the scenes make less enthusiastic claims. Therefore evidence linking audience opinion to changes in casting or storylines can help to clarify the picture. For example, r.a.t.s. members organized a letter writing campaign to protest the show's rapid repression of the fact that the "redeemed" Powell Lord was just as much a rapist as his two frat brothers, a campaign that was followed by a storyline reproblematizing Powell's role in the rape by focusing on his repression of guilt and the violent consequences of that repression. Some net members are also convinced that soap writers "lurk," perhaps gathering ideas for future plots and characters and definitely exploring viewer opinion of new characters, couples, plotlines, glaring continuity or soap history mistakes, and so on. Again, there is some evidence to support this contention. For example, the actress playing Natalie Dillon (she of summer-in-a-well fame) was replaced in the spring of 1993 by a new actress. The net loathed the replacement from the start, which is not uncommon, but the group never did warm up to her, referring to her even months after her debut as "NewNotNat" and "Tweety" (sadly, she resembled the cartoon canary). After only a few months and no formal letter writing campaign, NewNotNat fell victim to a fatal car crash and has not been heard from since. Initially skeptical of writers' lurking, many new network members write in after a few months, proclaiming themselves convinced. Besides the countless times that r.a.t.s. nicknames or in-jokes have suddenly appeared in the mouths of show characters, more sustained network discussions will find echoes on the show.[24]

After discovering r.a.t.s., I became increasingly interested in the group's discussions and wanted members' ideas on two questions: whether viewers find it important to watch or discuss shows with others, and whether they think audiences have any control over storylines. Therefore I posted these questions and asked for responses. Clearly this approach did not produce anything like a random sample. In fact, its biases closely resemble those of the magazine advertisement that Ien Ang used to gather the responses given as the basis for *Watching Dallas*, her study of the pleasures and purposes of the infamous nighttime soap opera. In both cases, besides the obvious slanting of a self-selected sample of respondents, there are problems of quantity and of the particular population from which respondents were hailed: in Ang's sample, a women's magazine; in my sample, a computer discussion group.[25] However, like Ang I am much less interested in quantitative measurement of soap audiences at this stage of audience research and much more compelled by viewers' subjective accounts of their viewing practices and pleasures. In addition, I had a kind of "control group" in that I could compare the responses I received with the overall discourse of the network discussion group as well as with the accumulated testimony of the many soap fans that I and other researchers have interviewed. Based on this comparison, their statements are representative. Here are some of their voices.

In response to the query about the importance of group discussion of shows, respondents agreed that interpretative communities are "VERY IMPORTANT!" (respondent's emphasis). One woman writes: "I never realized how important it was to have other people to talk about the soaps until I found r.a.t.s. I found a friend (or two) and we talk about other things, but when the soaps are on (we both do it real-time), we talk back and forth about the happenings on screen. I didn't used to talk to the TV, but I do that more now . . . even for non-soaps." So net activity has made this respondent a more active viewer in general, in a process extending beyond the soap community that gave rise to this new mode of interacting with television. Another says:

> I think it is a lot more fun to watch the soaps when you can discuss (or watch) with others. The times I have been the most involved in the soaps have been (1) in college, when a group of us would watch together on a big screen TV, and (2) now, when I have access to other people's opinions on r.a.t.s. There have been a few times when I was basically watching by myself . . . and I got so disgusted at stupid storylines or whatever that I quit watching for a while. In fact, I think this summer has been so boring . . . that I would have quit *AMC* again, if it were not for the fun of discussing the stupidity on the net.

This response is characteristic of soap fans in general: many (myself included) have ceased or decreased viewing when deprived of interaction with other viewers. The show *itself* is not the main focus of this viewer's interest, then, and she does not passively accept "stupid storylines". Rather, she would choose not to watch if necessary, but given the option prefers to continue watching while *ironicizing* the stories, which thus serve a quite different function than that intended by the network.

Another fan explains that "No one around me watches *AMC* on a regular basis . . . so I felt like I was on the veritable desert island when my r.a.t.s. ship came in! These folks are a great bunch, I'll tell you. It's a little community." This woman goes on to explain that she uses soaps as fuel for gossip with her husband: "Once, we were in the car for an HOUR and I realized we had not talked about anybody we knew personally . . . just the characters from *AMC* and some of my net.friends." This response forces me to extend my earlier argument that serial fiction serves to bond virtual strangers by providing a common circle of "acquaintances" about whom to gossip. Clearly such talk can enhance intimacy even between discussants who do know each other well.

Other respondents support the research of Brown, Hobson, and others by citing discussions at the office and watching with family members as important factors in their soap enjoyment. None felt that watching alone was as fulfilling as watching with others. One woman discusses the importance of new perspectives derived from soaptalk, attesting that they enrich her interpretation not only of the show but of "real" life as well: "By discussing plot twists and possible storylines, I get more involved with the show and I also get to hear other people's views on life. When people talk about Marty's rape on *One Life to Live*, they also talk about their own experiences, or experiences of people they know. Soaps allow people to live other lives safely." In the last sentence, this woman articulates with wonderful economy serials' ability to provide a nonthreatening space for acting out divisive social issues. Another explains, "I also like the different points-of-view on characters/situations. . . . I also think it's a great forum for other discussion too. I don't know if you were around for the big racism discussion that ensued after the Terrence episodes. . . . Being a white female, I gained a good deal of insight from other folks that get attitude just for being a different race. This is not a bunch of stereotypical bon-bon eaters in curlers watching the soap while the wash is spinning (does that even exist anymore?)"

Both these viewers praise soap opera's role in heightening public awareness of social issues. Significantly, however, they see this increased awareness as resulting not from mere soap watching but rather from the all-important activity of discussion of soap storylines and from the increased diversity of audiences.

In response to my second question about audience influence on soap opera, all but one respondent replied that fans do influence the shows. Some are strong believers, saying, for example, "I think the writers know they have to please the audience and one of the ways to judge if they are doing that is by reading and reacting to the mail they receive," or "YES! For some reason soaps are more paranoid than other TV shows about losing even one viewer" and "They probably do take fan letters seriously." Others offer qualified support, stating, for example, that "I think that the audience as a whole has some (small) impact on what the producers do" or "It looks like we affect things because most of the people who read r.a.t.s are smart enough to write soaps and probably come up with the same ideas (or better ideas) as the writers do."

In support of their belief that writers lurk on the net, respondents cited the way that r.a.t.s. nicknames and terminology mysteriously appear in the mouths of soap characters. Many also mentioned a recent and much discussed writer "blooper": a young girl who showed up in Pine Valley turned out to be Erica Kane's long-lost daughter. The product of a rape in Erica's early adolescence, she was put up for adoption and then utterly repressed; this is a retroactive storyline, since neither daughter nor rape had ever been mentioned before. Drawing on its collective knowledge of the history of *All My Children*, r.a.t.s.ers compiled a dateline for the show, fit this event into it, and emerged with the result that if Erica really did give birth when she was thirteen or fourteen (as we were told), and if Kendall was assumed to be seventeen or eighteen (she looked a bit younger and the actress playing her was only sixteen, but it is nice to give writers the benefit of the doubt), Erica must now be between thirty and thirty-two. Since the character has been on the show from its first episode in 1970, when she was in late adolescence, now she ought to be in her early forties at least, actress Susan Lucci's own age. Clearly the writers were insulting audience intelligence and ignoring the existence of viewers who have been watching since 1970 and could thus compare their own ages with Erica's. R.a.t.s.ers took great delight in calling these facts to the show's attention. A few weeks later (shows are taped roughly two weeks before airtime), writers began including gratuitous mentions of Kendall's age every few episodes: "I'll have champagne," she would say, "You know I like it, and I'm over twenty-one"; or "I *am* twenty-three, after all." At first, viewers were pleased by the correction, but these extradiegetic comments quickly became tiresome, to such an extent that an updater finally exploded, "This seems especially unnecessary since we're also expected to believe that this twenty-three-year-old is intensely competitive with a nine-year-old child—her half-sister—and works to sabotage her at every turn."

Case Study: Redeeming the Rapist

> *When you look in Todd's eyes, you can see that there's no heart or soul
> in there anymore. He's made a pact with the devil, sold his soul to the
> devil. He can find a way out when there's no way to be found, he keeps
> going on, he keeps coming back, and there's nothing we can do about it.*
> —Marty, One Life to Live

> *Sorry, babe, but this door's locked—and you know what happens with
> you and me when we're behind locked doors.*
> —Todd, One Life to Live

To explore r.a.t.s.ers' interaction with a specific text, I will draw on the debate surrounding a storyline already discussed here, *One Life to Live*'s three-
year portrayal of the consequences of the gang-rape of Marty Saybrooke by
three fraternity boys. To summarize the story so far: in 1992, Marty Saybrooke
showed up in Llanview as a "poor little rich girl" orphaned by a car crash
and abandoned to the tender mercies of her socialite Aunt Kiki. On soaps,
most rich girls are also bad girls, and Marty was no exception; she drank, did
drugs, and tried to seduce the local minister. But in the spring of 1993, she
began to settle down. A few weeks later, Todd—with whom she had had sex
once, though she had refused more recently—took his revenge when he
found her drunk at Spring Fling. He raped her and incited two of his friends
to rape her as well. As in the stories of Billy, the homosexual teen trying to
come out to his friends and family, and Terrence, whose house was bombed
by white thugs, we focus on Marty's terrifying powerlessness in that situation and her consequent need to prove that "I can't go on being a victim. I
am going to take back control over my own life." Terrence and Marty's
storylines were initially flawed in that the racist thugs and two of the rapists
were demonized, their subjectivity denied in ways that tended to oversim-
plify the situations and thereby failed to capture the complex power relations underlying racism or violence toward women. The perpetrators of these
crimes were simply evil or out of control and therefore could be rejected
along with the mindsets they represent.

Marty's was a gang rape, so the figure of the rapist was split into three:
the evil instigator, the good resister, and the mediator between these polar-
ized figures. The instigator, Todd Manning, was transformed in the process
of raping Marty from a crude but still human character to a dehumanized
embodiment of rage. Set over against the absolute evil of Todd Manning was
the relative "good" of Powell Lord—like Dickens, soap writers sometimes
choose names dripping with symbolism—who initially resisted the rape,

urging his friends to let Marty go, but ultimately gave in to peer pressure. As mediator we had Zach Rosen, who never acquired much of an identity beyond his function as go-between.

As we have seen, serials are fascinated by the instability of identity— hence the recurrence of radical character transformations, returns from the dead, evil twins, and so on—and the splitting in this storyline enhances interrogation of the identity of the rapist. What becomes especially clear is that for these characters the act of rape is not about sex, about women, or even about Marty. It is about what takes place, as Eve Sedgwick would put it, *between men* and hence marks a departure in soap treatment of rape. As in the case of the Bradley Headstone/Eugene Wrayburn rivalry, the polarization this splitting produces marks a transition from realism to melodrama. Soap opera rapes draw on powerful archetypes, most dramatically the fight between good and evil, weak and strong, and soaps tend to configure these archetypes in ways that resemble their use in nineteenth-century melodrama to critique power relations, especially the oppression of the poor by the rich and of women by men. This particular storyline, though, polarizes not only the gap between rapist and raped but also the figure of the rapist himself. The show also departs from the rape paradigm not only by insisting on the essential "goodness" of Powell Lord—which many viewers have found hard to accept, considering that he *did* commit rape, a crime for which "peer pressure made me do it" is hardly an adequate (or even a physiologically possible) excuse—but even more startlingly by redeeming the evil Todd.

Initially, Todd was unequivocally bad: sullen, remorseless, charmless. Writers clearly had a terrific time camping up Todd as the embodiment of evil. Just before his incarceration, for example, he attempted to rape Marty again to punish her for "winning" the trial, and her friend Luna stopped him by whacking him with a crowbar, thus marking him with a nasty scar zigzagging across his right cheek. The camera loved to fetishize that scar as the symbol of his villainy, zooming in to linger on it at every opportunity (see fig. 3.6). The character seemed headed for a killing spree and then a quick end, but the actor playing Todd, Roger Howarth, is highly skilled and managed against all odds to add depth to a one-dimensional character. His popularity grew as a result, so the show's producers faced a conundrum. Todd had become the devil, but Howarth was boosting ratings. Executive producer Susan Bedsow Horgan and head writer Michael Malone chose a solution that proved highly controversial: they set out to complicate their one-dimensional rapist.

After Powell Lord (who finally confessed, attempted suicide, and was publicly forgiven by Marty herself) was sentenced to only three months in

Fig. 3.6: The symbolic scar. © 1996 Ann Limongello/ABC, Inc.

jail while Todd and Zach each received eight-year sentences, Todd, as furious as many viewers about Powell's light sentence, vowed he would be out in three months also.[26] His character veered increasingly toward the demonic, and he succeeded in making good his threat to escape by drugging himself, waking from a coma to leap from a speeding ambulance, and then reviving himself again by stabbing a knife through his hand while rolling his eyes heavenward and exulting, "Pain. Pain is good." By this point in the narrative, such excess had become characteristic, with Howarth camping up the villainy for all he was worth and many fans responding enthusiastically. After escaping, Todd returned to Llanview to stalk Nora Gannon, the attorney who had refused to defend him once she learned that he was guilty. He then attempted to rape Marty for the third time, killed Marty's boyfriend Suede, kidnapped an ingenue named Rebecca, went on the lam with her, stole a car, was found by police and shot in the chest, fell off a bridge into a freezing river in far upstate New York, was washed downstream among the ice floes, crawled out again, lay on the bank for a few episodes while the camera panned slowly up his apparently lifeless body, regained consciousness, began walking, and immediately saw a sign saying, "Llanview, PA, 50 miles."

After Todd's third or fourth miraculous escape and recovery, fans began calling him the Terminator or alternatively the Energizer Bunny, nicknames reflecting fan recognition of the fact that Todd had clearly crossed the border separating realistic soap character from the villain appropriated from nineteenth-century melodrama and Gothic traditions. In apparent contradiction but in clear response to the actor's growing popularity, writers simultaneously began to "deepen" the character by, for example, emphasizing his tenderness toward the innocent Rebecca and including flashbacks and testimony of his father's brutality toward him. We were therefore encouraged to read a causal narrative—"abusive father produces abusive child"—into the scenario. However, as many fans noted, this reading does not historicize the problem but simply removes the cause of violence one step. In the absence of any analysis of social, political, and economic factors, "my abusive father made me do it" just demonizes the father rather than the son.

In the spring of 1994, one year after the rape, Todd began to be "redeemed" (soap fan parlance for the process of turning a "bad" character into a "good" one, thus allowing that character to become incorporated into the community). Since Todd had crossed so far into absolute villainy, this transformation has required a whole arsenal of heavy symbolic weaponry. As far as I know, it is unprecedented for a rapist to be redeemed in exactly this way. Traditional soap narrative treatment of rapists must be seen in relation to soaps' initially female writers and viewers and their early constructions of masculinity, the "wheelchair syndrome" for example. Generally, soap men commit rape as a result of a long-standing rage and/or need to control. The rape does not function as a turning point in character development, then, but as a culmination, an act after which the character slides quickly into irredeemable villainy. Rape has been the one unforgivable crime. Thus, the rapist often wreaks havoc on the entire soap community for the duration of a ratings sweep and is then either committed to life imprisonment and/or sent away (like Ross Chandler, *All My Children*) or very often killed off by one of the characters he has hurt (like Will Cortlandt, also *All My Children*). In either case, the rapist is shunted off the show, never to return.

There are precedents for redemption of actors considered too popular to be written off the show, the most famous of which is the Luke and Laura storyline on *General Hospital*.[27] Luke Spencer stalked Laura and then raped her, but since the couple proved overwhelmingly popular, writers rewrote past history to the extent that as far as Luke and Laura themselves are concerned, the rape was "semi-consensual" (whatever that means). Interestingly, though, the treatment of this exception actually underscores the strength of the rule: the fact that the rape had to be erased from collective memory indicates that in the minds of the writers, a rapist *could not* become a good character and therefore the rape itself had to be denied and dissolved. What is more, viewers so vehemently and publicly expressed their horror at the thought that *One Life To Live* might be heading in such a direction that the executive producer issued a statement (published in *Soap Opera Digest*) to the effect that a Luke/Laura style romance—explicitly so labeled—between Todd and Marty was "absolutely, categorically out of the question."[28]

The writers who redeemed Todd included an unusually high number of male writers (eight men and three women were on the team during much of this storyline) and were led by head writer and novelist Michael Malone (since replaced by Jean Passanante), known for his "Dickensian" plots. Malone's nineteenth-century influences are overt and conscious in the redemption of Todd; for example, in a *Village Voice* article he compared Rebecca's decision to marry Powell rather than Todd to Cathy's decision to marry Edgar Linton rather than Heathcliff (Aug. 16, 1994). More disturbingly, in a *TV Guide* article focusing on the recent pattern of rapists redeemed (June 1994), he claims: "The bond between the woman and the violator is a great, historical tradition in fiction and in films. . . . Rudolph Valentino, Humphrey Bogart, Kirk Douglas, and Clark Gable all began as totally irredeemable villains. . . . You certainly don't want to say that these women want to be raped or that they are drawn to violence, because that's not true. But they *are* responding to the intensity of passion and an actor who lets you inside the torment. Some [women] believe they can be swept up in that passion and still turn it good. They think, 'With *me*, he'd be different.'"[29] The article's author, Michael Logan, pushes home the subtext here by stating, "Let's call a spade a spade: There is a very large contingent of American female soap viewers who find something very attractive about rapists." It is hardly necessary to mention that actual "female soap viewers" were furious at being so categorized. The response of one woman to the r.a.t.s. group will stand for many. "This is such a stupid statement," she says, in response to Logan's generalization. "Speaking only for myself, I don't like Todd because he's a rapist. I like Todd because Roger Howarth is a great actor. Powell and Zach raped Marty too, and I'm not a bit fond of either one of them."[30]

In working to recuperate Todd for the purpose of future storylines and ratings, the team used four techniques drawn from the conventions of Victorian sentimental fiction. First, we learn about Todd's unhappy childhood and specifically about his love for his mother and the cruelty of his wealthy, domineering, abusive father. Second, Todd repents and begins visiting a church to confess both past misdeeds and present impulses (to murder Powell, for example—something also high on many fans' agenda). Third, we see his "pure" love for an innocent and highly religious virgin, Rebecca, who by "believing in him" helps him to express his rage against his father. This relationship is one that many viewers found particularly hard to swallow, given both Todd's earlier predilection for raping any woman who ran across his path and Rebecca's open-mouthed passivity. With her pre-Raphaelite curls, "drooping head," and inarticulate cries, Rebecca is almost a caricature of Dickens's more sentimental and less felicitous heroines. Visually, the scenes between Todd and Rebecca are heavily iconic: symbolic representations include the Virgin, the Mother, and also the feminization (with heavy homage to Freud) of Todd himself as, for example, he opens Rebecca purse, reminisces about his mother's purse, and then attempts to use women's makeup to hide the scar of a violent masculinity.

A fourth and crucial weapon used in Todd's redemption is his friendship with two children, Sarah and C.J., who find him hiding in their garden shed. This subplot bears an uncanny (and almost certainly deliberate, given Malone's affection for nineteenth-century literature) resemblance to the monster's narrative in Mary Shelley's *Frankenstein*. Shelley's monster describes his rescue of a drowning young girl, which is misunderstood as an attack on her; he also tells of sadly watching, from his hideout in an outbuilding, two happy, innocent children going about their lives. Similarly, from his post in the toolshed Todd rescues the children's teenage cousin Jessica, who is being accosted by an older boy; he also mournfully watches the family's activities, longs to be part of them, and spends his time carving toys for the two children. After the children accidentally discover him, Todd convinces them to keep his secret and to bring him food by telling them that he is a genie on the run from an evil master (figs. 3.7 and 3.8). The stories he tells them function as clear metaphors for his feelings about his father. For example, one day when C.J. asks him why he looks sad, he replies, "Every genie wants the same thing, you know? We all want our masters to smile, and care about us. We all want to grow up to be just like our masters. But some masters, C.J., some masters they don't deserve genies. They hit them, and they punish them, and they send them away . . . and they tell them that they're stupid, and worthless. And after a while, the genies start to think that they *are* stupid. And maybe they are . . . 'cause they just want the masters to care about them. They never will." Interestingly, even while constructing such consciously touching scenes the directors seem aware that viewers may be disturbed by watching small children in contact with a character who has so successfully been established as evil. These scenes make extensive use of unusual visual techniques, shooting from the children's perspective down on a crouching Todd to diminish the threat he poses when he is with them and using shots from the ground up as well as zooming in on the scar to increase the threat when he is alone. For many viewers, the final, damningly

Figs. 3.7 & 3.8: The iconography of redemption: Todd with C.J. (Tyler Noyes) and Sarah (Courtney Chase).

obvious blow in this battle to redeem Todd was the writers' choice to have Todd save the life of the woman he'd raped, Marty, by rescuing her and one of the children he'd befriended after a car accident (see fig. 3.9).

Does the unprecedented handling of this rape storyline simply reflect a need to recycle an old story in a new way, or does it reflect important shifts in soap narrative as a result of the newly male-dominated writing team on *One Life to Live*? A partial answer can be found in viewer reaction. Responses were violently split along lines reflecting attitudes toward gender relations as well as soaps' own split between narrative realism and fantasy. Some viewers loathed Todd and were furious that the writers seem to be intending to keep him on the show. For example, one r.a.t.s.er writes, "I think it would be a real kick in the head to anyone who's ever been raped to have them show something like [Rebecca falling in love with Todd, and Todd staying on the show to be involved with her] . . . I know that's been done in the past, but hopefully things have changed since Luke and Laura"[31](Jan. 28, 1994). This writer clearly values soaps' long-standing respect for independent, strong women. In addition, she prefers a realistic treatment of rape storylines and privileges soaps' social realism over their fantasy. Conversely, a male fan who seems to prefer fantasy says, "I don't care where [Todd] goes . . . just as long as he keeps coming back. One of soapdom's greatest tricks is to keep bringing villains back from the dead. . . . a few years back, *One Life to Live* ran the same route with Jamie whatshisname. That guy was even more evil than Todd" (Feb. 11, 1994).

Clarifying the underlying issues involved in Todd's redemption, another fan points out:

> The writers are sort of playing mind games on us with this character. He's been talking a lot about his mom lately, and it looks like they might try to redeem him rather than kill him. I *might* be able to go along with that, even though he raped Marty. BUT, he tried to rape her again—twice! That's pretty hard to forgive, and pretty hard for a character to overcome, I think. But I still think Todd is one of the most interesting and well-acted characters I've seen in a long time, and I really enjoy his scenes. Maybe they'll wound him, he'll be taken to the hospital, and they'll find out a brain tumor was causing all of his aggression. Then they can remove it . . . and he'll be Mr. Nice Guy. Hey, anything could happen! [Jan. 22, 1994]

These last two writers clearly appreciate the fantastic conventions of serial fiction, chief among them the interrogation of identity that over the years has produced tropes such as radical character changes (fig. 3.10). However, the last commentator is both conflicted and disturbed by the too easy leap from narrative realism to fantasy: she appreciates Roger Howarth's skill as well as the complexity of the character but does not want past violence to be forgotten.

Fig. 3.9: Todd rescuing Marty. © 1996 Ann Limongello/ABC, Inc.

My own response to this storyline is equally ambivalent. On the one hand, Todd's redemption certainly conveys one of the most important lessons of soapdom: never leap to conclusions about people based on race, class, appearance, rumor, or even fact, because it is impossible to understand the Other without understanding the history that has shaped him or her. On the other hand, using powerful narrative and visual techniques to mobilize sympathy for a man who has raped at least three women, attempted to rape several others, killed a man, and so on seems dubious at best. The narrative weight placed on Rebecca's role in Todd's redemption, for example, seems to encourage both female and male fantasies about the power of a "good woman" to save a man from his own violent impulses.

Given actor Howarth's popularity—a result not of his onscreen persona but of his undeniable acting ability, praised even by Todd haters—it seemed doubtful that producers would respond to the minority of fans who wanted Todd off the show. But a combination of fan response and the actor himself impelled producers to add a new twist to the storyline. Roger Howarth, who works with his wife in a rape crisis center, was disgusted by his redemption. In published interviews he stated that he had been hired to play an evil rapist, was horrified when the redemption process began, and decided to quit when the writers would not listen to his protests. A contract dispute followed, only resolved by Howarth's promise not to appear on a competing

Fig. 3.10: The mirror scene: Todd interrogates his identity. © 1996 Ann Limongello/ABC, Inc.

soap for two years. He remained on the show while writers worked to write him out, finally achieved by the old ploy of sending him off a cliff in a car. In the spring of 1996, we saw him lying on the coast of Ireland, fingers twitching to tell fans (in a less than subtle manner) that Todd would return when all the furor had died down. Tune in tomorrow. . . .

All such controversial storylines spur active debate over the issues involved, the realism of the writers' depiction, and possible resolutions to the story. These televisual explorations of power relations are, then, valuable as they promote discussion, and even more valuable if they do respond to viewers. Countering the traditional view of soaps as pernicious, mindless entertainment, Nochimson, Allen, and others have argued that they have enormous potential to effect social change. Supporters of soap operas cite their socially relevant storylines as well as their creation of that rare mass-cultural entity, a female-dominated narrative that refuses to privilege teleology or closure, does privilege interpersonal relations and communication, and allows even female protagonists space to develop newly defined identities. In addition to these factors, I would argue that soaps are ground breaking most of all in the community of viewers they produce.

Plots like Janet the evil twin and Todd's radical character transformation synchronize with both soap meaning and production exigencies. Forced into awareness of all points of view (including the economic), all sides of the story, all possible shifts in history and memory, soap viewers are refused the luxury not only of teleology but also of unchanged judgments on characters and past histories, of an absolute morality. Almost all soaps include drug addicts, prostitutes, and so on who are introduced as "bad," play the role of villain or villainess for months or even years, and then are gradually redeemed, usually through the love or friendship of central "good" characters and almost always after a fleshing out of past history that explains present nastiness. This narrative trajectory works in reverse in the case of minority characters: introduced as simplistically "good," black or Asian or gay characters survive a trial period as victims of the misguided prejudice of longstanding characters, gradually become incorporated into the soap world (again through links with established inhabitants), and only then are allowed to have a few faults. In both cases, though, one of the crucial lessons is awareness of the complexity of personality and of social context and acknowledgment of the possibility of change. Ideal texts in this age of flexible production since they are continually remaking themselves to suit both consumers and context, soaps underscore the cultural specificity of interpretation as well as the process of formation of identity. They teach that every action, every subplot, every character will ultimately be intertwined and balanced. There is no such thing as isolated action, or freedom from consequences, on the soaps. Paradoxically, given the obsession with industry "scoops" discussed earlier, they explore a world in which knowledge is not sufficient—or even necessarily valuable. They reverse the standard equation of knowledge with power.

The appeal of this subversion can be attributed in part to demographics. The disenfranchised make up a large part of the soap audience (because it is the unemployed, the ill or injured, women, and students who tend to be at home in the daytime), and to a viewer who cannot find a job, for example, subversion of the superiority of those "in the know" can have a powerful appeal. The flip side, of course, is the anxiety inevitably produced (in both viewers and characters) by the unreliability of knowledge and the ambiguity of its possession, serial elements that (as we have noted in the cases of the Dickens reader Henry Crabb Robinson and the comics reader George) parallel the random and contingent feel of the actual, as opposed to the idealized, workings of the "information economy" and the commodification of knowledge. Soaps underscore the impossibility of fixed interpretations and stable truths. But in whose interests does this indeterminacy work? Are producers betraying their obligation to viewers by the careless recycling of worn-out plots and resuscitation of characters long abandoned to the garbage barges of television history, even if this approach comes at the cost of a "forgetting" of soap history that is of crucial importance to long-term viewers? Or can we see this syndrome as an advance: soap narratives refuse easy answers, require constant reinterpretation, and admit the existence of limits (of plot, character configurations, identities), thus demanding heightened imaginative interaction from both creators and audiences.

Humor, Irony, and Self-Reflexivity

> *"Well my goodness, lucky Natalie. She falls into a well, she finds the only singles well in America."*
> —Erica Kane, on being told that Dimitri
> (who rescued Natalie from her well) is one of the
> Eastern Seaboard's most eligible bachelors

"The soap opera is never funny about anything . . . but why are soaps so relentlessly *serious*?"[32] This quotation, from a 1987 study of television genres, indicates the critical myopia of those who allow canonical condescension to interfere with experiencing texts as they actually work in the viewing context. Fortunately, cultural critics increasingly acknowledge their own enjoyment of mass texts; investment in mass culture has become a strength to be explored rather than an impossibility or a repressed that has yet to return. Personal as well as critical engagement with texts certainly brings its own problems, but surely an acknowledged, if unresolved, affinity with fans is preferable to the impossible "ideal" of critical distance in analyzing the pleasures of a mass Other.

To respond to the complaint quoted above, many shows do now incorporate generic commentary. For example, one-liners on the absurd coincidences of the genre abound, as in Erica Kane's comment on the fabulous fortuity of her old nemesis Natalie being stumbled upon—in a well, no less—by the handsome, wealthy, and available Bachelor #1 Dimitri Marrick. Most soaps now include (intentional) camp humor, slapstick, and irony as an integral part of narrative strategy. If they do not, fans impose their own ironic readings of relentlessly serious storylines like Natalie-in-the-well (r.a.t.s.ers engaged in a long debate as to where exactly this woman managed to relieve herself during weeks in a tiny well—a topic that exposes both tragedy's need to elide bodily functions and this particular storyline's unintentional slippage from tragedy to bathos). As the TV generation acquires control over the industry that saturated its childhood, television begins to comment on its own conventions, memory, and history. Since the form has become so critically visible over the past ten years, soap watching (like all media-related experiences) has become increasingly self-conscious and thus increasingly humorous.

Its vexed relation to more prestigious forms like Hollywood movies inspired the following self-parody. First, a bit of the background usually needed to understand soap jokes. Many daytime TV actors still make periodic pilgrimages to Hollywood, where they attempt to break into "real" acting, and actors and viewers alike are well aware of the status and economics involved in making the transition from daytime TV to the silver screen. Playing on this real-life cliché, *All My Children* set up a one-liner based on the trials (both real and televisual) of Tad Martin (played by Michael Knight). Having fallen off a bridge in 1990, Tad was washed downriver and presumed dead. Viewers knew better, however, since we alone watched him amnesiacally amble off into the sunset. And that was the last we heard of Tad for three years, during which—as most viewers also knew from soap magazines or from each other—Knight made a less than successful effort to make a movie career for himself. In July 1991, a stranger showed up at Dixie's (Tad's widow's) door, telling her that Tad had been spotted alive. "Where?" she asked, and was told, "In Hollywood."

As this example indicates and as I have shown above, one particularly active soap pleasure is the complex game of following both a show and external media sources like fan magazines to acquire the cultural capital necessary to untangle soap history, predict plot moves (or scenes or lines), and verbally narrate the absurd complexity of a single subplot (complete with crucial digressions into each involved character's inordinately complicated past). Viewers match wits with producers in an oddly collaborative competition. This active fandom has influenced form in forcing producers to become increasingly self-conscious about soap as a genre. Many shows now incorporate generic commentary in the form of camp scenes and characters, elaborate, parodic flashbacks and fantasies drawn from pop culture icons, and (as in *One Life to Live*, or—a r.a.t.s. member tells me—*Loving*, on which characters have been known to watch *All My Children*, set in neighboring Pine Valley) the weaving of "soaps within the soap" into the narrative web. An obvious example is *OLTL*'s soap "Fraternity Row," now sadly defunct. In June 1989, Megan, the star of "Fraternity Row," began fueling up for the Daisy Awards in which she competed against stars from such top-rated daytime dramas as "All Or Nothing," "The Wild and the Wealthy," and my personal favorite, "Day After Tomorrow." The Daisy show aired on June 29, just like the Daytime Emmy Awards, and was hosted by Robin Leach. Many viewers reported the Daisys to be infinitely better produced than the Emmys, with more interesting costumes and choreography and superior entertainment value. As an added bonus, Daisy viewers were treated to behind-the-scenes glimpses of Megan locked in a meat freezer by Spring Skye, her competition for best actress. All this is pure pleasure, but at the same time it acknowledges pleasure's absurdity as well as the very real issues of power, economics, and cutthroat competition that form the inescapable base of the culture industry.

Lynn Joyrich, who believes that feminists can recuperate television in ways similar to those in which cinema has been legitimated as a subject worthy of serious scholarly attention, argues that "film melodrama has been able to call attention to the contradictions in our class and gender system through its use of formal conventions which stand as ironic commentaries on otherwise conventional narratives. By reading TV melodramas against the grain and providing our own ironic commentaries, feminist criticisms may continue to bring out the contradictions of the TV age. . . . Such work might then make more apparent the sites of stress and contradiction in postmodern culture, its construction and deconstruction of the terms of gender and consumption, so that the boundaries thus drawn may be stretched in new directions" (147). Joyrich rightly calls for critics to provide such ironic commentaries. However, most soap critics ignore the fact that such arguments have informal parallels among both audiences and producers, who are now very much aware of soaps' reputation for social relevance[33] and of its potential for irony or parody. Both fans and shows already provide their *own* commentaries. Soaps take their responsibility for dealing with sites of social stress and contradiction very seriously and do so through both humor and straight drama.

Several (*All My Children, One Life to Live, General Hospital,* and *Santa Barbara* are perhaps the most explicitly ironic) must now be read at least partly "against the grain," since they provoke and expose their own contradictions by incorporating ironic commentaries on soap as form. Besides *Fraternity Row,* examples of genre self-parody include characters such as Bunny the Mafia transvestite (*Santa Barbara*) or Phoebe the histrionic socialite and Cecily the trust fund feminist (both from *All My Children*). These and other longtime soap favorites use intentionally ironic or "over-the-top" acting styles to deflate the one-dimensional character type they portray, whether villainess, patriarch, or working-class woman with a heart of gold—Erica Kane, Palmer Cortlandt, or Opal Cortlandt.

In addition to humorous self-reflexivity, most soaps interact extratextually with contemporary news, current events, and urgent social issues, running at least one "relevant" storyline at any given time to respond explicitly to, for example, cultural contradictions in ideologies of race, sexual orientation, gender, or power. As discussed earlier, recent storylines include an exploration of homosexuality and AIDS, a yearlong treatment of racism, and a year and a half exploration of gang-rape and its consequences for both survivor and perpetrator. Other recent topics include incest and child abuse, alcoholism and drug abuse, drunk driving, interracial romance, sexist and racist job discrimination, and single parenthood. Many of these episodes included hotline numbers flashed onscreen during the show or public service announcements like the one running before *All My Children* (February 1992) that featured the show's teen members urging talk, not violence, in settling racial issues.

As usual, Erica Kane will have the last word on *All My Children*. A recent seduction—an attempt to recycle a previously trashed romance with Jackson Montgomery—takes place under the auspices of Pine Valley's campaign to block the aptly named Mar View landfill. Learning that Jackson is on the antilandfill committee, Erica suddenly realizes how deeply she cares about our planet. As they work together on a fund-raising campaign, she articulates her seduction of Jack through an impassioned defense of environmentalism (her rhetoric is so convincing that it eventually sweeps Erica herself away on its green tide, and she becomes an authentic, and effective, social activist, but that is another story). Leaning toward Jack, Erica stares into his eyes and breathes, "The solution is so simple . . . and absolutely life-affirming, you know what I mean? Because most people feel that they are so small and insignificant. But the truth is that every one of us has the ability, within us, together, we have it in us to absolutely change the world." While speaking, Erica becomes increasingly passionate. She has convinced herself: she *can* rekindle her relationship with Jack; she *can* stop the landfill from destroying Pine Valley. The two goals become fused. Showing us how serial recycling intersects with both narrative ecology and the narrative of twentieth-century ecology—and, not incidentally, how political change starts with the personal, another message of soap opera—Erica makes environmentalism sexy.

And what is more, she is right. If Erica Kane, soap seductress, can convincingly explain the importance of the environment not only to Jack but to sixty million Americans—and more important, if mass concern with the environment can spur the ABC writing team to incorporate green storylines (however cynical their motivation) that impel more mass concern as audiences discuss the show—surely this means that we, not just "viewers" but participants in cultural production, can acquire still more of a voice. These fictional events work to increase public awareness of environmental issues and sexual violence, and they do so not by preaching at a passive, voiceless audience but by spurring active debate over the ways such issues are represented on television and over their intersection with viewers' own lives.

Of course, these examples of soap opera's social responsibility and self-ironicizing commentary do not mean that the form has become the only totally self-conscious, nonideological text going: far from it. It is interesting, for example, that "over-the-top" or intentionally parodied characters are generally either wealthy, powerful, and snobbish or lower-class buffoons. The middle classes, which networks still perceive as their primary audience, are generally treated "straight." And soaps' reprehensibly few minority characters invariably receive kid-glove treatment, their storylines handled with a desperate seriousness that underscores the urgent need across the media to incorporate more varied perspectives on all races.

Also, despite soap producers' very real interest in viewer opinion and despite viewers' very active role in choosing how to use texts in their daily lives, it is important to emphasize that however much audiences may influence a particular text, control over the production agenda remains firmly in the hands of networks, producers, and advertisers. As David Morley rightly points out, "In acknowledging audiences as active in a range of ways as they integrate what they see and hear into their domestic lives, we should not romanticize or exaggerate the audience's creative freedoms. There is a difference between power over a text and power over an agenda" (1980, 34). ABC production executives have told me, for example, that while networks do monitor audience response and opinions carefully, strong negative response to a storyline does not necessarily alter it: if viewers are engaged enough to respond angrily, they are engaged enough to keep watching. Only when *no* response comes in will axes definitely fall. So, again, the relation between soap texts and soap audiences is a double-edged one. Although the daytime serial does seem to be one of the few mass-cultural forms where viewers feel at least some degree of power over the agenda—a confidence that producers insistently (though how sincerely remains open to question) support—the kind of power they wield is a highly mediated one. By investigating ways in which networks respond to audience desire and working to expand them, we encourage a more actively hegemonic mass-cultural production.

Tune In Tomorrow

> *Look, it's up to you. Can you accept the status quo for a while longer, or should we just end things right now?*
>
> —All My Children

In the past ten years Tania Modleski, Robert Allen, Sandy Flitterman-Lewis, and others have reclaimed the previously denigrated soap opera as a viable and valuable narrative form. Two factors enabled this relative legitimization:

feminist recuperation of condemned "women's fiction" and (in a move politically influenced by feminist rewriting of the canon) institutionalization of
mass culture within the academy. Modleski cites Horace Newcomb, who
suggests that daytime drama's televisual and narrative conventions "represent in some ways the furthest advance of T.V. art." Because of the small,
intimate televisuals discussed above, soaps' narrative space is far better suited
to the small screen so intimately inserted into our private lives than are, say,
adventure series.

Modleski (1982) proposes a focus on exactly those qualities that make
the genre an alternative pleasure directed at women. Discussing soaps' fantasy fulfilling function, she explains that "it is important to recognize that
soap opera allays *real* anxieties, satisfies *real* needs and desires, even while it
may distort them. The fantasy of community is not only a real desire (as
opposed to the 'false' ones mass culture is always accused of trumping up), it
is a salutary one. As feminists, we have a responsibility to devise ways of
meeting these needs that are more creative, honest, and interesting than the
ones mass culture has supplied. Otherwise, the search for tomorrow threatens to go on, endlessly" (108–9). Her approach here speaks for the compelling Marxist/feminist modification of the Frankfurt School's cultural imperi-
alism. She not only insists on the valuable qualities of the existing form but
asserts our power to change and improve it.

I would like, however, to revise the "we" with responsibility to transform televisual texts. Power lies in the hands not just of feminist academics
but of audiences themselves: the nonworking women often perceived as the
typical soap audience as well as the large numbers of professional women,
adolescents, unemployed, people of color (20 percent), and men (30 percent) who form its actual audience. Because of its serial production process,
enormously high rate of output, and vast audiences, soap opera is of necessity collaboratively created, incorporating ideas from many different sources.
Monitoring—and at least partially satisfying—audience desire is a crucial
part of production already, and the institutionalization of audience response
within the production process seems to be on the rise. As we have seen,
networks do hype their responsiveness, but at least some degree of direct
response can be seen not only in storylines and casting decisions but in the
makeup of the shows themselves. Changing demographics led directly to
increases in minority characters, especially Latinos and African Americans,
and inscription of issues such as AIDS, drug addiction, interracial couples,
and homosexuality long before these became hot tickets at the box office. In
a mediated, negotiated way, then, soaps already provide a kind of community, both in the collaborative production and consumption practices and in
the negotiated space between the two.

The deep interpenetration of fictional themes and everyday lives that has marked serial fiction as a genre from Dickens's time to the present also makes soap opera a powerful forum for exposure and debate of social and political questions. Because of their resistance to closure and their development of a textual system privileging not an individual hero or heroine but a community, soaps have been seen as deconstructing the patriarchal emphasis on telos and the individual. Nochimson argues that if soap opera as a genre becomes more aware of its own power "to dramatize the full spectrum of social and sexual difference" and "the historical influence on self" (39), it will be able to accomplish much more than it has already. I would agree that this awareness is necessary, since increased attention may prevent the kind of closing off of complexity that occurs when a true menace—racism, rape—irrupts within the usually multivocal world of the soaps.

Nochimson also points out that "we must ponder the strength of desire in creators and spectators that has caused a narrative with a feminine structure to survive in a male-dominated society," and concludes that the rejection of soaps which refuses "normal discussion" and "intellectual curiosity" about soap opera, allowing only the level of the commercial discourse of soap fanzines and gossip, comes from "dark, unexamined panic about gender difference" (199). Although Nochimson certainly understands the history, structure, and motivations of soap opera, I disagree with her conclusions here. First, the kind of questioning, impassioned analysis she seeks already exists and is proliferating constantly on computer networks. Second, the source of denial here is not simply panic about gender difference, just as serial structure is not solely "feminine" and its power does not derive simply from its antiteleological narrative structure and deconstruction of traditional female roles within patriarchal structures. These are important factors, of course, but the difference goes further than this, to inflect serial construction of subjectivity and identity on all levels.

Serial history from Dickens onward inscribes a narrative of the absence, elision, stereotypical inclusion, and gradual visibility of populations marginalized not only by gender but also by race, class, and sexual preference. In addition, later serials' refusal of closure, recycling of characters and plots, and fluid construction of temporality allow them to explore shifting identities in ways not possible in more traditional narrative spaces. Thematically, then, serials act out over time historical moments in the political economy of sex, race, and class roles within cultural production. And they do this within a narrative structure privileging difference over homogeneity, understanding over rejection, open-endedness over closure.

Recent intensification of sites of social stress and conflict may explain, at least in part, soaps' increased problematizing of generic codes and conventions.

By mocking patriarchs and socialites or ironicizing male chauvinism by means of mafia cross-dressers, camped-up Elvis fantasies, or (on a more serious level) depicting a male cop saved by the black female partner he initially refused to work with, soaps deflate the power of class, gender, and race boundaries.[34] Of course, Erica's environmental phase will not stop real-life Mar Views from being built, the sympathetic depiction of a popular black character as the victim of sex and race discrimination in the workplace will not affect civil rights legislation, and the fact that a character has an abortion shown to be, for many reasons, the best possible choice for her does not mean that the Supreme Court will uphold the right to choose. But soap opera's multiple perspectives on highly charged issues make the form capable of providing the first step toward increased tolerance for others: a forum for public discussion of the issues involved. Generic televisual codes, which refuse the subject/object positioning that structures classic Hollywood cinematography by constructing the viewer simultaneously as voyeur and participant, possessor of knowledge and investigator, increase soaps' potential for exposing all sides of political issues. And this characteristic is also true for the serial genre as a whole, as becomes clear in examining the latest incarnation of the serial form: on-line serials.

As discussed in the introduction to this book, Roger Hagedorn argues that serialization has historically been used as a kind of lure to help defuse the anxiety surrounding a new medium. The power of the serial to attract and hold an audience works to acclimatize potential consumers to the medium, helping to ensure the popularity and thus the profitability of new technologies. Hagedorn's theory is perhaps best supported by the fact that in the last few years producers have begun appropriating serial power to develop an audience for the latest mass-media technology: computer networks. This latest incarnation of serial fiction demonstrates not only the genre's centrality to the history of mass culture but also its potential ability to respond more clearly and directly than most mass-cultural forms to an audience whose activities include collaborative discussion groups, prediction, metacommentary, parody, rewriting, and creation of new storylines. All these strategies culminate not only in soap discussion groups on the Internet, America Online, and other services but even more directly in these networks' becoming forums for on-line serials, some authored by fans. The World Wide Web's soap opera home page provides links to soap information resources, news groups, and discussion groups maintained by fans as well as to a selection of on-line serials that has grown from six to thirty-three available texts between 1994 and 1996.[35]

These serials serve a range of purposes. They can be created by fans, intended to increase traffic on a particular site or to serve as vehicles for advertising, or impelled by the pure pleasure of the genre. One of the more interesting is ALT.DAYS, a fan-created alternative to NBC's *Days of Our Lives,* started in April 1993 by fans dissatisfied with the direction taken by the show's writing team. The on-line soap's alternative storylines take control over characters and storylines away from writers, allowing fans to preserve what they see as the integrity of long-term characters and to tackle issues too controversial for the networks to touch. There is also a wave of serials aiming for a self-consciously young and hip audience. These include "East Village" and "The Spot," which won this year's First Annual Cool Site of the Year Awards, also known as the Webbys. As on-line versions of MTV's "Real World," "East Village" and "The Spot" follow the trials and tribulations of a fictionalized group of young adults, the first, obviously, in New York, the second in a California beach house. "East Village" is especially imaginative, not only for its use of visuals and sound but for implementing, for example, a peculiarly on-line version of the fan club: readers can choose to become part of one particular character's in-group, thus receiving advance information about that character. Loyalty to one's in-group is enforced by the fact that each reader can only join one such group.

Another quite creative serial, Starwave Corporation's "Until Tomorrow," runs on the Starwave web site, which contains a mix of news and entertainment services. The serial works as a kind of pilot to increase awareness of the site's services, which are currently free but will be charged for once the number of "hits" per day indicates a loyal consumer base.[36] The corporation also intends to increase profits by attracting sponsors who will buy advertising space. Proof of high levels of traffic will obviously increase the site's marketability for potential advertisers as well as for the PR firm's clients. Not surprisingly, this use is common for net serials. Another example is the thin and ad-dominated "As the Web Turns" produced by the Colorado PR firm Metzger Associates and including gratuitous references to its various clients, including the Colorado Ballet and the Isle of Man.

Like TV soaps, some on-line serials are used as vehicles for advertising. The *New York Times* area of the America Online (AOL) service contains three separate storylines collectively known as "Parallel Lives." The concept came from a small advertising company, Gauthier and Gilden, who contacted the *Times* to propose writing a serial to be printed in the newspaper itself. Since the *Times* was in the process of setting up its AOL site, it suggested that Gauthier and Gilden create an on-line serial instead. Nabisco agreed to sponsor the project as a pilot exploration of advertising on the 'net. A menu contains seven items: four advertising areas, three storylines, and one area with general information about the stories. Clicking on the "about Parallel Lives" icon leads to a summary of the three concurrent storylines: "Urban

Studies" follows a group of upscale Manhattanites, conveniently entangled in romance, apparent heart attacks, and murder from the moment we meet them; "One Point Seven" introduces a middle-class African-American family plunged into earthquakes and adoption issues; and "A Boy and His Dog" exposes the Lynchland lurking beneath an apparently tranquil small town surface. The general information area introducing these stories tells us: "'Parallel Lives' is interactive. You can send us comments and story ideas via the message board and e-mail areas. We want to hear from you!" At the same time, we are informed that "'Parallel Lives' is sponsored by Nabisco. You can click on Nabisco's product icons on the 'Parallel Lives' screen for useful articles, recipes and more." Clicking on one of these four icons leads to recipes using or information about one of four Nabisco products and related advice ranging from entertaining to dog care.

Author Mark Gauthier received a flood of responses to his stories. For example, one reader of "Urban Studies" wrote to berate him for failing to include any nonwhite characters. When Gauthier steered him toward "One Point Seven," he wrote back to congratulate the author on creating the most authentic portrayal of African-American life this reader had seen in the media. Since Gauthier describes himself as "the whitest guy on the planet," the high praise is ironic at best. On the other hand, the reader's ability to convey to the author of an ongoing storyline his desire to read stories reflecting the diversity of American life speaks to the enormous potential of the serial form. At their best, serials can allow audiences to participate in the creative process by urging serious treatment of social issues, suggesting storylines, demanding diversity.

The "Parallel Lives" pilot seems to have proved very successful on a number of fronts. Gauthier is pleased with the interest his stories have generated and finds the immediate response very gratifying. The international dissemination of the serials means that he has received up to two hundred e-mails a day from readers, and feedback includes praise for his character development and storylines as well as suggestions for plot developments. In addition, the success of this first venture into cyberserials led to a new contract for Gauthier and Gilden, for their second series of fictions, to run on the Microsoft Network from February 1996.[37]

The sponsors were also pleased with the pilot. Despite the fact that the area was so deeply buried in the *Times* site, news spread by word of mouth, and people who had entered the area once were likely to return. That the storylines were the draw here was proved by a "spike" in the number of hits on Monday evenings when new episodes were posted. In addition, visitors hit the storylines and the advertising areas in about equal numbers, so the serial was effective as a draw for advertising. The average time spent within the serial area was 5 minutes 26 seconds, a high average for web sites. To confirm its effectiveness in advertising, Nabisco set up "mail hooks" within the advertising areas and included free offers such as coupons, recipe booklets, and so on. The success of these hooks proved a high level of reader responsiveness to on-line advertising. It is both ironic and interesting how closely this strategy parallels that used by Procter and Gamble to check the effectiveness of their soap opera as an advertising vehicle in 1931.

Although I have not interviewed readers of this serial, the amount of mail it generated indicates that the audience enjoyed both the form and the author's request for feedback. In addition, readers demonstrated the same desire for control over their fictions that many serial audiences manifest: they established an alternate storyline, "Parallel Parallel Lives," created and written by fans who disagreed with the choices made by the writer himself.

On-line serial producers have, then, combined the production, profit-generating, and audience-response techniques developed by earlier incarnations of the serial genre into a range of new forms. In linking serials like "Parallel Lives" to the larger context of serial production, one element is immediately apparent: the translation to new media has produced essential changes in the economic exigencies of serial production. In the case of these new on-line soaps, polling techniques have not yet been established; as we just saw, when Nabisco wanted to check its site's effectiveness as an advertising spot it simply recycled techniques developed for 1930s radio soaps. But widespread anxiety about controlling and legislating commercial use of the information highway, as well as widespread fantasies about the profits that may ensue, have the potential at least to work to the advantage of consumers who seek a voice in shaping the fictions they enjoy.

Given that serializers since Dickens have tended to shape their fictions over time to reflect the input of audiences, it is ironic that the one serial convention "Parallel Lives" does *not* make use of is this kind of collaboration between author and readers. At their best, serials not only provide a public forum for working through issues of immediate concern to their audiences but also become increasingly interactive, with writers working to incorporate audience suggestions into the production process. Gauthier, writer of "Parallel Lives," says that this interaction is his ultimate vision, but he has encountered two snags so far. First, the thirteen-week limit of his pilot project meant that the episodes were actually scripted before going on-line, a problem that will obviously be solved by the shift to long-term serials. Second, the prospect of using readers' ideas to generate (presumably profitable) storylines raises questions of intellectual property. In fact, a lawyer advising the *New York Times* website insisted that Gauthier and Gilden print a notice stating that all ideas sent to them became the property of the firm. This difficulty, too, will have to be resolved in the near future, as the issue of ownership of on-line ideas is codified.

All this discussion is not to celebrate on-line serial fiction as utopian cultural form but simply to suggest the need, in the face of the transmigration of serialized fiction into yet another medium, to revise long-standing misperceptions of serial audiences and to attend to the ways its model, negotiated as it may be, offers possibilities for increasing audience involvement with all forms of mass media. International communities of media audiences, exchanging information and working together to affect the narratives created by existent networks, have already developed on the 'net, and the potential for developing new, interactive ways of telling stories to reflect and thus shape our lives is obviously immense.

In this study, I have discussed ways in which serials mutate, taking on new themes, characters, messages, even media in response to the demands and available technologies of successive ages. In addition to its narrative suitability to the small screen, there is another way in which the serial genre represents Newcomb's "furthest advance in TV art." Soap opera's recent cultural visibility is no accident. With its quick cuts, multiple and competing voices, multiracial characters, and sudden alterations of plotlines in response to shifts in viewer interest or current events, the serial form epitomizes the post-Fordist world of "just in time" production, goods manufactured in small, easily alterable lots to satisfy a saturated, trend-prone consumer market. These characteristics, so often derided by critics, mean that serials have an essential role to play in shifting attitudes toward mass audiences. The form's responsiveness encourages audiences to become especially vocal and visible, and close attention to the voices of these readers and viewers can help to reverse conventional views of serial repetition (of plotlines, situations, and character types) as mindless and purposeless—and as consumed by similarly vacuous audiences—and increase appreciation of the pleasures of the text within the narrative of serial transformation across the media. Serial producers and consumers actively appropriate what has long been perceived as a junk genre and recycle it, transforming it to satisfy audience desire for a collaborative narrative experience. Because of their continued accountability to consumers, inscribing responsiveness to audiences within the production process, serials may offer cultural models for material transformation, models that come not from the directives of academic critics, not from marginal pockets of cultural resistance, but from within mass culture itself as a result of the influence of fans' voices over time. By engaging with the history of serial fiction and using the lessons of that history to work with these new serials, we join the process of creating a past that allows a viable future.

Notes

Introduction

1. Arnold, Sermon IV: "Moral Thoughtfulness" (text from Col. 1:9), 28; published in *Sermons*. This condemnation was both preached to the boys themselves and published in a collected edition of Arnold's sermons.

2. It is impossible to estimate how effective his remonstrances were in affecting attitudes toward reading. We know from retrospective, fictionalized testimony in *Tom Brown's Schooldays* that the doctor was equivalent to God in the nostalgic eyes of former Rugby boys; nevertheless, in that novel East "luxuriously devour[s]" an early number of *Pickwick*, "which was just coming out," and reads bits aloud to Tom without mention of the dread doctor's prohibition. Possibly East had missed chapel on the crucial Sunday.

3. Gramsci, "Serial Novels," in *Selections from Cultural Writings*, ed. Forgacs and Nowell-Smith, 34.

4. Although work on genre is ongoing across the media, the most innovative developments have occurred in film and television studies.

5. Benjamin's critique probably refers to the traditional rather than the serial novel, although Benjamin does discuss serials.

6. Most notably in the excellent and wide-ranging studies by Kathleen Tillotson, John Sutherland, J. Don Vann, and of course George Ford; also see the collaborative work of Linda Hughes and Michael Lund.

7. This figure is taken from the CBS media exposé "48 Hours: Behind the Soaps," which aired August 18, 1989.

8. "Television's Hottest Show," *Newsweek*, Sept. 28, 1981, 60. So far I have been unable to obtain more recent figures from the networks.

1. Mutual Friends: The Development of the Mass Serial

1. Serial publication of fiction (as opposed to nonfiction) has a slightly different history. Vann, *Victorian Novels in Serial*, provides a brief but careful recapitulation of the economic impetus behind part-published novels, which began not with the issue of texts in individual parts but with the reprinting of novels as filler in newspapers to enable evasion of the newspaper tax by making the papers long enough to qualify as

tax-free "pamphlets." In 1724, Parliament caught on to the scam and regulated the tax code. But the public, says Vann, "had developed a taste for serial fiction. . . . Henceforth publishers used serialization as a means of maintaining their readership" (1). Serial publication was, then, associated with the novel from its inception and helped to increase the readership of the new form by making it accessible to a wider audience. However, there were major differences between eighteenth- and nineteenth-century serialization of fiction. Eighteenth-century circulations were much smaller, and the novels were generally reprints although not always. The first magazine-published new novel was Tobias Smollett's *Sir Lancelot Greaves* (1760–61, in *British Magazine*), and the successive volumes of Samuel Richardson's *Clarissa* produced high levels of anticipation while readers waited for successive parts.

2. The novels of Richardson, Frances Burney, and Henry Fielding, best-sellers of the time and the closest eighteenth-century analogues to Dickens, Thackeray, and Braddon and other popular authors of the nineteenth century, sold between 2,000 and 6,000 copies in the first year, as compared with 40,000 to 50,000 per *part* for Dickens's novels. The usual number published per edition was from 750 for "serious" books to 1,250 for circulating-library novels (see Altick, *The English Common Reader*, 49; and Williams, *The Long Revolution*, 164).

3. Of course, the development of a mass audience would not have been possible at all without the extraordinary extent to which commodity prices dropped because of industrialization, thus increasing sales and, consequently, profits for capitalists. In 1814, the usual price of a complete novel (two or three volumes) was 15 to 18 shillings; this amount rose to 31 shillings 6 pence by 1840, but because of competition from part-published novels, fiction issued serially in magazines, and single-volume "cheap" reprints (as well as lower costs for labor and raw materials), the price had fallen to 8 shillings 4½ pence by 1853. The number of books published increased dramatically also: from an average of 372 per year at the end of the eighteenth century to 842 in 1828 to 2,500 in 1853 (Vincent, *Bread, Knowledge, and Freedom*, 115–16, and Altick, *The English Common Reader*, 263).

4. Quoted in Wicke, *Advertising Fictions*, 30.

5. In *Bread, Knowledge, and Freedom*, Vincent traces the concrete effects these material processes had on the working classes, as evidenced in working-class autobiographies—a new genre that significantly though not surprisingly also began in this era. Those born at the end of the eighteenth century lamented the dearth of cheap books, newspapers, periodicals, lectures, and so on, all of which had come into existence since their early struggles to educate themselves (113 and passim).

6. For the history of British serialization before Dickens, see Wiles, *Serial Publication*, and Robert D. Mayo, *The English Novel in the Magazines, 1740–1815* (Evanston: Northwestern University Press, 1962).

7. For this reading of events, see Sutherland's introduction to *The Annotated Dickens*.

8. From William Jerdan's *An Autobiography* (London: A. Hall, Virtue 1852); quoted in Tillotson, *Novels of the Eighteen-Forties*, 34.

9. [Richard Ford], "Oliver Twist," *Quarterly Review* 64 (June 1839), quoted in Philip Collins, *Dickens: The Critical Heritage*, 86. As we will see in the second chapter,

this parallel between texts and the mode of manufacture that produces both them and their readers is elaborated even further by comic strips, which can be seen metaphorically as Taylorist time-and-motion studies of narrative.

10. Unsigned review, "David Copperfield and Pendennis," *Prospective Review* (July 1851): 157–91, quoted in Phillip Collins, *Dickens: The Critical Heritage*, 264.

11. The publication schedules of periodicals reflect their target audience: "lowbrow" papers came out weekly, "highbrow" periodicals quarterly, middle-ground publications monthly, which implies a certain degree of class conditioning of attitudes toward time. On the other hand newspapers, serving a different function, actually reversed this pattern. "Respectable" papers appeared daily, but workers could not afford a daily outlay and tended to buy either a weekly newspaper or the weekend issue only, which produced a division in marketing and subject matter that continues today.

12. Of course, Dickens was not the only writer criticized for attempting to meddle with material conditions. In his famous harangue "The License of Modern Novelists" (*Edinburgh Review*, July 1857), James Fitzjames Stephen does slam Dickens for exercising "a very wide and a very pernicious political and social influence" by tackling "Poor Laws, or Imprisonment for Debt, or the Court of Chancery, or the harshness of Mill-Owners, or the stupidity of Parliament"; but he also lays into Charles Reade (objecting to his exposé of a boy's suicide while in prison) and Elizabeth Gaskell (who had recently been forced to retract "slurs" made against a woman supposedly involved with Branwell, in her biography of Charlotte Brontë). He remarks mockingly that "[Gaskell] seems to have thought, as Mr. Reade does, that it is part of the high commission of literature to try offences which elude the repression of the law" (all cited in Collins, *Dickens: The Critical Heritage*, 104, 125, 156).

13. Thus the Victorian serial parallels capitalism, while Caniff's *Terry and the Pirates* in its wartime incarnation echoes the U.S. obsession with remaking the world in its image, and soap opera has charted the American obsession with preserving the family and extended-family networks while allowing a fantasy of immortality and the endlessly new.

14. As we will see, serial reviews in periodicals reinforced this attitude by evaluating texts' worth in terms of the time and money required for their consumption as compared with their rewards—which may be social, sentimental, moral, and so forth.

15. For analysis of the politics of culture with specific reference to the ways debates over such concepts as "realism," "the individual," and social responsibility are reshaped within—and help to reshape—English novels from the 1830s to the 1860s, see Gallagher, *The Industrial Reformation of English Fiction*. For a mildly Marxist reading of the ways nineteenth-century narrative works to reconcile social malaise through language, see David, *Fictions of Resolution in Three Victorian Novels*. For a post-Watts discussion of the late-eighteenth-and early-nineteenth-century novel as "literally dramatiz[ing] a significant awareness of the individual's relationship to reality developing in the culture of the time," see Konigsberg, *Narrative Technique in the English Novel*, 9 and passim.

16. In my reading of Dickens's *Our Mutual Friend*, this hegemonic process is vividly illustrated by contradictions and disjunctions within the novel itself. Dickens

seeks to uphold widely held bourgeois values (especially the sanctity of the family, love, and motherhood, idealization of the child, and obsession with the purity of women) while challenging others (privileging of the moneyed class and the gentry, social control of the poor). Despite Dickens's reputation as "author of the people," in some ways his novels firmly uphold the status quo. For example, while he actively pursues social change, he tends to do so by demanding that the ruling classes enact reforms, rather than by aiding the disempowered to claim their rights.

17. Sept. 24, 1853; quoted in Philip Collins, *Dickens: The Critical Heritage,* 280.

18. This sense of connection is a function that television has taken on in our own time. See, for example, *A Day in the Life* of television, a massive ethnographic project undertaken by the BBC in 1988, which provides firsthand evidence that viewers watch the latest TV shows at least partly in order to have something to discuss with fellow workers, with whom they may otherwise have nothing in common.

19. Cited in Ackroyd, *Dickens' London,* 14.

20. For a discussion of these modes, see Kaplan's *Sacred Tears* and Tompkins's *Sensational Designs.*

21. Rose's call for a history of audiences is an important one. However, the conclusion of his own preliminary study—that "trash" had little impact on readers and can at most "communicate simple formulas" ("Rereading the English Common Reader," 61), while "'great' books . . . burst the boundaries of the mind" (62)—is simplistic.

22. Open University Unit 26, "Hard Times and Culture," 140.

23. "The Unknown Public," *Household Words* (Aug. 21, 1858): 217. Patten, *Charles Dickens and His Publishers*, finds no record that the large lending libraries (which accounted for up to 90 percent of the average three-decker's sales) purchased part-issued works (219). If true, this discovery can be seen as a kind of negative evidence for Dickens's working-class popularity. Given the sheer volume of sales of his works and the relatively small percentage of middle and upper classes within the population, if lending libraries were not buying him, then the working classes must have been.

24. It is crucial, for example, that today, when consumption of television is perceived as a private—or at most a family—activity, soap opera viewers go out of their way to form communities of viewers by arranging schedules around each other, watching taped shows while discussing them on the phone, or stealing time from work or lunch breaks to connect to computer-network discussion groups.

25. For an account of the ways working-class readers managed to acquire texts, see Vincent, *Bread, Knowledge, and Freedom*, chap. 6. Vincent also points out that Dickens's industrial novels helped create the genre of working-class autobiography since they "began to show how it was possible to incorporate the lowest elements of society into the highest form of literature. Burn dedicated the first edition of his autobiography to Dickens, and Green explained that he was provoked into writing by inaccuracies in Dickens' portrayal of cheap-jacks" (23).

26. Letter to Forster; quoted in Phillip Collins, "Dickens's Public Readings," 125.

27. Against this entry, the author later noted, "Done in Our Mutual."

28. The trope of drowning becomes central to other novels of the 1860s; for example, this serial advertised on the first page of the cheap newspaper *News of the*

World (June 5), in a format designed to fool readers, at first, into thinking it an actual "found drowned" notice: FOUND DROWNED. . . , the body of A FEMALE. She was elegantly attired, and evidently of superior rank." And below this notice the "real" advertisement proclaimed that "Blue Band: or, Female Detectives of London" would be issued in *Home Magazine.*

29. Sutherland, "Chips off the Block," in *Dickens and Other Victorians,* ed. Shattock, 117. Of course, some of these arguments hold true for magazine publication as well, but there the profits had to be split among a much larger number.

30. Schachterle, "*Oliver Twist* and Its Serial Predecessors," discusses the structural and thematic differences in part-issue versus magazine serials, most of which he attributed to the shorter installments and (sometimes) the pressures of weekly parts necessary for magazine publication (1–13).

31. Chapman and Hall accounts to Dickens.

32. Patten, *Charles Dickens and His Publishers,* reads the evidence differently: "Altogether Dickens made well over £12,000 from a serial on which Chapman and Hall lost £700" (308).

33. Chapman and Hall accounts to Dickens. Chief among advertising sites were the railway stalls of W.H. Smith House, where Chapman and Hall rented three hundred double crown frames and thirty long frames for four months each—important in indicating the increasing role of both the wholesaler and nationwide distribution in disposing of books.

34. Hatton and Cleaver, *Bibliography of Periodical Works,* 343–70.

35. By Philip Collins, Catherine Gallagher, Kathleen Tillotson, John Sutherland, and Linda Hughes and Michael Lund, among many others.

36. In the case of *Our Mutual Friend,* these include the frequent articles on garbage and industrial waste appearing previously to and contemporaneously with the novel or the constant pieces on paupers turned away from poorhouses and dying in the street or—like Betty Higden—actually preferring to do so rather than enter the infamous workhouses. Similarly, in our own time sensational news stories not only parallel similarly sensational soap story lines, but may—as in the O.J. Simpson trial—actually preempt soap coverage, thus replacing soaps in daily conversations among fans as well as in more formalized discussion formats such as computer bulletin boards.

37. From Smith, *Charles Reade,* 129; quoted in Altick, *The Presence of the Present,* 80.

38. Wilkie Collins, *No Name,* ch. 8, quoted in Altick, *The Presence of the Present,* 81.

39. Dickens responds to the charge in *Household Words,* Aug. 1, 1857.

40. For other accounts of women "passing" as men in the same time period, see "A Female Marine," *Reynolds's Newspaper,* Nov. 6, 1864, 6; "Singular Case of a Female Assuming Masculine Attire," *Reynolds's Newspaper,* July 23, 1865; and "Extraordinary Case," *London Sunday Times* Sept. 23, 1865, 7.

41. As Cotsell, *Companion to Our Mutual Friend,* points out, the novel's central plots are based on two plays by James Sheridan Knowles: *The Hunchback* (1832), in which "a young woman . . . is taught the value of true love by her guardian's pretence that he has become mercenary," and *The Daughter* (1837), in which "the daughter of a wrecker . . . is deceived into believing that her father murders someone who has been wrecked" (4).

42. Despite his reputation as "author of the people," throughout his career Dickens codes characters by their speech in reactionary rather than realistic ways. Middle-class characters speak the "Queen's English," lower-class ones either cockney or a country dialect. However, select members of the poor (either those actually of "gentle" birth, such as Oliver Twist, or those intended to be recuperated into the middle class, such as Lizzie Hexam) speak a language they could not possibly have learned in their apparent habitus. This inconsistency reveals Dickens's essentially middle-class worldview and intended audience: it was apparently impossible for him to envision a central, noncaricatured character expressing his or her thoughts in the language of the lower classes, which was itself automatically coded as humorous.

43. *London Sunday Times*, Jan. 29, 1865, 7, and June 4, 1865, 7; *Reynolds's Newspaper*, Jan. 8, 1865, 4.

44. This connection was inspired by Rohan McWilliam's paper "The Family Romance of the Tichborne Claimant: Radicalism and the Mid-Victorian Melodramatic Imagination," delivered at the Age of Equipoise? conference, Leeds Centre for Victorian Studies, Leeds, U.K., July 14–17, 1996.

45. Perhaps most explicit is the narrative aside in chapter 17 of *Oliver Twist*: "I am anxious to disclaim at once the slightest desire to tantalise my readers by leaving young Oliver Twist in situations of doubt and difficulty, and then flying off at a tangent to impertinent matters, which have nothing to do with him" (106 n. 3).

46. "Charles Dickens," *National Magazine*, no date (1845–1851?); in *Dickens Annual* 83.

47. J. Hillis Miller, *Charles Dickens*, 210, 292; quoted in Metz, "Artistic Reclamation of Waste," 60.

48. J. Hillis Miller, *Charles Dickens*, 279–327; cited in Brattin and Hornback, *Our Mutual Friend: An Annotated Bibliography*, 80.

49. Edward Johnson, *Charles Dickens: An Introduction to His Novels*, 1969; cited in Brattin and Hornback, *Our Mutual Friend: An Annotated Bibliography*, 143.

2. Terry's Expert Readers: The Rise of the Continuity Comic

1. "'Oliver Twist' by Boz," *Quarterly Review* (June 1839), 89.

2. For an analysis of the development of conventions, see Barker, *Comics*, 9–10, and Kunzle, *History of the Comic Strip*, especially the chapter "Movement Before Movies: The Language of the Comic Strip."

3. For an intriguing analysis of Fordism, see Rosenthal, "Jacked In," 80 and passim.

4. Comics are still considered by readers as essential to many papers, and editors acknowledge the need to respond to readers' demands. For example, during the paper shortage of 1973, one editor deleted all nonnews features but had to reinstate the comics because "we got the most reaction from readers of the bridge columns and the comics" (cited in Walker, *Backstage at the Strips*, 23). And in 1991, a *New York Times* story reported the response of *Washington Post* readers to the paper's dropping of three of its strips: "The Post invited readers to vent their opinions on comic strips and received 15,000 calls and 2,000 letters, most of them passionate

declarations of love for favorite strips or scathing attacks on comics thought to be rivals for the available space. . . . 'Everyone reads comic strips,' said Jay Kennedy, comics editor" (Jones, "To Papers, Funnies Are No Joke," D1).

5. Papers still do keep an in-house "bullpen" (the new but still derogatory term for "stable") or comic art department, which might include, for example, an editor (who makes sure, among other things, that strips do not violate local political or moral standards), several artists for lettering and repairs postedit, a benday person (to glue the dots that add depth to grey areas), two colorists, and a scheduler. But the artists themselves generally sign with syndicates (King Features is the largest), which now control three thousand features, five hundred of which are cartoons. Each paper pays from five dollars to five hundred dollars per week per strip, revenues that the syndicate and the cartoonist split fifty-fifty. Syndicates generally own strip copyrights, but artists who manage to retain rights can profit enormously; Charles Schultz, for example, earned an estimated $26 million in 1991.

6. One early comic strip deliberately plays on collapsing the two media: Ed Wheelan's *Minute Movies*, a Hearst-owned production begun in 1918, paralleled the development of silent films by establishing a stock company of actors and directors and moving from "cliff-hangers" and stage melodramas to adaptations of classic works of literature.

7. John Fell, *Film and the Narrative Tradition*; quoted in Inge, "*Comics as Culture*," 144.

8. Unless otherwise noted, all letters are from the Caniff Archive, Ohio State University, Columbus, Ohio.

9. Quoted in Sheridan, *Comics and Their Creators*, 158.

10. On the other hand, newspaper strips tended to be produced by older men, many (like Caniff) exempt from the draft, and therefore opportunities for female newspaper-strip artists were fewer—though wartime certainly improved conditions for women even in the newspaper industry, as in most other workplaces.

11. The longevity of "Terry" meant that stereotyping became increasingly taboo over the course of its run. By its last years, as we will see, the "screwy Chinese" character, Connie, a caricature of Americans' perception of Asians, had been replaced by the handsome, barely identifiably ethnic officer Bucky Wing.

3. The Future of the Serial Form

1. Unless otherwise noted, this and all subsequent offset quotations are selected from recent *All My Children* and *One Life to Live* episodes.

2. This relation to time has, of course, in turn been complicated by technological developments—VCRs, for example—which will be discussed later in this section.

3. See Stedman, *The Serials*, chap. 1.

4. Reinforcing VCR domination of the soap experience, the Jan. 23 issue of *Soap Digest* featured a full-page ad for pink-labeled videocassettes with matching cases reading "All My Soaps . . . Your special tape for recording soap operas." The *Soap Digest* table of contents also reflects the new primacy of video, including as it

does a weekly feature called the "VCR alert," which keeps viewers informed about upcoming soap highlights (weddings, deaths, location shoots) that viewers will want to tape and save for repeated viewing.

5. However, it is important to emphasize that the essential structure of the soap opera, developed under earlier conditions of production, at least so far maintains its peculiar relation to narrative time. VCR-addicted viewers wishing to save those special soap moments have difficulty doing so because of the sheer volume of output: the storage space required for even a month's worth of episodes is considerable, as is the cost of videotapes. Most viewers have a single tape on which they record each day's episode, taping over it after viewing.

6. Michael Malone, head writer of *One Life to Live*, unwittingly epitomized this condescension toward Nixon when accepting the 1994 Daytime Emmy Award for "best writing team." He thanked Nixon for "creat[ing] the world that we live in" and then added, "If Charles Dickens is the father of daytime, she's his daughter, and we're very proud to be among her children."

7. These figures were true at the time of analysis (spring 1994); however, writing teams change constantly.

8. This function was unwittingly acknowledged by the press coverage of the Anita Hill/Clarence Thomas case. Repeatedly and derogatorily labeled a "soap opera," the case did in fact serve the discursive function of actual soaps, making issues of race and sexual harassment the focus of nationwide debate. The parallel is even more striking in that network soaps were preempted and replaced by coverage of the hearings. Unfortunately, these "hearings" were not a space free from consequences.

9. See, for example, Fiske, "The Cultural Economy of Fandom," in *The Adoring Audience*, ed. Lewis, as well as other essays in the same collection; see also Jenkins, *Textual Poachers*.

10. Frenier, "Seventh and Eighth Graders 'Read' Daytime Soap Operas," in *Staying Tuned*, ed Frentz, 65; author's emphasis.

11. A wedding, divorce, operation, birth can stretch over weeks of episodes, though this tendency is changing as daytime television increasingly incorporates elements of adventure series, prime-time soaps, MTV, and other televisual genres.

12. Maurice Valency, *The Flower and the Castle*, cited in Quigley, *The Modern Stage*, 71.

13. Hence Marcia Kinder's suggestion that the "open-ended, slow paced, multiclimaxed" soap form is "in tune with patterns of female sexuality" (quoted in Modleski, *Loving with a Vengeance*, 98)—though I think it is important to move beyond essentialist explanations of serial narrative appeal, especially given the fact that the soap audience is now 30 percent male.

14. For an exposition of Lacanian feminist film theory, see Silverman, *The Subject of Semiotics*, 158 and passim.

15. This topic will be discussed in detail in the following two sections of this chapter.

16. Quoted in Pond, "Shades of Change," 26.

17. Above examples are from the *All My Children* fans on the Usenet soap discussion group rec.arts.television.soaps. The master list of "soap rules" is divided into eight sections: "special exemptions to Pine Valley laws," "laws applicable to families in Pine Valley," "finance in Pine Valley," and so on.

18. Classes for new or would-be soap stars teach the "freeze" technique, among other soap-specific skills.

19. Jane Feuer, in her "Narrative Form in American Network Television," draws on and extends Ellis's discussion, stressing the psychological positioning of the viewer in each form and arguing that the dominant model of a "cinema apparatus" does not work for television, whose implied spectator is not "the isolated, immobilized pre-Oedipal individual described by Metz and Baudry in their metapsychology of the cinema, but rather a post-Oedipal, fully socialized family member" (101–113).

20. January 10, 1992. David Canary plays twin brothers Adam and Stuart Chandler on *All My Children*.

21. Many thanks to the anonymous former viewer mail department employee who volunteered to waylay a number of letters (after quantitative and qualitative analysis by the department) and forward them to me in 1989.

22. To determine letter-writers' awareness of *All My Children* as constructed text, I looked for references to the distinction between the actor and the character he/she portrays; the importance of actors' contract negotiations, soap opera conventions, and competition with other soaps in determining story lines; and awareness of viewer power—as rulers of the ratings—over *AMC* writers and producers.

23. Quoted with permission of the author.

24. Nicknames are the prime example, as are characters apparently commenting on fans' discussions of them; for example, a character named Charlie—dubbed "choppers" by the net due to his large teeth— asked why another character did not like him: "Is it because my teeth are too big, or what?"

25. I received 15 responses to my query.

26. As mentioned earlier, soon after the rape the character Powell Lord was depicted as unproblematically "good": he apologized for his role in the rape, was forgiven, and had apparently put the whole thing behind him. Viewers were appalled by this facile dismissal of Powell's part in the crime. They complained to each other on the net, wrote individual letters to the show, and finally (July 1994) collaborated on a letter to producers; they began, diplomatically, by praising the show's earlier handling of the story line, but then argued that Powell's overnight redemption was both offensive and untenable. A month later, Powell and his friends suddenly "realized" that he had repressed his role in the rape too quickly, and he began participating in therapy. Fan complaints continued, however, and Powell eventually took over the "monster" role in the story line, as what he had repressed consumed his personality. He became a serial rapist and was written off the show in short order.

27. Other redeemed rapists include Jack Deveraux and Lawrence Alamain on *Days of Our Lives*, and Roger Thorpe on *Guiding Light*.

28. *Soap Opera Digest*, Aug. 2, 1994; quoted from a r.a.t.s. post, July 17, 1994.

29. Michael Logan, "Rapists: Unlikely Heartthrobs." *TVGuide*, June 18, 1994.

30. r.a.t.s. post, June 20, 1994.

31. These and all other fan comments have been quoted, with permission when contact could be made with their authors, from posts to the Usenet rec.arts.tv.soaps bulletin board.

32. Berman, *How Television Sees Its Audience*, 73.

33. Or what were originally dubbed "Agnes Nixon stories"; Nixon created *All My Children* and *One Life to Live*, both now known as ground-breaking shows.

34. Although soaps do occasionally tackle racism, their approach is very different and fairly problematic. In the example cited here, for example, the male officer is also black, so the issue of race is essentially silenced.

35. Soap home page: http://members.aol.com/soaplinks/index.html

ALT.DAYS: http://www.io.com/~jlc/alt_days/

As the Web Turns: http://metzger.internet-plaza.net/soap/

As the WWWeb Turns: http://www.rubyslippers.com/sadtuna/asturns.html

East Village: http://www.theeastvillage.com/

The Spot: http://www.thespot.com

Until Tomorrow: http://www.starwave.com

36. The Starwave "Frequently Asked Questions" area states that "each service will always include a free area with lots of great content. Over time, each service will also include some 'premium' areas for which there will be modest fees."

37. Mark Gauthier, personal telephone interview, October 20, 1995. All information about the production and reception of "Parallel Lives" was obtained during this interview.

Bibliography

Archives

Caniff, Milton. Papers. Ohio State University, Columbus, OH.
Chapman and Hall accounts 1862–1870. Courtesy of the Forster-Dyce Collection, box 18.3. Victoria and Albert Museum, London.
Dickens Annual Scrapbooks. Courtesy of the Dickens House Museum, London.

General Works

Adorno, Theodor, and Max Horkheimer. 1986. *Dialectic of Enlightenment*. Trans. John Cumming. New York: Continuum.
Barrett, M., P. Corrigan, A. Kuhn, & J. Wolff, eds. 1979. *Ideology and Cultural Production*. London: Croom Helm.
Beniger, James R. 1986. *The Control Revolution: Technological and Economic Origins of the Information Society*. Cambridge: Harvard Univ. Press.
Benjamin, Walter. 1968. "Some Motifs in Baudelaire." In *Charles Baudelaire: A Lyric Poet in the Era of High Capitalism*. Trans. Harry Zohn. Reprint. 1985. London: Verso.
———. 1969. "The Storyteller" and "The Work of Art in the Age of Mechanical Reproduction." In *Illuminations*, ed. Hanna Arendt, trans. Harry Zohn. New York: Schocken Books.
———. 1986. *Reflections*. Ed. Peter Demetz, trans. Edmund Jephcott. New York: Schocken Books.
Berman, Ronald. 1987. *How Television Sees Its Audience*. Newbury Park, Calif.: Sage Publications.
Bourdieu, Pierre. 1984. *Distinction: A Social Critique of the Judgement of Taste*. trans. R. Nice, Cambridge: Harvard Univ. Press.
Brooks, Peter. 1976. *The Melodramatic Imagination*. Reprint 1985. New York: Columbia Univ. Press.
Clarke, J., C. Critcher and R. Johnson, eds. 1979. *Working Class Culture: Studies in History and Theory*. London: Hutchinson University Library.
de Lauretis, Teresa. 1987. *Technologies of Gender: Essays on Theory, Film, and Fiction*. Bloomington: Indiana Univ. Press.

Doane, Mary Ann. 1987. *The Desire to Desire: the Woman's Film of the 1940s*. Bloomington: Indiana Univ. Press.

Doray, Bernard. 1988. *From Taylorism to Fordism: A Rational Madness*. Trans. David Macey. London: Free Association Books.

Douglas, Ann. 1977. *The Feminization of American Culture*. New York: Knopf.

Eisenstein, Sergei. 1967. "Dickens, Griffith, and the Film Today." In *Film Form and the Film Sense*. Ed. and trans. Jay Leyda. Cleveland: World Publishing.

Ewen, Stuart. 1976. *Captains of Consciousness: Advertising and the Social Roots of the Consumer Culture*. New York: McGraw Hill.

Fiske, John. 1989. "Moments of Television: Neither the Text nor the Audience." In *Remote Control: Television, Audiences, and Cultural Power*, ed. Seiter et al. New York: Routledge.

———. 1992. "The Cultural Economy of Fandom." In *The Adoring Audience: Fan Culture and Popular Media*, ed. Lisa A. Lewis. New York: Routledge.

Fox, Richard Wightman, and T.J. Jackson Lears, eds. 1983. *The Culture of Consumption*. New York: Pantheon Books.

Geertz, Clifford. 1975. *The Interpretation of Cultures*. London: Hutchinson.

Gendron, Bernard. 1986. "Theodor Adorno Meets the Cadillacs." In *Studies in Entertainment: Critical Approaches to Mass Culture*, ed. Tania Modleski. Bloomington: Indiana Univ. Press.

Gramsci, Antonio. 1971. "Americanism and Fordism." In *Selections from the Prison Notebooks*. Ed. and trans. Quintin Hoare and Geoffrey Nowell Smith. New York: International Publishers.

Gramsci, Antonio. 1985. *Selections from Cultural Writings*. Ed. David Forgacs and Geoffrey Nowell Smith, trans. William Boelhower. trans. London: Lawrence and Wishart.

Hagedorn, Roger. 1988. "Technology and Economic Exploitation: The Serial as a Form of Narrative Presentation." *Wide Angle* 10, no. 4: 4–12.

Jameson, Fredric. 1971. *Marxism and Form*. Princeton: Princeton Univ. Press.

———. 1981. *The Political Unconscious: Narrative as a Socially Symbolic Act*. Ithaca: Cornell Univ. Press.

Jenkins, Henry. 1992. *Textual Poachers: Television Fans and Participatory Culture*. New York: Routledge.

Kaplan, E. Ann. 1987. *Rocking Around the Clock: Music Television, Postmodernism, and Consumer Culture*. New York: Methuen.

Kern, Stephen. 1983. *The Culture of Time and Space, 1880–1918*. Cambridge: Harvard Univ. Press.

Lacan, Jacques. 1968. *The Language of the Self*. Ed. Anthony Wilden. Baltimore: Johns Hopkins Press.

Leavis, Q.D. 1932. *Fiction and the Reading Public*. Reprint. 1968. London: Chatto and Windus.

Lewis, Lisa A., ed. 1992. *The Adoring Audience: Fan Culture and Popular Media*. New York: Routledge.

Macherey, Pierre. 1978. *A Theory of Literary Production*. Trans. G. Wall. London: Routledge and Kegan Paul.

Mumford, Lewis. 1934. *Technics and Civilization*. New York: Harcourt, Brace, and World.

Mursell, James L. 1936. *Streamline Your Mind*. Philadelphia: J.B. Lippincott.

Neale, Stephen. 1980. *Genre*. London: British Film Institute.

———. 1990. "Questions of Genre." *Screen* 31:1 (spring 1990): 45–66.

Radway, Janice. 1984. *Reading the Romance: Women, Patriarchy, and Popular Literature*. Reprint. 1991. Chapel Hill: Univ. of North Carolina Press.

Rosenthal, Pam. 1991. "Jacked In: Fordism, Cyberpunk, Marxism." *Socialist Review* 21:1 (Jan.-March 1991): 79–103.

Stallybrass, Peter, and Allon White. 1986. *The Politics and Poetics of Transgression*. Ithaca: Cornell Univ. Press.

Stedman, Raymond William. 1971. *The Serials: Suspense and Drama by Installment*. Norman: Univ. of Oklahoma Press.

Todorov, Tzvetan. 1973. *The Fantastic*. Trans. Richard Howard. Cleveland: Press of Case Western Reserve University.

———. 1990. *Genres in Discourse*. Trans. Catherine Porter. Cambridge: Cambridge Univ. Press.

Weeks, Jeffrey. 1981. *Sex, Politics, and Society*. New York: Longman.

Wicke, Jennifer. 1988. *Advertising Fictions: Literature, Advertisement, and Social Reading*. New York: Columbia Univ. Press.

Williams, Raymond. 1958. *Culture and Society, 1780–1950*. Reprint. 1983. New York: Columbia Univ. Press.

———. 1961. *The Long Revolution*. London: Chatto and Windus.

———. 1973. *The Country and the City*. New York: Oxford Univ. Press.

———. 1975. *Television: Technology and Cultural Forms*. New York: Schocken Books.

———. 1977. *Marxism and Literature*. New York: Oxford Univ. Press.

Worpole, Ken. 1984. *Reading by Numbers*. London: Comedia Publishing Group.

The Nineteenth Century Novel

Ackroyd, Peter. 1987. *Dickens' London*. London: Headline.

Altick, Richard D. 1957. *The English Common Reader: A Social History of the Mass Reading Public, 1800–1900*. Chicago: Univ. of Chicago Press.

———. 1991. *The Presence of the Present*. Columbus: Ohio State Univ. Press.

Arnold, Thomas. 1878. *Sermons*. London: Longmans, Green.

Bentley, Nicolas, Nina Burgis, and Michael Slater. 1990. *The Dickens Index*. New York: Oxford Univ. Press.

Blake, Andrew. 1989. *Reading Victorian Fiction: The Cultural Context and Ideological Content of the Nineteenth-Century Novel*. Basingstoke: Macmillan.

Brattin, Joel A., and Bert G. Hornback. 1984. *Our Mutual Friend: An Annotated Bibliography*. New York: Garland.

Butt, John. 1969. *Pope, Dickens, and Others*. Edinburgh: Edinburgh Univ. Press.

Butt, John, and Kathleen Tillotson. 1957. *Dickens at Work*. London: Methuen.

Carlisle, Janice. 1981. *The Sense of an Audience*. Athens: Univ. of Georgia Press.

Chesterton, G.K. 1911. *Appreciations and Criticisms of the Works of Charles Dickens*. London: J.M. Dent and Sons.

Churchill, R.C. 1979. "The Monthly Dickens and the Weekly Dickens." *Contemporary Review* 234 (Feb.): 97–128.

Collins, Philip. 1962. *Dickens and Crime*. New York: St. Martin's.

———. 1969. "Dickens's Public Readings." *Studies in the Novel* 1:2 (summer): 118–132.

———, ed. 1971. *Dickens: The Critical Heritage*. London: Routledge and Kegan Paul.

———. 1972. "Reading Aloud: A Victorian Metier." Lincoln, U.K.: Tennyson Research Centre, Tennyson society. Tennyson Society Monographs #5.

Collins, Wilkie. 1862. *No Name*. London: Sampson Low.

Coolidge, Archibald C., Jr. 1967. *Charles Dickens as Serial Novelist*. Ames: Iowa State Univ. Press.

Cotsell, Michael. 1986. *The Companion to Our Mutual Friend*. London: Allen and Unwin.

Cruse, Amy. 1935. *The Victorians and Their Books*. London: Allen and Unwin.

Cvetkovich, Ann. 1992. *Mixed Feelings: Feminism, Mass Culture, and Victorian Sensationalism*. New Brunswick, N.J.: Rutgers Univ. Press.

Darwin, Bernard. 1930. *The Dickens Advertiser*. New York: Macmillan.

David, Deirdre. 1981. *Fictions of Resolution in Three Victorian Novels*. New York: Columbia Univ. Press.

Dickens, Charles. 1972. *Letters and Writings, 1844–1855*. Princeton: Princeton Univ. Press.

Dickens, Charles. n.d. *Household Words*. London: Bradbury and Evans.

———. 1966. *Oliver Twist*. Oxford: Clarendon Press.

———. 1967. *Little Dorrit*. London: Penguin.

———. 1989. *Our Mutual Friend*. New York: Oxford Univ. Press World's Classics.

Feltes, Norman N. 1986. *Modes of Production of Victorian Novels*. Chicago: Univ. of Chicago Press.

Flint, Kate, ed. 1987. *The Victorian Novelist: Social Problems and Social Change*. London: Croom Helm.

Ford, George H. 1955. *Dickens and His Readers*. reprint 1965. New York: Norton.

Forster, John. 1875. *Life of Charles Dickens*. London: Chapman and Hall.

Gallagher, Catherine. 1985. *The Industrial Reformation of English Fiction*. Chicago: Univ. of Chicago Press.

Gissing, George. 1924. *Charles Dickens*. New York: Dodd, Mead and Co.

Hamer, Mary. 1987. *Writing by Numbers: Trollope's Serial Fiction*. Cambridge: Cambridge Univ. Press.

Harden, Edgar F. 1979. *The Emergence of Thackeray's Serial Fiction*. Athens: Univ. of Georgia Press.

Hatton, Thomas, and Arthur Cleaver. 1933. *A Bibliography of the Periodical Works of Charles Dickens*. London: Chapman and Hall.

Horton, Susan R. 1981. *The Reader in the Dickens World*. London: Macmillan.

Hughes, Linda K., and Michael Lund. 1991. *The Victorian Serial*. Charlottesville: Univ. Press of Virginia.

James, Louis. 1963. *Fiction for the Working Man: 1830–1850*. New York: Oxford Univ. Press.

Kaplan, Fred. 1987. *Sacred Tears: Sentimentality in Victorian Literature*. Princeton: Princeton Univ. Press.

Konigsberg, Ira. 1985. *Narrative Technique in the English Novel: Defoe to Austen.* Hamden, Conn: Archon Books.

Lovell, Terry. 1987. *Consuming Fiction.* London: Verso.

Mayhew, Henry. 1864. *London Labour and the London Poor.* London: C. Griffin.

McKendrick, Neil, John Brewer, and J.H. Plumb, eds. 1982. "The Birth of a Consumer Society." In *The Birth of a Consumer Society: the Commercialization of Eighteenth-Century England.* Bloomington: Indiana Univ. Press.

Metz, Nancy Aycock. 1979. "The Artistic Reclamation of Waste in *Our Mutual Friend.*" *Nineteenth Century Fiction* 34:1 (June): 59–72.

Miller, D.A. 1988. *The Novel and the Police.* Berkeley: Univ. of California Press.

Miller, J. Hillis. 1958. *Charles Dickens: The World of His Novels.* Cambridge: Harvard Univ. Press.

Mundhenk, Rosemary. 1979. "The Education of the Reader in *Our Mutual Friend.*" *Nineteenth Century Fiction* 34:1 (June): 41–58.

Newspaper Press Directory. 1864. London: C. Mitchell.

Patten, Robert. 1978. *Charles Dickens and His Publishers.* Oxford: Clarendon Press.

Plumb, J.H. 1982. "The Commercialization of Leisure in Eighteenth-Century England." In *The Birth of a Consumer Society: The Commercialization of Eighteenth-Century England,* ed. McKendrick et al. Bloomington: Indiana Univ. Press.

Robinson, Henry Crabb. 1938. *Henry Crabb Robinson on Books and Their Writers,* ed. Edith Morley. London: J.M. Dent and sons.

Rose, Jonathan. 1992. "Rereading the English Common Reader: A Preface to a History of Audiences." *Journal of the History of Ideas* 53:47–70.

Schacterle, Lance. 1974. "*Oliver Twist* and Its Serial Predecessors." *Dickens Studies Annual* 3:1–13.

Schlicke, Paul. 1985. *Dickens and Popular Entertainment.* London: Allen and Unwin.

Sedgwick, Eve Kosofsky. 1985. *Between Men: English Literature and Male Homosocial Desire.* New York: Columbia Univ. Press.

Shattock, Joanne, ed. 1988. *Dickens and Other Victorians.* Basingstoke: Macmillan.

Shea, F.X. 1968. "Mr. Venus Observed: The Plot Change in *Our Mutual Friend.*" *Papers on Language and Literature* 4:2 (spring): 170–181.

Smith, Elton. 1976. *Charles Reade.* Boston: Twayne Publishers.

Sutherland, John A. 1976. *Victorian Novelists and Publishers.* London: Athlone Press.

———. 1988. "Chips Off the Block: Dickens's Serialising Imitators." In *Dickens and Other Victorians.* ed. Joanne Shattock. Basingstoke: Macmillan.

Thackeray, William Makepeace. 1853–55. *The Newcomes.* London: Bradbury and Evans.

Tillotson, Kathleen. 1954. *Novels of the Eighteen-Forties.* New York: Oxford Univ. Press.

Tompkins, Jane. 1985. *Sensational Designs: The Cultural Work of American Fiction.* New York: Oxford Univ. Press.

Vann, J. Don. 1985. *Victorian Novels in Serial.* New York: The Modern Language Association of America.

Vicinus, Martha, ed. 1977. *A Widening Sphere: Changing Roles of Victorian Women.* Bloomington: Indiana Univ. Press.

Vincent, David. 1981. *Bread, Knowledge, and Freedom.* London: Europa Publications.

Watt, Ian. 1957. *The Rise of the Novel.* London: Chatto and Windus.

Waugh, Arthur. 1931. *A Hundred Years of Publishing.* London: Chapman and Hall.

Welch, Charles H. 1960. *An Autobiography.* Banstead, U.K.: Berean Publishing Trust.

Wiles, R.M. 1957. *Serial Publication in England Before 1750.* Cambridge: Cambridge Univ. Press.

Williams, Raymond. 1970. *The English Novel from Dickens to Lawrence.* London: Chatto and Windus.

Comics

Adams, John Paul, Rick Marschall, and T. Nantier. 1981. *Milton Caniff, Rembrandt of the Comic Strip.* Jackson Heights, New York: Flying Buttress Publications.

Banta, Martha. 1993. *Taylored Lives: Narrative Productions in the Age of Taylor, Veblen, and Ford.* Chicago: University of Chicago Press.

Barker, Martin. 1984. *A Haunt of Fears.* London: Pluto Press.

———. 1989. *Comics: Ideology, Power, and the Critics.* Manchester: Manchester Univ. Press.

Berger, Arthur Asa. 1974. *The Comic-Stripped American.* Baltimore: Penguin Books.

Blackbeard, Bill, and Martin Williams, eds. 1977. *The Smithsonian Collection of Newspaper Comics.* Washington, D.C.: Smithsonian Institution Press.

Caniff, Milton. 1984–1987. *Terry and the Pirates.* Jackson Heights, New York: Flying Buttress Classics Library.

———. 1987. *Male Call, 1942–1946: Featuring Miss Lace,* ed. Peter Poplaski. Princeton, Wisc.: Kitchen Sink Press.

Caswell, Lucy Shelton. 1986. *The Festival of Cartoon Art.* Columbus: Ohio State Univ. Libraries (illustrated catalogue of exhibition).

Cohen, Stanley. 1973. "The Failure of the American Mind." In *Perspectives on 20th Century America,* ed. Otis L. Graham, Jr. New York: Dodd, Mead.

Couperie, Pierre, Maurice Horn, Proto Destefanis, Edouarel Froncois, Claude Moliterni, Gérald Gassiot-Talabot. 1968. *A History of the Comic Strip.* Trans. Eileen B. Hennessy. New York: Crown Publishers.

Dorf, Shel, ed. 1987. *Milton Caniff's America.* Forestville, Calif.: Eclipse Books.

Dorfman, Ariel, and Armand Mattelart. 1984. *How to Read Donald Duck: Imperialist Ideology in the Disney Comic.* Trans. David Kunzle. 2d ed. New York: International General.

Eisner, Will. 1985. *Comics & Sequential Art.* Tamarac, Fla.: Poorhouse Press.

Goulart, Ron. 1975. *The Adventurous Decade.* New Rochelle, N.Y.: Arlington House.

Gilbert, James. 1986. *A Cycle of Outrage: America's Reaction to the Juvenile Delinquent in the 1950s.* New York: Oxford Univ. Press.

Hardy, Charles, and Gail F. Stern, eds. 1986. *Ethnic Images in the Comics.* Philadelphia: The Balch Institute for Ethnic Studies.

Inge, M. Thomas 1979. "Comics as Culture." *Journal of Popular Culture* 12 (spring). Special issue.

Jones, Alex S. 1991. "To Papers, Funnies Are No Joke." *New York Times,* April 8, 1991, D1.

Kunzle, David. 1990. *The History of the Comic Strip: The Nineteenth Century.* Berkeley: Univ. of California Press.

Lupoff, Dick, and Don Thompson, eds. 1970. *All in Color for a Dime.* New Rochelle, N.Y.: Arlington House.

Marschall, Richard. 1989. *America's Greatest Comic-Strip Artists.* New York: Abbeville Press.

Morrison, Miriam E. 1978. "The Perceived Impact of Terry and the Pirates During the War Years, 1939–1945, as Reflected in the General Correspondence of Milton Caniff." Unpublished thesis, Ohio State University, Columbus.

O'Brien, Frank M. 1928. *The Story of The Sun.* New York: D. Appleton.

O'Sullivan, Judith. 1971. *The Art of the Comic Strip.* College Park, Md.: University of Maryland, Department of Art.

Reitberger, Reinhold, and Wolfgang Fuchs. 1972. *Comics: Anatomy of a Mass Medium.* Trans. Nadia Fowler. Boston: Little, Brown.

Robbins, Trina, and catherine yronwode. 1985. *Women and the Comics.* Guerneville, Calif.: Eclipse Books.

Robinson, Jerry. 1974. *The Comics.* New York: G.P. Putnam's Sons.

Science Research Associates. 1956. *The Sunday Comics: A Socio-Psychological Study with Attendant Advertising Implications.* Chicago [no publisher].

Scott, Randall W. 1988. *Comic Books and Strips: An Information Sourcebook.* Phoenix: Oryx Press.

Seldes, Gilbert. 1924. *The 7 Lively Arts.* Reprint. 1957. New York: Sagamore Press.

Sheridan, Martin. 1942. *Comics and Their Creators.* Boston: Hale, Cushman and Flint.

Silbermann, Alphons, and H.D. Dyroff, eds. 1986. *Comics and Visual Culture: Research Studies from Ten Countries.* New York: K.G. Saur.

Uslan, Michael, ed. 1979. *America at War: The Best of DC War Comics.* New York: Simon and Schuster.

Walker, Mort. 1975. *Backstage at the Strips.* New York: Mason/Charter.

Wertham, Fredric. 1954. *Seduction of the Innocent.* New York: Rinehart.

Wheelan, Ed. 1977. *Minute Movies.* The Hyperion Library of Classic American Comic Strips. Westport, Conn.: Hyperion.

Yronwode, Catherine. 1987. "Tribute." In *Milton Caniff's America*, ed. Shel Dorf. Forestville, Calif.: Eclipse Books.

Zimmerman, Carla B. 1986. "From Chop-Chop to Wu Cheng: The Evolution of the Chinese Character in *Blackhawk* Comic Books." In *Ethnic Images in the Comics*, ed. Charles Hardy and Gail F. Stern. New York: Balch Institute for Ethnic Studies.

Soap Opera

Allen, Robert. 1992. "Audience-Oriented Criticism and Television." In *Channels of Discourse, Reassembled*, ed. Robert C. Allen. Chapel Hill: Univ. of North Carolina Press.

Allen, Robert C. 1985. *Speaking of Soap Operas.* Chapel Hill: Univ. of North Carolina Press.

————. 1989. "Bursting Bubbles: 'Soap Opera,' Audiences, and the Limits of Genre." In *Remote Control: Television, Audiences, and Cultural Power*, ed. Ellen Seiter et al. New York: Routledge.

Ang, Ien. 1985. *Watching Dallas*. New York: Methuen.

————. 1991. *Desperately Seeking the Audience*. New York: Routledge.

Brown, Mary Ellen. 1994. *Soap Opera and Women's Talk: The Pleasure of Resistance*. Thousand Oaks, Calif.: Sage.

Buckman, Peter. 1985. *All for Love: A Study on Soap Opera*. Salem, N.H.: Salem House.

Cantor, Muriel, and Suzanne Pingree. 1983. *The Soap Opera*. Beverly Hills, Calif.: Sage.

Carveth, Rodney Andrew. 1992. "Exploring the Effects of 'Love in the Afternoon': Does Soap Opera Viewing Create Perceptions of a Promiscuous World?" In *Staying Tuned: Contemporary Soap Opera Criticism*, ed. Suzanne Frentz. Bowling Green, Ohio: Bowling Green State Univ. Popular Press.

Cassata, Mary, and Thomas Skill. 1983. *Life on Daytime Television*. Norwood, N.J.: Ablex.

Cubitt, Sean. 1991. *Timeshift: On Video Culture*. New York: Routledge.

Ellis, John. 1982. *Visible Fictions*. London: Routledge & Kegan Paul.

Feuer, Jane. 1986. "Narrative Form in American Network Television." In *High Theory/Low Culture: Analysing Popular Television and Film*, ed. Colin MacCabe. Manchester: Manchester Univ. Press.

Flitterman, Sandy. 1983. "The Real Soap Operas: Television Commercials." In *Regarding Television: Critical Approaches—An Anthology*, ed. E. Ann Kaplan. Frederick, M.: University Publications of America.

Frenier, Mariam Darce. 1992. "Seventh and Eighth Graders 'Read' Daytime Soap Operas." In *Staying Tuned: Contemporary Soap Opera Criticism*, ed. Suzanne Frentz. Bowling Green, Ohio: Bowling Green State Univ. Press.

Frentz, Suzanne, ed. 1992. *Staying Tuned: Contemporary Soap Opera Criticism*. Bowling Green, Ohio: Bowling Green State Univ. Press.

Frentz, Suzanne, and Bonnie Ketter, 1992. "Everyday Sex in Everyday Drama." In *Staying Tuned: Contemporary Soap Opera Criticism*, ed. Suzanne Frentz. Bowling Green, Ohio: Bowling Green State Univ. Press.

Intintoli, Michael James. 1984. *Taking Soaps Seriously*. New York: Praeger.

Joyrich, Lynn. 1986. "All That Television Allows: TV Melodrama, Postmodernism and Consumer Culture." *Camera Obscura* 16:129–54.

LaGuardia, Robert. 1983. *Soap World*. New York: Arbor House.

Modleski, Tania. 1979. "The Search for Tomorrow in Today's Soap Operas." *Film Quarterly* 33, no. 1:12–21.

————. 1982. *Loving with a Vengeance: Mass-Produced Fantasies for Women*. Hamden, Conn.: Archon Books.

————, ed. 1986. *Studies in Entertainment: Critical Approaches to Mass Culture*. Bloomington: Indiana Univ. Press.

Morley, David. 1980. *The Nationwide Audience: Structure and Decoding*. London: British Film Institute.

———. 1986. *Family Television: Cultural Power and Domestic Leisure*. London: Comedia Publishing Group.

Newcomb, Horace. 1974. *TV: The Most Popular Art*. New York: Anchor.

Nochimson, Martha. 1992. *No End to Her: Soap Opera and the Female Subject*. Berkeley: Univ. of California Press.

Pond, Steve. 1990. "Shades of Change." *US* (May 28): 20–26.

Porter, Dennis. 1982. "Soap Time: Thoughts on a Commodity Art Form." In *Television: The Critical View*, 3d ed., ed. Horace Newcomb. New York: Oxford Univ. Press.

Quigley, Austin E. 1985. *The Modern Stage and Other Worlds*. New York: Methuen.

Seiter, Ellen, Hans Borchers, Gabriele Kreutzner and Eva-Marie Warth, eds. 1990. "Don't Treat us Like We're So Stupid and Naive: Towards an Ethnography of Soap Opera Viewers." In *Remote Control: Television, Audiences, and Cultural Power*. London: Routledge, Chapman and Hall.

Silverman, Kaja. 1983. *The Subject of Semiotics*. New York: Oxford Univ. Press.

Soares, Manuela. 1978. *The Soap Opera Book*. New York: Harmony Books.

Spigel, Lynn. 1985. "Detours in the Search for Tomorrow: Tania Modleski's *Loving with a Vengeance*." *Camera Obscura* 13–14 (spring-summer): 215–34.

Stone, Laurie. 1994. "Coming clean: A Soap character Who Can't Be Laundered." In *Village Voice*. Aug. 16, 1994, 38.

Thurber, James. 1970 (orig. 1948). "Soapland." In *The Beast in Me and Other Animals*. New York: Harcourt Brace Jovanovich.

Timberg, Bernard. 1984. "The Rhetoric of the Camera in Television Soap Opera." In *Television: The Critical View*, ed. Horace Newcomb. New York: Oxford Univ. Press.

Wakefield, Dan. 1976. *All Her Children*. New York: Avon Books.

Waters, H.F. 1981. "Television's Hottest Show." *Newsweek*, Sept. 28, 60–66.

Williams, Carol Trayner. 1992. *"It's Time for My Story": Soap Opera Sources, Structure, and Response*. Wesport, Conn.: Praeger.

Index